# BOB DOLE
## AMERICAN POLITICAL PHOENIX

S T A N L E Y   G.   H I L T O N

CB

CONTEMPORARY
BOOKS

CHICAGO · NEW YORK

**Library of Congress Cataloging-in-Publication Data**

Hilton, Stanley C.
   Bob Dole : American political phoenix / Stanley G. Hilton.
      p.   cm.
   Includes index.
   ISBN 0-8092-4561-2 : $18.95
   1. Dole, Robert J., 1923-      .   2. Legislators—United States—
Biography.   2. United States.   Congress.   Senate—Biography.
4. Presidential candidates—United States—Biography.      I. Title.
E840.8.D64HJ55     1988
973.927'092'4—dc19
[B]                                                          88-6877
                                                               CIP

For E.G., C.K.O., and K.V.K., for sharing a vision

Published by Contemporary Books, Inc.
180 North Michigan Avenue, Chicago, Illinois 60601
Manufactured in the United States of America
Library of Congress Catalog Card Number: 88-6877
International Standard Book Number: 0-8092-4561-2

Published simultaneously in Canada by Beaverbooks, Ltd.
195 Allstate Parkway, Valleywood Business Park
Markham, Ontario L3R 4T8 Canada

# CONTENTS

# PREFACE

The idea for this book germinated when I was working as a Senate aide to Bob Dole during his ill-fated 1980 presidential campaign. I felt then, and still feel now, that Dole is a truly unique person with the potential to become a great president, but whose true story is largely unknown to the American people. I believe that this story can be told only by someone who has worked for Dole and is therefore in a position to shed light on his character, motivation, and phenomenal drive to succeed.

I began researching this book in the fall of 1982, convinced that Dole would one day be a serious contender for the American presidency. That day is now at hand.

In an election year, the public can expect saturation coverage of the candidates. The candidates themselves fight desperately for media attention, newspaper interviews, and television appearances that will help put across the image they have chosen to project. For the front-runners, there will be the inevitable campaign autobiographies, carefully sanitized to present their records and qualifications in the rosiest light.

Yet in all this deluge of information and hype, there is, I feel, a deplorable paucity of objective biographies. This is due in large part to the reluctance of the men and women who know the candidate best—his current or former aides—to go on record with a detailed account of the character and performance of their former boss.

In Dole's case, the media seems fascinated with the seemingly paradoxical and contradictory traits shown over the many years of his career. Countless articles and television programs have raised the questions, "Are there two Bob Doles? Is there a dark side and a bright side to this man? Is Bob Dole a moderate or a conservative? Is he compassionate or bitter? Would he make a good president? And does he have any vision?"

*Bob Dole: American Political Phoenix* is an attempt to answer such questions.

My research assistant and I have attempted on numerous occasions to obtain an interview with Senator Dole but have never received a response. This is unfortunate, for I offered Dole the opportunity to present his side of the story on numerous incidents and issues raised in this biography. As far as I am aware, he made no efforts to stop or hinder this book from being written and published, but he provided no encouragement either.

This book is an attempt to present Dole's life in an objective, fair, and balanced way—to analyze and discuss all sides of his personality and record, the good and the bad, the admirable traits and the flaws. In writing this book, I have drawn from my own personal experience in working with Dole, as well as from the recollections of numerous persons who have known him at various stages in his life. My research assistant and I have interviewed more than two hundred persons, and I have carefully read virtually every major newspaper and magazine article written about Bob Dole since the beginning of his political career. I have examined the files on Dole at the Kansas State Historical Society Library in Topeka, Kansas, as well as government documents and other material.

In hopes that this biography will serve to enlighten and entertain the reader at a critical time when America must choose its next president, I present this account of a truly unique man who has the potential to become an outstanding and interesting president of the United States.

March, 1988
San Francisco, California

# ACKNOWLEDGMENTS

I would like to take this opportunity to express my appreciation to the many people who generously contributed to this book, and who provided great support and encouragement. I would especially like to acknowledge Eugene DeForrest, my research assistant who conducted many interviews with Bob Dole's siblings and early friends from his hometown of Russell, Kansas, and who assisted me in the drafting of some chapters and in editing and structuring this book. His comments and suggestions brought a fresh perspective to many aspects of the book.

Special thanks must also go to Russell Townsley, publisher of the *Russell Daily News* and the *Russell Record*. Mr. Townsley has known Dole for more than forty years, particularly during the early and formative years of his political career as Russell county attorney, and generously helped my research assistant and me in setting up interviews with Russellians. He also provided many of the original photographs of young Bob Dole that appear in this book. I am particularly grateful for his assistance in reaching Mrs. Phyllis Macey, Bob Dole's ex-wife, for our interviews with her. Kenny Dole, Gloria Dole, Dean Banker, Bub Dawson, John Woelk, and Polly Bales also deserve special thanks.

My thanks go also to the present and past colleagues and associates of Bob Dole who, for reasons of their own, have requested anonymity. Though their names do not appear in this book, their insights were invaluable. I also thank Al Nencioni and Devereaux Jennings for their gracious and graphic descriptions of World War II and Professor James David Barber for his valuable insights into the presidential character.

The staffs of the Kansas State Historical Society Library in Topeka; the Russell, Kansas, Public Library; and the Kansas City, Kansas, Public Library were unfailingly helpful, as was Mr. Larry Vos of the Wichita Information Service. For their generous and courteous assistance I am deeply grateful.

I would also like to thank Bernard Shir-Cliff, my editor at Contemporary Books, Inc., for his encouragement and advice and my literary agent, Peter Miller, for his indefatigability in seeking and finding the right publisher.

Finally, I wish to express special thanks to Kathy Willhoite and the entire staff at Contemporary Books, Inc., for their expert and tireless assistance in the preparation of the text and for their dedication, which kept them on the job through long days and weekends to bring my book to press in record time.

# 1
# BOB DOLE
# AND THE
# AMERICAN DREAM

For nearly two decades, Senator Bob Dole has been a towering figure on the national political scene—a prince of the United States Senate and the Republican Party and a major national political force in shaping legislation. Widely touted as the most effective Senate majority leader since Lyndon B. Johnson, hailed by the national press and a growing string of admirers as the next president of the United States, Dole has nonetheless been condemned as a "Jekyll-Hyde" figure by a major Washington civil rights lobbyist, has been called "a disaster" by a major conservative guru and fund-raiser, and has presided over a Senate plagued by legislative stalemate and partisan bickering. Criticized by civil rights leaders and then hailed as the savior of a major civil rights law,[1] alternately labeled a conservative and a moderate, a hawk and a dove, a champion of the oppressed and a minion of big business, Dole has presented the nation with a contradictory portrait, one of a political and personal chameleon, a "Zelig of American politics."

[1]Dole was credited with saving the Voting Rights Act of 1982 by sponsoring a major amendment in the Senate.

1

As a major Republican candidate for president in 1988, Bob Dole has come a long way from the dusty streets of tiny Russell, Kansas, where he was born on July 22, 1923. Nearly killed by Nazi troops just three weeks before the end of World War II in Europe, Dole has risen to become the most prominent handicapped politician since Franklin D. Roosevelt, despite—or perhaps because of—a permanently crippled right arm and gnarled hand. He has risen through the ranks in the House of Representatives and the Senate to become GOP national chairman in 1971, the Republican vice presidential candidate in 1976, chairman of the powerful Senate Finance Committee and Senate majority leader in the 1980s, and a familiar face in millions of homes.

Consumed by an all-pervasive, fierce personal ambition that he visualizes as a perpetual campaign to climb all the rungs on the ladder of success, Bob Dole is an incarnation of the American Dream, a truly self-made man, a political Horatio Alger whose entire adult life has been an attempt to prove the myth that in this country anyone can become president. Born to modest circumstances, he has become a millionaire as well as a towering national political figure.

In an age when workaholism seems a necessary attribute to millions of people, Bob Dole is the consummate workaholic, a man who, in the words of a close friend, "is always driving at 75 mph when everyone else is going at 55." Habitually putting in twelve- to eighteen-hour days, never taking a prolonged vacation, and lacking any outside interests or hobbies whatsoever, Dole is like an airplane with faulty landing gear, which must forever remain in the air for fear of crashing to the ground. He is a man obsessed by the "how" of his ambition, but oblivious to the "why," a man so consumed by politics that he leaves virtually no time for any other pursuit, a man whose first marriage broke up allegedly because of his obsession with work and whose second marriage has survived because his new wife is as obsessed with work and ambition as he is.[2]

---

[2]Dole married Phyllis Holden in June 1948 and was divorced in January 1972. He married Mary Elizabeth Hanford in December 1975.

Americans have always had a fondness for myths, and the myth of Robert and Elizabeth Dole as the perfect insider power couple is potently attractive. The senator and his would-be first lady have paraded before television cameras countless times in the past decade, and the nation has been titillated by the vision of the Doles as the epitome of the successful dual-career couple of the eighties. As a U.S. senator husband and a cabinet officer wife (Elizabeth served as secretary of transportation from 1983 to 1987), the couple is a historical first, and they appear to be consummate insiders who seem to have mastered the game and whose next logical step can only lead to the White House.

Bob Dole would have us believe that his public image as a Washington insider is also the reality and that one need look no further in order to find the most qualified and experienced candidate for president. Indeed, if Americans are looking for a president who knows how to make the government run, Dole may well be their man. But doubts linger about what Dole really stands for, about who the real Bob Dole is, and about what Bob Dole's America would be like both in vision and in fact.

In actuality, the story of Bob Dole is the story of a lifelong outsider acting as an insider, desperately wanting to be liked by everyone but fearing rejection and ridicule, angry toward the world for having deprived him of a good arm and condemning him to be, in his own eyes, something less than a whole person. It is a tale of a man forever searching for an identity, blithely slipping in and out of widely disparate political and personal roles in order to be liked and successful. And it is the story of a man with a chronic need to challenge and test himself, to overcome overwhelming odds in self-manufactured crises, flirting with disasters in order to emerge, like the mythical phoenix, ever stronger and with a greater sense of self-worth.

To millions of Americans, the indelible image of Bob Dole is that of the acid-tongued, sardonic "hatchet man" who established his image in the national consciousness on an October night in 1976 when, as President Gerald Ford's running mate, he declared in a nationally televised debate that all of America's wars in this century were "Democrat wars," an outrageous comment that prompted his opponent, Walter Mondale, to declare that "Dole has richly earned his reputation as a hatchet man tonight." The sobriquet *hatchet man,* which was justified by Dole's harsh and acerbic performance throughout the campaign, has clung to his neck like an albatross over the years, despite his concerted effort to soften his image.

Dole's negative public image has been modified considerably in recent years, thanks to skillful revamping and an adoring national press corps that, in startling contrast to its former contempt for him, has generally touted him as a prospective president since 1981, when he became chairman of the Senate Finance Committee.

The transformation of Dole from hatchet man to statesman has been one of the most remarkable public relations feats of modern times. The media's effusive praise has led to widespread public belief that there is a new Dole, a mellowed Dole, an enlightened Dole. In an age when the media have essentially replaced political parties as kingmakers in presidential elections, Dole's wholehearted endorsement by his former nemesis, the press, may well prove sufficient to put him into the White House. Certainly it has contributed significantly to his support among college-educated "yuppie" voters who admire his ambition, efficiency, and emotional coolness.

But disturbing questions remain about the validity of repackaging a man once thought to be too mean and sarcastic to succeed to the mantle of Washington and Lincoln. One must ask whether it is really possible for a man well into his sixties to transform himself into a fundamentally different person overnight. Can a man really change his character, which is based on his life experiences? Is Dole merely a master at assuming different identities, a shrewd navigator skilled at sensing the direction of the political wind?[3] Should a national leader have a consistent ideology and personal-

---

[3]Senator Nancy Kassebaum of Kansas, co-chairman of Dole's 1980 presidential campaign, recently said: "Bob waits to see which way the wind is blowing. . . . There's always a question: Does he have a vision? You won't see him creating an agenda." (Subsequently, however, she wrote a letter to the *Times* saying she had been quoted out of context.) Martin Tolchin and Jeff Gerth, "The Contradictions of Bob Dole," *New York Times Magazine,* November 8, 1987.

ity in order to steer the ship of state on a steady course? And how important is predictability in a potential president?

On the eve of Dole's announcement for the 1988 Republican presidential nomination, *Newsweek* magazine spoke of his "contradictory character," while the *New York Times* discussed his "contradictions" and *Time* decried his lack of clear vision for the country. The validity and significance of these critiques will ultimately be decided by voters, but they deserve careful scrutiny.

Dole is, essentially, a lone eagle, as he has been described by his Senate colleagues. He is a man with a fiercely independent nature who resents being told what to do by anyone, from his own staff to contributors to his political action committee to President Reagan. Referred to as an "unguided missile" during his abortive vice presidential campaign twelve years ago, he is a solitary man who generally does as his own mind tells him and who cannot stand either to delegate or to obey authority. Widely reputed to be a difficult boss to work for, with a high staff turnover, he is stingy with praise and generous with criticism, cold and aloof—yet witty and charming.

Dole is a talented, natural comedian who has said that were he not in politics, he would like to sit in place of Johnny Carson as host of the "Tonight" show. Yet he is moody as well, and his humor often has a sarcastic, acerbic bite to it, aimed at another person's hide. Like Kansas weather, his mood can shift rapidly from brilliant sunshine to a ferocious tornado. At times, Dole can be so droll and self-deprecating that he appears to be an eccentric. The next minute, however, he may take himself so seriously that he views events in Manichaean terms, thunders against his opponents, and lashes out at scapegoats and whipping boys, speaking of being "betrayed" and "executed" by "gutless wonders" and acting as if his very life depended on winning.

As a boy, before he lost the use of his arm, Dole was obsessed with personal physical strength and with beating everyone else in competition. After his crippling injury, he channeled this obsession into politics, which he sees as an extension of the playing field and the battlefield. In politics, he has always been the supreme tactician, concerned primarily with beating the opposition rather than with enacting a particular agenda.

Dole is a man who cannot stand to lose and who must constantly prove himself a winner. As he stated so accurately in a recent argument on the Senate floor (where he felt his authority as majority leader was being challenged by Minority Leader Robert Byrd), "I don't come here to lose!" and, "I didn't become majority leader in order to be dictated to by the minority." After the two most crushing electoral defeats of his life (for vice president in 1976 and for president in 1980), he lashed out at his staff and opponents. In campaigns, he has often been a real slasher, cutting off his opponents at the knees with relish.

But in the Senate, where compromise with diverse factions is the language of winning, he has shown a knack for forging deals with legislators of all parties and ideologies. Here, his lack of a clear ideology has proven to be a plus, enabling him to shepherd many pieces of important legislation through Congress at a rate more impressive than that of any politician since Lyndon Johnson thirty years ago.

Dole's reputation as a Senate wheeler-dealer, which has earned him kudos from the national press, would seem to augur auspiciously for him as a president, and he has tried to base his candidacy almost entirely on his record, running an intensely personal campaign aimed at proving that he is the most qualified candidate to lead the nation. But questions about his so-called dark side linger.

He is the man who was once so fanatically loyal to Richard Nixon that he earned the moniker "Nixon's Doberman pinscher" and prompted the famous line "If you like Richard Nixon, you'll love Bob Dole." Yet even Nixon himself criticized Dole as being too "abrasive" and too much of a "one-man band," and he dismissed Dole as GOP chairman and replaced him with the slavishly obedient George Bush.

So striking are the contradictions in Dole that he has been compared to political figures as diverse as Nixon and FDR, has been branded a comedian and a gunslinger, a populist and a conservative, a mean-spirited man and a man with a heart of gold.

Who the real Bob Dole is, and what his agenda for America may be, can be gleaned from a study of his life and of the experiences that shaped him into what he is today.

On the eve of his announcement for the 1988 GOP presidential nomination, Dole was asked on national television why he was running for president. His reply, typically vague and vintage Dole, was "to make a difference." When asked what his vision for the country was, he replied that he wanted to create "greater opportunity" for people, especially the underdogs of society, with whom he identifies.

But these reasons alone—making a difference and creating greater opportunity—do not justify the stupendous emotional, personal, and financial cost of running for president of the United States, and that leaves us wondering what the *real* reason is for his presidential ambition.

Perhaps more than any other politician since Richard Nixon and Ed Muskie, Dole has been characterized in the media as having an overwhelming desire to be elected president. Having worked directly for him in the Senate while he was running his first presidential campaign, I can attest to the accuracy of this perception and can offer the opinion that Dole's tremendous drive to reach the top derives from factors in his background and his personality.

The equally ambitious drive of his wife, Elizabeth, which adds fuel to Dole's own fire of ambition, is an essential component of the Dole phenomenon. There was considerable truth to the mock-serious campaign buttons that read "Dole & Dole in '88," which sprouted up during the 1984 GOP convention in Dallas. In a real sense, the Doles are a team of fierce competitors, so obsessed with the desire to win for winning's sake, and so consumed by a flurry of work, that they have not found the time to think about why they really do want to wind up in the White House.

In an age when a politician must avoid appearing too ambitious, for fear of scaring off the electorate, Bob Dole has only thinly veiled his drive. His inability to clearly and coherently articulate a genuine policy rationale for his candidacy is a serious shortcoming and has led to criticism that he lacks a vision.

To one who has worked for Dole, the vision void is a logical consequence of a certain character trait, namely the fear of going out on a limb and taking the lead on a specific issue. The Bob Dole I knew was very indecisive when it came to sticking his neck out and, in his words, "leading a platoon" and thereby possibly serving as "cannon fodder."

While much has been made of the beneficial psychological consequences of Dole's war injury (giving him a fierce drive and determination to succeed), little has been said of its deleterious consequences. His wartime experience, in some ways, has made Dole a very cautious, gun-shy individual when it comes to "leading a platoon" on a controversial issue. Perhaps because his leading a squad of troops nearly killed him over forty years ago, he has been reluctant to place himself in a similar advance position of danger ever since. It is for this reason that he is, in many ways, a political sailboat, always moving in the direction of the prevailing wind and unwilling to expose himself to the danger of defeat and disaster that might befall a Goldwater or a Reagan—ideologues who are willing to risk defeat in order to promote a particular cause and who place the cause above their own personal goals.

Bob Dole has never been a rigid ideologue, and he never will be. He has shown a remarkable adaptability and willingness to change; in order to survive, he has shifted with the political wind. Therein lie both his strength and his weakness. He may be an ideal candidate for getting things done and making government work, and his presidency might well prove to be a welcome relief from the stalemate between Congress and the White House that we have seen in the last few presidencies. It may be, in fact, that Dole's qualities parallel those of the nation at large and that his pragmatic eclecticism and so-called realism would make him a good president.

Nonetheless, in the case of Dole we must ask: Is there a consistent character behind all these myths? If there is, what is it, and what would it mean for the nation if Bob Dole should finally achieve his life's crowning ambition?

# 2
# BOB DOLE COUNTRY, U.S.A.

Thirty miles from the spot where Bob Dole was born, a sign by the road reads: YOU ARE HALFWAY BETWEEN PARADISE AND THE GARDEN OF EDEN.[1] The colorful names of the towns and way stations stand in stark contrast to the flat terrain that stretches away as far as the eye can see. This is the heart of the Kansas wheat land, the exact geographical center of the continental United States.

Here at America's epicenter, the land appears so ordinary that it is extraordinary. As you drive past the town of Paradise (which, believe it or not, once had a mayor named Mr. Angel) and head into the ocean of wheat, dotted by occasional oil rigs and farmhouses, the miles and miles of golden grain remind you that you are in the heart of America's breadbasket, the largest wheat-producing state, and one of the last vestiges of rural America, where tiny towns with odd names like Paradise, Lucas, and Luray pop up on the horizon and then fade away like mirages.

In the early nineteenth century, this part of the country was

[1]The town of Luray is halfway between the town of Paradise and the Garden of Eden, a striking collection of concrete statues depicting Garden of Eden biblical figures and other subjects, in the town of Lucas.

9

called the Great American Desert, a vast, empty, treeless land with the wind blowing ceaselessly out of the west in an unbroken sweep from the mountains of Colorado. It was never a desert, and today it is a remarkably productive land, a world unto itself, whose true soul can be discerned in the Kansas state motto: *ad astra, per aspera*—"to the stars, through difficulties."

Not so coincidentally, this state motto happens to be the presidential campaign theme of Bob Dole, whose roots are deeply implanted in this soil, the land where he was born. Located 240 miles west of Kansas City, just off Interstate 70, at the intersection of U.S. Routes 40 and 281, the hometown of Bob Dole is clearly marked by four huge billboard signs proudly proclaiming: WELCOME TO BOB DOLE COUNTRY: RUSSELL, KANSAS. Bold and brazen in their patriotic red, white, and blue insignia, they stand like silent sentinels at each of the four approaches to the town, making certain that everyone who enters knows that this is the home of Kansas's favorite son.

"Bob Dole is Russell, and Russell is Bob Dole!" a townsman told me proudly, and Dole was there on November 9, 1987, to announce his candidacy for the GOP presidential nomination in this community of 5,600 souls.

Dole brought back with him from his desk in Washington the same cigar box that the townspeople had used to collect $1,800 in donations to pay for his postwar surgery forty years before. The cigar box had stood on the counter of Dawson's Drug Store, where Bob had once worked as a soda jerk, and has been his most prized possession since it was presented to him, filled with money in 1947. The army had abandoned him and refused to pay for his surgery, but the people of Russell came through, and Dole never forgot. Now, as he announced his presidential campaign, he was presented with the same cigar box at the same drugstore, this time containing much more than $1,800 for his presidential campaign. Their native son and local hero had returned home, and the people of Russell had come through again.

This reenactment of the cigar box offering served as a symbolic reaffirmation of the bond between Dole and the people of Russell. Anyone walking through the streets could feel the adulation for him. It is a degree of hero worship approaching a cult of personality and is extraordinary to behold. From the huge billboards to the plaque before the courthouse, Dole is commemorated as a hero of larger-than-life proportions.

People in Russell still remember Dole as the indefatigable high school honor student who played basketball, football, and track after school, worked late into the night at Dawson's Drug Store, and jogged every morning at 5:30 A.M. They remember the man in motion at all times, the runner who could never stop, the workaholic human machine, the magnificent athlete who had gone off to war and returned an emaciated bag of bones with a Dachau victim's look. And they remember the phoenixlike resurgence of this tall, saturnine hero with the handsome Humphrey Bogart face and the withered right arm, who refused to admit that he was handicapped, with the indomitable spirit that refused to go down.

The legend of Bob Dole lives on in Russell, and no man is more aware of it than Dole himself. It is no surprise that he has continued to return to Russell, time and time again, like a machine recharging its batteries by plugging into their power source. To understand Dole, one must understand Russell.

The town lived by "gritty prairie values" such as the importance of hard work and obedience. "When Bob grew up in the twenties and thirties, he was surrounded by doers, achievers here in Russell," says Dean Banker, a third-generation clothier in Russell who used to fit Bob's father with 42–32 overalls. There were men like A. E. Seeley of "the Lucky Seven," a group of local bold and competitive entrepreneurs who had taken the risk of drilling for oil in a hitherto barren land, 10 miles north of town and 155 miles from the nearest producing wells. These men risked their capital and their reputations to go out drilling for oil, and Bob was deeply impressed by them, as he was by numerous other wildcat drillers who brought in the first oil well in Russell and spurred a major oil boom destined to make the Sunflower State one of the largest oil-producing state in the union, thus boosting the Kansas economy.

"Competition is the lifeblood of this town," a lifelong Russell resident told me. "Even our sense of humor is based on competition; the idea is to get the last word in, by trading light banter, trying to be the most clever, the fastest wit, the guy who gets the most laughs." Dole, whose caustic humor was honed in the streets of Russell, displayed this sense of wit brilliantly in national politics, but his joking was mistaken for meanness and contributed to his hatchet man image. In Russell, such humor is called "one-upmanship." Frankness to the point of being blunt is also a common characteristic among Russell's citizens. The town's unofficial motto is: "Tell it like it is."

The town's competitive ethic was closely related to its strong work ethic; a man's worth was determined by the ferocity and success of his effort. "There's no such thing as a free lunch in Russell," his brother Kenny Dole says. "You gotta make the effort, you gotta go at least halfway, and the town will then welcome you with open arms," Dean Banker says. "There's a certain charisma to this town, a vibration. People who have lived here all their lives can sense it. It never leaves them. It's in their blood."

As Bob was growing up there, Russell was growing as well. The population was 1,969 in 1920, was 4,819 by 1940, and reached its peak of 6,483 in 1950.

The energy and competitive spirit of the town were not the only influences bearing on young Bob. An even more powerful influence was the daily example set by his own parents, who provided a magnificent daily demonstration of the competitive work ethic in action, and Bob soaked up their example as a sponge soaks up water.

Robert Joseph Dole was born in a two-room white house near the Union Pacific railroad tracks on Russell's Maple Street,[2] to Doran and Bina (pronounced "Bye-na"), Dole, a pair of lifelong Russell residents who had been married in 1921 with a reception inside Doran's own White Front Cafe. The second eldest of four children, two sons and two daughters,[3] Bob was the only one destined to go to college and to leave the Russell area for far greater horizons than those to which he was born in 1923.

Doran's and Bina's own families had been in Russell almost as long as the town itself, which was founded in 1871 by a group of immigrants from Ripon, Wisconsin—by coincidence, birthplace of the Republican Party. Bina's father, Joe Talbott, arrived in Russell

---

[2]The house, razed in 1976, was located a block away from the house at 1035 North Maple Street, where Dole grew up—and which he still owns.
[3]Bob was born two years after his sister, Gloria, and fourteen months before his brother, Kenny. His second sister, Norma Jean, was born in 1925.

County from Rising Sun, Indiana, in 1901 and was a farmer and an itinerant butcher who went from farm to farm slaughtering hogs and other animals. He married Elva Mitchell, fathered twelve children, and lived until 1960, the year Bob Dole was first elected to Congress.

Bob's paternal grandparents arrived in Russell shortly after the town had been founded. Robert Grant Dole, a farmer, later lost his property during the Great Depression and wound up on welfare. Doran was born in 1900, served in the Army Medical Corps in World War I, bought the White Front Cafe at 833 Main Street at the age of nineteen, and married Bina Talbott two years later. He was a hearty, muscular man who stood almost six feet tall and had a fierce independent streak, an entrepreneurial spirit, and a low-key sense of humor that worked wonders with farmers and patrons.

"Doran always had a smile on his face," recalls Dean Banker. Doran was a workaholic, a perfectionist, and a strikingly consistent man in everything he did. "Pop woke up at five o'clock in the morning every day," Bob's sister Gloria recalls. "And, when his feet hit the floor, everyone else's had better, too." Doran didn't get home until late in the evening, often near midnight. "He missed only one day of work in forty years," Kenny recalls. "When he wasn't working, he was serving as a volunteer firefighter—he finally retired at the age of seventy-four—or he was out at someone's home, watching a sick person all night, and when he wasn't doing that, he was out hunting or fishing." Discipline was left up to Bina, who occasionally dispensed it with a belt or switch on Saturday afternoons, according to Bob.

When Bob was growing up in the 1920s, Doran started a cream and egg station around the corner from his cafe. There he would sit for the next fifty years, acting as middleman between Russell County farmers, local merchants, and nearby creameries. The station, at one point called Dole's Produce, became a town crossroads, a focal point for business and social contact. Typically, farmers would bring in cream, produce, chickens, and eggs, and Doran would pay them with cash or by barter, sometimes exchanging utensils, tools, scrip, coupons for a drawing, vouchers redeemable at Banker's department store, or IOUs.

Doran seems to have impressed the people of Russell as a dynamo who would not quit. G. B. "Bub" Dawson recalls walking to work with his brother at 7:30 each morning, "and we'd always see the light on at Doran's cream and egg station." At night, Doran's light would still be on when the lights in every other business in town were out. "There might be someone coming down the street to do business," Doran would say and wait until the last light went out and he had satisfied himself that there was no point in staying open any longer.

Bob took Doran's example seriously. One day, Doran asked Bob to pick up some medicine at the local drugstore. Bob got there too early in the morning, before opening time. Rather than go home empty-handed, the sleepy Bob stayed outside the drugstore to be sure he would be there when it opened. When Doran went to fetch him a half hour later (4:00 A.M.), the druggist recalls, "there was Bob, all curled up, asleep in the doorway." Years later, when Bob had his own office as county attorney and later as congressman and senator, people would remember seeing his office light on long after everyone else's windows were dark. Like Doran, Bob would live by the slogan "First in, last out."

In his flurry of work, Doran was home so seldom that he seemed more like a guest than a full-time resident, and when he was home, he was silent. "He didn't give out praise," Gloria says of their father. "You just were expected to do your work, and that was that. You didn't get a pat on the head from Dad." When Bob recently attributed to his father the maxim "There are doers and stewers," Kenny remarked, "I doubt that Dad said that; he wasn't home long enough to say anything like that. I think that's Bob's own saying."

Bob himself tells the following story of "Silent Doran," the parsimonious praise-giver. "Kenny and I trimmed all the grass in our yard, just perfectly, to please Dad. It took us a week. Dad looked at it and said, 'Not bad—not good, but not bad.' "

The similarity between father and son is striking. In later years, Bob would display the same workaholic pattern of activity, and the same closemouthed reluctance to praise another person for a job well done. When I worked for him, I was struck by his general failure to praise any staffers (except before constituents and other visitors), even for working long hours and securing important victories for him on bills passed in the Senate. Jo-Anne Coe, his assistant for over twenty years, confirmed that "he doesn't praise people." And Phyllis, Bob's first wife, was hurt by the fact that, like Doran, Bob seldom got home before midnight and was out of the house by 5:00 A.M., behavior that led to their divorce.

It is no coincidence that Bob kept a photograph of his father, in overalls, on the wall near his desk in his Senate office. Nor is it coincidental that, when asked on national television which U.S. presidents' portraits he would hang up in the Oval Office if elected president, he replied: "I'd hang up a picture of my parents—of my father in his overalls."

It was at Doran's cream and egg station that young Bob got his first lessons in the art of politics. Watching his affable and popular dad make clever deals with farmers and merchants every day, the bashful young Dole picked up the skills he would later master as a U.S. senator and national politician.

"Doran would empathize with every farmer who came into his station," Dean Banker recalls of Bob's father. "During the Great Depression and Dust Bowl of the 'Dirty Thirties,' when the price of wheat plummeted, the farmers would come in and rail against 'the interests' who 'rigged' the price of wheat. Doran would nod in agreement, smile, and commiserate with them. 'You know, I think maybe you got a point there,' he would say." And Bob, standing behind his dad, would take it all in. Doran would listen and listen for hours to the farmers, thereby setting an example for Bob, who would also become a great listener, always looking for, in his phrase, "bright ideas" and forever willing to "make a deal."

Influence by example was not limited to the paternal side of the family. Dole's mother, Bina, had an industrious and work-oriented personality as unusual as her name. In the 1930s, when women were expected to limit themselves to kitchen, children, and church, Bina broke with tradition and went into business for herself as a roving saleswoman for Singer sewing machines. She was a seamstress who struck upon the brilliant (and hitherto unheard of) idea of offering sewing lessons to anyone who bought a Singer sewing machine from her. "I think she started the first sewing classes in the country," Kenny recalls. "She was always traveling around, selling machines, and she traveled all over Kansas.

"She even sold the products received from her patrons to Dad, at his cream and egg station," Kenny says, explaining that Doran would buy the products from his wife, with cash, and would then try to sell them to the farmers and merchants who came into his station. "Mom and Dad had a partnership," Kenny insists.

Bina impressed Bob with a saying he later echoed in his career: " 'Can't' never could do anything," she would say. If you set your mind to winning, self-reliance and aggressiveness would bring success, and that was that. Bob, stubbornly determined to succeed, would remember the lesson.

In addition to selling sewing machines and teaching, Bina Dole made clothes for her four children. Like Doran, she had a seemingly inexhaustible reservoir of energy.[4] Unlike Doran, she seemed affectionate and warm, and she was particularly close to her elder son. "Bob was very close to her," sister Gloria recalls. "Even when he went to Washington, he used to call her once every week at least."

The degree of Bob's affection for Bina can be discerned from the sparkle in his eyes in a photograph taken on her birthday in 1983. In another photograph taken in front of the U.S. Capitol building in Washington on January 10, 1963, when Bob's parents came to visit him as congressman, Bob can be seen standing one step below his parents so that he appears shorter than they, when in fact he was taller than both of them. These photos reveal much about the man and the unusually strong admiration he felt for his parents.

What is most striking about the Dole family, apart from its devotion to work, is the almost total lack of strong emotion, intense conflict, or hostility. Bob received no praise from his parents, but he experienced virtually no anger either. His siblings cannot recall any notable arguments or spankings. Instead they recall their parents as silent work machines who communicated the values of perfection and work through example. In such a family, one didn't gain affection just for being *oneself*; rather, one gained admiration and respect by *being a hard worker*.

In such a family environment, Bob became conditioned to seek admiration more than affection and to earn it by outdoing himself in hard, competitive work. Perhaps he sought to outdo his father

---

[4]When Bob was running for office, Bina worked hard on his campaigns, nailing his posters on trees, hosting tea parties, and touring the state for him, up through 1976.

as well, in order to get the approval of the man he admired.

Yet neither his brother nor his two sisters ever approached his fanatical ambition or work habits. Kenny became an oil-lease broker, and Gloria opened a beauty shop, both in Russell, where they remain to this day; sister Norma Jean married in nearby Derby, where she lives today and declines to talk to the press. Kenny recently joked that "there ought to be a club called 'Brothers Anonymous,' " accurately describing his status when compared to Bob's.

From a psychological standpoint, the question is: Why was Bob the only member of the family to go to college and mount a lifelong quest to become president of the United States? Might this have something to do with his being the elder son in a family where the father was usually out to work? Bob may well have felt a keen sense of competition with Doran, a desire to prove himself stronger, more industrious, and more successful.

The impact of Doran and Bina's influence on their son must be viewed against the backdrop of the Depression and the great Dust Bowl drought that scourged Kansas during Bob's formative teenage years. When the stock market crashed in October 1929, Bob was only six years old. As the Great Depression rolled into Kansas, it had a devastating impact on the local economy, lowering demand and prices for wheat, oil, and other goods. The terrible drought of the "Dirty Thirties" exacerbated the economic woes. Throughout Kansas, Texas, and Oklahoma, hot winds swept across the parched fields, raising clouds of dust and darkening the sky each day by 4:00 in the afternoon until the land was one great Dust Bowl where nothing grew. The dust wiped out wheat fields, poisoned cows and other livestock, and even killed thousands of people with "dust pneumonia."

"The Dust Bowl and the Depression hit us with a double whammy," recalls Dean Banker. "It got so bad, they actually found a cow with a plant growing inside its belly. The cow had swallowed so much dust that a seed had actually germinated inside its stomach." Bob Dole, like most people, helped his parents place rags underneath their doorjambs and put a wet rag into his mouth when he went outside, when the dust storms became particularly strong.

Despite the hardships brought on by the Dust Bowl and the

Great Depression, Doran Dole managed to keep his cream and egg station, and Bina continued to sell sewing machines. "Everybody's got to eat and everybody's got to wear clothes," Bob later said of this period.

"Everybody was poor, even if they didn't know it," says Russell Townsley, publisher of the *Russell Daily News*. "There was really no social class structure in Russell, never had been," he adds. "Sure, there were disparities in wealth, but people didn't ever segregate themselves into exclusive classes; it was never a question of one social class refusing to talk to you because you were 'below' them or anything like that. Russell was just like one big family; people cared after you in those days. If you needed help, if you needed to borrow some money or some clothes or food, if you were sick, people would chip in and help out."

"Russell is an extended family," Bob's brother Kenny says. Dean Banker agrees. "If you tried to use your talents and met us halfway, we'd all chip in and help; that's how it was here in the thirties."

Bob recalled on national television that in the 1930s "there really weren't lots of wealthy families in Russell. Poverty is a relative thing. I remember my clothes were handed down to my brother Ken, and Gloria's were handed down to Norma Jean. My father had an old car."

Dole's family was never down-and-out; his parents were never unemployed, and he himself found ample opportunities to work after school in the drugstore and the cream and egg station. "Bob's father was a merchant," explains John Woelk, who lived in Russell in the thirties and later helped get Bob started in politics. "The merchants were rather middle-class in those days. During the Depression, those hardest hit were the workers, who lost their jobs; next were the farmers, with wheat at twenty-five cents a bushel; then came the merchants, like Doran Dole." Woelk considered Dole's family actually "upper-middle-class" compared to other families at the time. The house in which Bob grew up is physically quite impressive for Russell. It is quite large, and, though it has been remodeled in recent years, it must have been a status symbol of sorts for Doran Dole and his family.

Dean Banker, however, describes the Dole family as "lower-middle-class." Bob's brother Kenny, however, remembers his family's situation as even more desperate. "Every time Bob and I walked to school, we looked around for pieces of old cardboard on the street so we could put it inside our shoes and cover the holes," he recalls.

One year, about 1937, the Doles were forced to rent the main floor of their home to oil companies, which used it to house oil workers who were then drilling in the fields. The Doles, who needed the rent in order to survive, moved into the basement of their own home, a situation that was particularly humiliating for Bob and Kenny. "I was ashamed to go to school every day," Kenny says, adding that he never learned the details about the renting because "Mom and Dad didn't discuss finances with us."

Bob and his family were poor during the Depression, but they were not as poor as the millions of unemployed in the big cities of America. Bob tasted hard times, but not so hard as to make him bitter toward the rich or susceptible to the wave of populist oratory coming over the radio. He identified with Russell as an extended family, a small heartland community sufficient unto itself. He was not politically active and showed little interest in the great ideological debates raging over populism, capitalism, and other "isms" of the day.

His parents were Democrats,[5] however, and Bob was treated to frequent doses of populist rhetoric from the down-and-out farmers who visited his father's cream and egg station and who launched into long-winded diatribes about the evils of the "system" and the "Wall Street weasels" who "fixed the market." From Doran, who empathized with the farmers, Bob picked up certain populist sympathies that would reappear later in his political career, when he would side with "the little man" against "the interests."

Populism had always found fertile political soil in Kansas. Ever since wheat had first been planted in the state in 1874,[6] homespun "hayseed" orators had taken to the plains and the prairies like

---

[5]In Bob and Elizabeth's 1988 book, *The Doles: Unlimited Partners*, Bob says that his parents were originally Republicans, became Democrats when Bob was young, then switched back to the GOP when Bob ran for county attorney in 1952.
[6]Wheat was introduced to Kansas in 1874 by a contingent of Mennonites who brought Turkey Red wheat from the Russian Ukraine.

itinerant missionaries, preaching the virtues and rights of the common man and denouncing capitalism. The Great Drought of the 1890s had savaged the hitherto productive wheat fields, embittering Kansas farmers and filling their minds with thoughts of conspiracy and demands for government action to alleviate their distress.

Forty miles from Russell, in the tiny town of Lucas, a Civil War veteran named S. P. Dinsmoor invented a unique formula for concrete, sculpted a striking collection of statues, and placed them for public view in what he called "The Garden of Eden." One of those statuary groups depicts "Capitalism" smashing "Labor," a basic theme of populism.

Since the turn of the century, populist orators like "Sockless" Jerry Simpson and Mary Elizabeth Lease rumbled through Kansas with fiery tongues. Genuine wallbangers, they told hungry-eyed farmers that "Wall Street owns the country. It is no longer a government of the people, by the people, and for the people, but a government of Wall Street, by Wall Street, and for Wall Street. The great common people of this country are slaves, and monopoly is the master."

Bob Dole grew up hearing tales of the old populists, and he would go hear populists speak when they came to town. Though he took the populists' message with a grain of salt, he was sympathetic to their basic theme, which was "Us against Them." Many years later, when he began denouncing banks and corporations for their greed, when he sounded the clarion call for tax increases aimed at the rich, and when he denounced George Bush as the Rockefeller candidate, he bared his populist fangs. At the pinnacle of American politics, he would still consider himself an outsider running against "the interests," even while presenting himself, ironically, as the ultimate insider as a presidential candidate in 1988. He would always recognize a proper role for the government to play in aiding distressed farmers, poor people, and other minorities, contrary to the prevailing *laissez-faire* mood of his own Republican Party.

But in the thirties, Bob was too involved with sports, work, and school to take an active interest in politics. Bob's acquaintances from this early period remember him as popular but "hard to get close to," a hard-working young man who wanted to be liked and thirsted for recognition and admiration, far more so than his class-mates. He has continued to yearn for, and work hard for, public admiration all his life—perhaps to make up for the lack of praise and affection he experienced at home.

Hauling cream cans for his father helped Bob build up a show-piece of a muscular body and led him into a peculiar obsession with physical strength. He began jogging around Russell at 5:30 in the morning, every morning, and continued to do so for as long as anyone can remember. "Nobody else ran at 5:30 in the morning," Banker recalls, "except Bob. You could always see him running through the streets, like a messenger, a man going someplace. He was huffing and puffing, going at it, like a man in a hurry . . . that and basketball and football and track . . . he wanted to be a Charles Atlas." He became a "magnificent physical specimen," according to brother Kenny. By the time he was a teenager in Russell High School, he was six feet, two inches tall and weighed 190 pounds, all of it muscle. "He was a Rambo before that name was invented," a townsman explains. He ran while delivering newspapers and handbills, too, and never seemed out of breath.

From early boyhood, Bob demonstrated that he was marching to the tune of a different drummer, whose beat reverberated inside his mind and drove him to ever new limits of exertion. To Bob, the name of the game was competition, and the goal was to beat everyone else in sight at everything he attempted. His high school basketball coach, Harold Elliott, remembered Bob as "not the best athlete, but a fierce competitor. If you told him to climb a wall, he'd climb the wall." George Baxter, Bob's high school football coach, remembered a game in the late 1930s in which Bob "threw and caught his own pass and scored a touchdown." When asked later why he had played quarterback and receiver simultaneously, according to Baxter, Bob replied somewhat sheepishly, "I guess the ball just stuck to my hands."

This football incident was a forecast of Bob's later behavior as senator and presidential candidate. When I worked for him in the Senate, he repeatedly asked the question "Do I have to throw and catch my own passes?" as he furiously chided staffers for failing to live up to his high expectations, and he sacked one campaign manager after another for failing to "catch his passes."

Being a football star made Bob an instant hero in Russell. "In

Russell during the 1930s, the most important thing to everybody was to beat Hays High," according to Dean Banker. "Everyone in town came out to see the high school games," Banker explained, "because in those days there were no professional or college teams in the area, and the rivalry between Russell and Hays High was the most important topic of discussion, more important than the price of wheat." For weeks, people would be heard in the streets of Russell discussing the game in which Dole had been the hero.

In high school, Bob also had a job at Dawson's Drug Store, where he worked for a dollar a day, wore ice-cream-white trousers and coat, and helped the pharmacist fill prescriptions and dispense sodas and Coke at the store's fountain. There, while meeting doctors who came in to fill prescriptions, he developed an interest in becoming a country doctor himself.

Because doctors had great prestige and a guaranteed income even in bad times, Dole aspired to join their ranks. He began asking questions of the doctors who came into the drugstore, and he listened to their answers. "He saw that in the hard times the doctors were always the best-dressed men in town, the most respected members of the community, and the most secure," a friend recalls. "Bob was fascinated with the power over life and death that doctors had and with the fact that they were the most respected men. He wanted to be like them. He wanted to be liked."

Across the floor from the prescription stand at the drugstore, Bob was busy acquiring many of the social and political skills he would later utilize to the hilt as a politician. "The soda fountain at our drugstore was the social center of town in those days," Bub Dawson recalls. "It was the town watering hole. Every afternoon, it would fill up with school kids and shoppers who stopped to have a Coke or some ice cream or food. Bob had a real following then. Kids and other people liked him; he got along well with people of all ages. He would come in after practicing football and basketball after school, and he would work until ten or eleven at night. I think he picked up a lot of his humor, his bantering wit, at the soda fountain . . . but he was hard to get close to." The soda fountain job helped Bob overcome his shyness as he learned how to aggressively assault patrons with his put-down humor. "The Dawson brothers, Chet and Bub, would always insult patrons," Bob recalled. "I thought I'd add in a few jibes to make sure they got what they paid for." This humor was to develop into a talent that Bob would later use—both to his benefit and to his detriment—in his political career.

Dole worked as much in school as out. Alice Mills, who was principal of his school in the thirties, recalled in the town newspaper, "He was not a leader or a follower—he was independent. When called upon [in class], he was always ready with the answer. He was not a show-off, nor did he seek special attention. He was alert and dependable, and he always looked right—exceedingly neat."

Mabel Lacey, Bob's seventh-grade English teacher, told the paper that he was a "splendid student. He always paid attention. Bob was there to learn what was before him. He was better than any of the others in his class, and I never saw anyone who didn't like him. He was always already in the classroom when I got there."

Faith Dumler, Bob's high school Spanish teacher, echoed these praises in the *Russell Record*, remembering Bob as "a leader among the kids. He was well liked. I don't remember him dating. Bob and one of his very good friends, Bud Smith, who was killed in action, were both so good-looking. Bob was lots of fun. He had that banter wit that he still has, [that] put-down wit [that's] a prevalent area-type humor."

Bob's talents as a put-down comedian are remembered in Russell. A typical example is given by Faith Dumler: "Someone remarked they had just been to a beauty shop, and Dole would quip, 'Oh, you didn't get waited on, did you?' "

This put-down wit does indeed seem to be quite prevalent among Russellians. In Russell, the target of Dole's humor would generally counter with an even stronger joke-insult, and a blow-by-blow game of one-upmanship would ensue, at the soda fountain or in the courthouse. But in the world outside of Russell, Dole's barbs would often be resented and taken very personally. They can be charming and amusing, if one knows him and realizes he's just kidding. However, as his first wife, Phyllis, remarked, "When he started using that wit around people who didn't know him, he offended. But once you know him, you're not offended by it."

Typically, from my firsthand experience while working for him in the Senate, Dole would walk through his office, approach a staffer, and say something like "You planning on returning that suit to the Salvation Army after work?" or "What sixth-grader did you pay to write this speech?" or "That double-breasted suit was very popular during the Depression." When he practiced law in Russell, Dole would typically walk up to opposing counsel after a court appearance and snicker, "You sure you got a law degree? . . . When are you planning on taking Civil Procedure I?" And, if a rival praised him, he retorted: "I must have done something wrong."

With his talents in humor, scholastics, and athletics, the versatile Dole continued to challenge himself in the thirties. He got several other jobs, dug ditches for a while, and continued loading and hauling cream cans at his father's cream and egg station.[7]

In addition to his other jobs and activities, Dole managed to work as sports editor for the Russell High School newspaper, the *Pony Express*.

There was always something in Bob that yearned to break through the confines of his family's social station. At night, he listened longingly to the rumble of the transcontinental Union Pacific passenger trains hurtling through Russell to Denver or Kansas City. The train tracks, just two blocks from Bob's house, were a gateway to an exciting, unknown world calling to him far from beyond the confines of tiny Russell.

In the summer of 1941, Dole graduated from Russell High School, a member of the National Honor Society and a star athlete en route to Kansas University in Lawrence, which he entered in the fall as a freshman in the class of '45.

"Our parents could give him only $65 for the whole year at KU," brother Kenny recalls. "So, he had to get a loan on his own." Resourceful and clever as always, Bob asked the local Russell banker, George Deines, to lend him $300 and promised to work as a waiter when he got to Lawrence. According to Kenny Dole, Deines lent him the $300 and presented it to him along with the

---

[7]Doran Dole maintained his cream and egg station until the late 1940s, when such stations gradually faded away in the face of competition from large companies and farms. Doran then became an employee of the Norris Grain Company, managing its grain elevator next door to his cream and egg station, until he retired.

advice to wear a hat because "guys who move up in the world always wore hats."

He went off to KU with his best friend, Bud Smith, sporting his fedora and wearing his suit. He joined a fraternity, worked as a waiter to earn his keep, and pursued pre-med undergraduate classes. He also tried out and made the team in football, basketball, and track, but found the competition at KU far keener than at Russell High School. "I realized I wasn't quite the athlete I thought I was," Dole later admitted. His performance drooped, both on the playing field and in the classroom. Unable to adjust to the reality that he was not the best, he became carefree, a mediocre student.

Track became his true love at KU, the individual achievement best suiting his own temperament. He came very close to breaking an indoor track record for the quarter-mile at the university, competing even harder than he had at Russell High and earning block letters for his college sweater. As high school coach George Baxter said, "Bob never competed in the easy track events." He went in for the 440- and 880-yard events and continued his pattern of jogging alone at 5:30 every morning.

To Bob Dole, running in the early morning mist of Lawrence in the fall of 1941, the war raging in Europe seemed a million miles away. As far as he could see, the future looked bright. He would sweep through KU and medical school and then become a respected and secure country doctor.

# 3

# "THAT DAMN ARMY ALMOST KILLED HIM"

On December 7, 1941, the intense, hard young man with the powerful legs who had come within an ace of breaking a Kansas University indoor track record was busy pursuing his own personal agenda when Japanese planes attacked U.S. naval forces at Pearl Harbor. The following day, President Franklin D. Roosevelt asked Congress for a declaration of war.

Half a world away, back in Lawrence, Kansas, KU freshman track star Bob Dole, who had never been seriously interested in politics, listened to these world-shaking events on the radio, between track-basketball-football practice sessions and classes.

In the Midwest, isolationist sentiment had always run very high, and long before the day of infamy there had been a widespread suspicion (with, it turned out, considerable justification) that FDR was secretly maneuvering to get the country into the war. Though his parents were Democrats and admirers of FDR, Dole had tasted a hefty menu of anti-Roosevelt sentiment in his youth and had heard the president referred to as "King Franklin" (a reference to Roosevelt's serving an unprecedented third term in office starting in 1941) and as a tool of socialism (a reference to his New Deal egalitarian programs) and other foreign "isms." Because FDR was so closely identified with the distant, "Eastern Establishment" government, he was a particular target of populist wrath in Kansas. The farmers who had suffered in the Dust Bowl and Depression had been very bitter toward FDR, and this animosity had extended to his foreign policy as well.

To the apolitical young Dole, who had never seen a mountain or an ocean, the war seemed far away indeed. Having lived all his life in homogeneous and insular Kansas, 1,500 miles from either coast, Dole was unconcerned by geopolitical realities and the storm raging in Europe and the Pacific. What mattered to him was something far more tangible and immediate: winning his letters in college sports and doing well in his premed studies, then going on to Kansas University Medical School and becoming a country a doctor, "so I'll always have a roof over my head and a floor under my feet."

Though self-centered and obsessed with beating the competition in sports and school, Dole was intensely patriotic. He had grown up in a town that would one day boast the largest lifetime VFW membership in the world and had provided one of the cofounders of the American Legion.[1] He had grown up hearing Woodrow Wilson's doughboys regaling Russell with tales of heroism, physical bravery, and "militarized athletics" on the European battlefields. His ears had perked up and his eyes had sparkled as he'd listened to glamorous tales of thrilling combat and all-important victory in World War I. He'd spent many nights on the prairie dreaming of the glory of fighting and wondering whether he would ever get the chance to prove his physical prowess on some distant battlefield.

Though his country had been suddenly thrust into a world war on two fronts, Dole's primary concern was still finishing his studies at KU. He stayed in school, finishing his freshman year in May 1942 and earning a creditable record in his premed studies, while thousands of boys his age were either enlisting in the armed forces

[1]Dean Banker's father, Waldo.

or being drafted. In the summer of 1942, nineteen-year-old Bob lived at home in Russell and worked odd jobs, preparing for his sophomore year at KU, but could hear the rumble of the Union Pacific passenger trains streaking past his house at night en route between coasts, carrying troops now as well as passengers in mufti, as the arsenal of democracy shifted into high gear for the war effort.

Bob was not doing well academically at KU. The dean called him into his office and told him, "You're not doing very well; you might be better off in the army." His words struck home.

Bob, who had been priding himself on being the only member of the Dole family to go to college, but who lacked sufficient motivation to truly excel in school, now realized he had to put his academic plans on ice. In the fall of 1942, Bob and his kid brother Kenny were convinced that they would be drafted by the army. With his fierce need to prove himself superior to everyone else in whatever he did, Bob was horrified at the thought of becoming a nameless nobody in the army, mixed in with the hoi polloi, the faceless masses of uneducated men of the U.S. war machine. The army would be a step down from KU, without doubt, unless Bob could rise above the mass of noncoms and become an officer.

Bob set out to find a way to serve the country as a gentleman officer. In his usual way of transforming apparent setbacks into personal victories, Bob saw a way of using the army as a means of furthering his medical training, by joining the medical corps.

In December 1942, while the ultimate outcome of the war was still very much in doubt, Bob enlisted in the U.S. Army's Enlisted Reserve Corps but spent the next six months finishing out his sophomore year at KU, far from the din of gunfire. Bob's kid brother, Kenny, also enlisted in the army, and the two were both called to duty in June 1943 and headed for army training in Texas.

The young, athletic gentleman-soldier who left Russell in the summer of 1943 would return three years later in a body cast, the withered shadow of a man destined to spend the rest of his life trying to recapture what he had left behind on that brilliant summer day. But this was the last thing on Bob's mind as he boarded the train and headed across the burning plains of Kansas and into the abyss of total war.

At first, the war seemed only a distant and far-off rumble. By the time Dole entered army training, the tide had already turned irreversibly against Hitler and his Japanese and Italian Axis partners. The great battles of Stalingrad, Moscow, and Midway had already taken place, and the ultimate outcome was in little doubt. Nonetheless, because of Roosevelt's insistence on unconditional surrender, and because of the fanatical and self-destructive obstinacy of the Axis warlords, there would be heavy fighting ahead for men like Dole, and he knew it. He would have chances to prove himself on the field of battle as he had in the playing fields of Russell and Lawrence.

Bob journeyed to Camp Barkley in Texas, where he trained for the Army Medical Corps, following in the footsteps of his father, who had been in the Army Medical Corps during World War I. After his stint at Camp Barkley, Bob went on to Brooklyn College in New York, studying engineering. Meanwhile, Kenny headed for the South Pacific, where he would remain for the war's duration.

In early 1944, Bob finished his classes at Brooklyn College, moved on to Camp Polk in Louisiana, and then trained as an antitank gunner at Kentucky's Fort Breckenridge. He then was accepted for Officer's Candidate School (OCS) and entered Fort Benning in Georgia with the rank of corporal.

Being in the Deep South for the first time in his life, Dole witnessed firsthand the crass discrimination being perpetrated against blacks. The strict segregation, ridiculing, and ostracizing of black Americans left an impression he would never forget. Forty years later, he could recall his feelings of disgust at seeing "nigras" getting catcalls, being kicked around and treated as subhumans. This was something he had never seen in Kansas, where blacks were a tiny part of the population and where redneck fever didn't run very high.

While Dole was training to become an officer, the Allies invaded Europe. On D-Day, June 6, 1944, the Allies launched the long-awaited second front under the unified supreme command of another Kansan Dole had heard much about—General Dwight David Eisenhower. By August, Paris had been liberated, the Third U.S. Army under General George Patton was driving across France, and a kind of festive, victorious spirit pervaded the U.S. Army as its forces tightened the noose on hapless Germany. On

July 20, in an assassination conspiracy, a group of German generals placed a bomb under Adolf Hitler's table, but the führer miraculously escaped death. With even the führer's own generals having turned against him, it seemed that the end of the war could not be far away.

Soon Rome was liberated, and the Germans retreated into the northern Italian mountains. Mussolini, having been deposed by his own Italians in 1943 and then reinstated by Hitler as a puppet, now directed shadow armies while the more fanatical Nazi troops continued to mount a fierce resistance to the Allies in the mountains.

Bob's OCS crash course training lasted three months, into the fall of 1944. On graduation from OCS as a second lieutenant, he found himself headed for Naples, Italy, on a troop ship that arrived shortly before Christmas. From Naples, Bob went to a replacement depot near Rome, where he awaited assignment to a combat unit.

It appeared for a while as if Dole might not see action. If the Germans collapsed, as seemed possible any day, the war might be over. Dole sat in the replacement pool like a juror sitting around waiting to be called for jury duty, awaiting assignment to replace some officer who had been killed or wounded.

He was a second lieutenant now, and he realized that in action second lieutenants held the most dangerous position of all, because they led their platoons into the thick of battle and were the most visible target to the enemy. "Second lieutenants were the real cannon fodder of World War II," says Al Nencioni, who was Dole's sergeant.

Dole got his chance to play second lieutenant for real on February 25, 1945, when he was assigned to I Company, Third Battalion, Eighty-Fifth Regiment, Tenth Mountain Division.

The Tenth Mountain Division, now fighting in the northern Apennine Mountains of Italy, was one of the most formidable fighting units in the U.S. Army. A year before Pearl Harbor, when Japan was menacing the Pacific and Germany was overrunning western Europe, the head of the National Ski Patrol, a man who was coincidentally named Charles Minot "Minnie" Dole (no relation to Bob) came up with the idea of establishing a unique elite army unit of mountain troops whose purpose would be to fight the Axis in places as diverse as Norway, Burma, and the Alps. Minnie Dole convinced the War Department to organize the mountain unit and began recruiting volunteers who were mostly experienced skiers and athletes, many of them from the ski slopes of New England, Utah, and Colorado.

One such recruit was Devereaux Jennings, a young skier from Utah who was destined to fight alongside Bob Dole in 1945 and was one of the first men to volunteer for the Mountain Division. Jennings emerged from the war unscathed and went on to compete in the 1948 Olympics. He has remained close to Dole since the war. In Bob's 1988 presidential campaign, he serves as national co-chairman of Veterans for Dole, a coalition of vets of all ages.

Al Nencioni, another soldier destined to fight alongside Dole, recalls that while still a high school student in his native Washington, D.C., "I saw a photograph of the ski troops on a Colorado mountain in *Parade* magazine in the *Washington Post*." Nencioni got the three letters of recommendation originally required and volunteered.

The mountain unit, originally called the Eighty-Seventh Regiment, first trained at Fort Harris, near Mount Rainier in the state of Washington, and then moved to Camp Hale in Colorado. The Eighty-Seventh Mountain Regiment eventually combined with the Eighty-Sixth and Eighty-Fifth and formed the Tenth Mountain Division, which arrived in Italy in late 1944.

The Tenth went into action in early 1945, in the Italian Apennines, and had just completed a successful battle against the Germans for Mount Belvedere when Bob Dole joined it as a replacement officer in late February 1945.

Dole was assigned to lead the second platoon of I Company and quickly found himself immersed in a highly motivated and potent unit, whose high morale seemed contagious. "We had the highest *esprit de corps* you could find," Nencioni recalls. "A lot of those guys were college guys; they'd been on their college skiing teams, including the captain of the Dartmouth skiing team. They had an *esprit de corps* from their school, and I think it just went right into the unit."

The men of I Company stood out in terms of both brawn and brains. "We had a lot of guys who were great big athletic, boxer types," says Nencioni, and they made Dole, who was then a second lieutenant, look almost "timid." Along with Jennings, another future Olympian, Ollie Manninen, was in the company, but there were also a lot of intelligent, college-educated athletes. "The first two regiments probably had the highest IQ of any infantry ever in the history of the army," Nencioni says. "They told us the regiment I was in had an [average] IQ of 122, which meant that everyone could go to OCS, but hardly any of them went because they wanted to stay enlisted."

Walt Galson, then an enlisted soldier who gave Dole a ride in his jeep, later remembered, "I was approached by an MP and told, 'Here's this young lieutenant fresh out of OCS; could you give him a lift?' He had only fuzz on his chin and seemed so young."

"He [Dole] came in as a replacement, which isn't easy," Dev Jennings recalls.[2] Jennings, who served directly under Dole as a sergeant in the Second Infantry platoon, and who was "very close" to Bob throughout his combat tour, recalls that the young Dole "started asking questions as soon as he got there. He really adapted himself and learned what was going on very quickly. He was always cool about things and very human. He never intimidated people or got outwardly tough. He was brave and very respected by the staff and the whole company. He was the best officer I ever had, he listened and really wanted to know what was going on. Before we made a move he'd call us up to come and take a look, and he'd show us what the plan was and make sure the communications were right and that we'd understood things."

From the time Dole joined the unit to the date on which he was wounded, April 14, I Company was "pretty much under fire all the time," Jennings says. Dole's troops were "subjected to artillery fire all night when you're in defensive positions and along ridges and when you're out on patrols. There wasn't any real time in between when it was 'sweet.' We didn't bivouac, we just lay there in the hole [at night]." I Company served as the spearhead of attack,

[2]According to Jennings, I Company began in early 1945 with 6 officers, 188 enlisted men, and 3 medics. By the time the company finished off the Germans in early May 1945, it had received the following replacements: 5 officers (including Dole), 181 enlisted men, and 4 medics—striking evidence of a huge casualty rate.

the forward troops who always pushed ahead of the rest of the army, often encountering Germans ensconced in dugouts on the sides of the rugged mountains.

Al Nencioni,[3] who handled mortars in the platoons, recalls Dole as a particularly brave officer who showed no hesitation in charging into combat. Nencioni and the other troops found they could trust Dole and rely on his judgment and bravery, "right down to the nitty-gritty. I'd rather have this guy [Dole] lead than a company of these other type of guys," Nencioni says to this day. Dole seemed to fit in well with the troops. "I think some of our *esprit de corps* rubbed off on him," Nencioni explains.

Nencioni's and Jennings's account of Dole as a courageous troop leader who asked a lot of questions and listened to make sure he understood everything that was going on presaged Dole's later behavior in the Senate, when he would seek to understand every detail of bills under discussion.

Dole's leadership qualities were an important ingredient in the Tenth Mountain Division's relentless drive to mop up the tail end of Hitler troops still clinging desperately to the mountains of northern Italy. The Tenth became legendary for never giving up a foot of ground it had captured and for being willing to sustain severe casualties in order to achieve its objectives. This relentless "Damn the torpedoes—full steam ahead!" quality paralleled Dole's own personality throughout his life. Dole would remain intensely loyal to the Tenth for the rest of his life, attending reunions forty years after the end of the war.

Despite the fact that they went into combat during the last four months of the war, Dole's unit saw some of the fiercest fighting in the European theater. "The battalion lost between 60 and 70 percent of the men," Nencioni recalls. Dole himself was slightly wounded in the leg in March and earned a purple heart, but he went right on fighting, leading his platoon as the Tenth launched Operation Craftsman, a massive assault on German positions in the Po Valley.

[3]Nencioni, who would suffer a concussion shortly after Dole's injury, went on to become an FBI agent for twenty-six years. Operating out of the Washington field office, he frequently visited with Dole during the latter's congressional tenure in the 1960s. A talented musician and composer, Nencioni won a music performance prize in Italy after the end of the war and went on to compose the FBI March.

In the early hours of April 14, 1945, a day that would be a turning point in Dole's life, American bombers began dumping their bombs over a German-held area not far from Bologna, in the hills along the Pra del Bianco valley.

Postponed for two days because of bad weather, the massive U.S. asssault was now about to begin in full fury. Dole and his platoon had camped along the ridge of a mountain during the night, when they received reinforcements. Their objective, on the morning of April 14, was to cross the valley and storm the German-held Hill 913, about a thousand yards away. Mines, concealed along the valley, posed a major hazard to the troops.

U.S. planes blasted the area with bombs until "the hill looked like a cloud of smoke filled with dust," according to Nencioni. "We didn't think it would be too bad, so we took off," he adds.

Dev Jennings, Dole's sergeant, recalls that "we jumped off at about 10:30 or 11:00 in the morning, on the front side under very heavy fire."

"Our objective [that day] was to go three miles," Nencioni recalls. The troops moved into the mine-loaded valley. "There was a hedgerow and other obstacles in the way," Al says. "When we got there, we were met with heavy artillery, machine-gun and sniper fire," says Jennings, who was leading his own squad to the right of Dole's unit when Dole's "got into trouble."

It was an ambush. The Nazis threw everything they had at the Yanks—machine guns, rifles, mortars, even a "rocket that was the first I'd ever seen," says Jennings. "It looked like a cigar."

Dole says he was filled with "raw anger" and a "protective instinct" for his comrades as he saw them go down like tenpins. He spotted a farmhouse near the base of Hill 913 from which Nazi gunfire crackled. According to technical sergeant Frank Carafa, the original orders called for Carafa to lead the men across the clearing while Dole was supposed to remain behind. But in his thirst for action, according to Carafa, Dole altered the orders and personally led a squad of men toward the enemy gunfire.

In the din of the assault, Dole saw his radioman go down, killed by German bullets. Dole hauled the radioman back into a hole, then charged out again when something suddenly hit Dole in the back and right shoulder.

"He was hit twice, I believe," Nencioni says. To this day, no one has ever determined exactly what hit Bob, whether it was bullets or mortar fragments. Dole went down.

Platoon sergeant Stanley Kuschick[4] ran to Sergeant Jennings, shouting, "The lieutenant's been hit!" Kuschick ordered Jennings to lead his squad to Dole's left flank, where help was badly needed.

According to Nencioni, Kuschick administered a shot of morphine to Dole, and then "he took Bob Dole's blood and made a big 'M' on his forehead, so nobody would give him any more morphine" (thereby preventing a dangerous overdose). Dole "didn't look good," Kuschick told Nencioni at the time, adding that he didn't know whether Dole would "make it or not."

The prevailing myth seems to be that Bob was left for dead or abandoned by his troops, and combat troops are trained to keep driving forward toward their objective and to leave the killed and wounded behind. But Kuschick ignored these rules and ordered a soldier who had been shot in the leg to stay with the fallen Dole until help arrived. Nencioni says, "Because our objective was three miles out, we had to keep going. So, in that sense, he [Dole] was 'abandoned.' "

The platoon, without Dole, made it to the top of Hill 913 that night, wondering what had become of its fallen lieutenant. It would not see him again until long after the end of the war.

The Tenth Mountain Division pushed on to crush the Germans and bring about the surrender of the Italian front commander at the Brenner Pass on May 2, 1945. According to Nencioni, the German commander, who had seen action on the eastern and western and Italian fronts, stated that the Tenth Mountain Division "was the best division he'd ever faced."

As for the wounded Dole, April 14 turned out to be an excruciatingly long and agonizing day. He lay alone on the battlefield in a semiconscious stupor, unable to feel his legs or arms, miles from any medical facility. As his whole past life raced before his mind's eye, he claims to have "seen" his dog, his parents, and childhood friends.

He might well have died that night had it not been for a wonder-

---

[4]Kuschick emerged from the war unscathed and returned to his father's chicken farm in New Jersey, eventually to become mayor of a New Jersey township.

ful stroke of luck. As dusk set in, a twenty-five-year-old U.S. Army private named Bill Roberts spotted him. Roberts, whose detail was about to march down a winding ten-mile road to an ambulance pickup spot, was leading seven German prisoners. He spotted Dole, noticed the red *M* on his forehead, and checked for signs of life. Dole was still breathing but paralyzed (two of his vertebrae had been crushed, and his right arm was a mangled, bloody mess).

Private Roberts ordered two German prisoners to carry Dole on a litter down the mountain road. Once, the small detail was shelled by the enemy. Later, a U.S. tank driver saw the Germans carrying the litter, thought they were enemy troops, and ordered his tank crew to fire. Roberts barely managed to countermand the order by identifying himself, and Dole's life was miraculously spared. Finally, Roberts's detail inched its way to the ambulance rendezvous, and Dole was driven to a medical aid station. "I think Jesus was with us that night," Roberts said forty years later when he learned for the first time that the nameless young lieutenant he had brought down the mountain on a litter that night was in fact Bob Dole.

Dole was treated at an army evacuation hospital and transported to a base hospital at Casablanca, Morocco. Dole's parents were informed of their son's injuries in a chilling telegram sent to them in Russell, by J. A. Ulio, the adjutant general, which stated:

THE SECRETARY OF WAR DESIRES ME TO EXPRESS HIS DEEP REGRET THAT YOUR SON 2LT DOLE ROBERT J WAS SERIOUSLY WOUNDED IN ITALY 14 APRIL 1945 PERIOD HOSPITAL SENDING YOU NEW ADDRESS.

Bob dictated letters to his parents from his hospital bed. A month later he was shipped to Florida in a body cast, "like furniture in a crate," as he would later recall.

After a brief stay at a Florida army hospital, a hospital train bore him home to Kansas, and he was admitted to the Winter General Hospital in Topeka. When his parents arranged to bring him home for a brief stay, the entire town was on hand to greet the wounded hero.

"He looked like someone who had just come out of Dachau,"

*U.S. Army telegram received by Doran Dole on May 3, 1945, notifying him that his son had been seriously wounded in Italy. (Courtesy of Russell Townsley and Kenny Dole.)*

said Bub Dawson, one of his Russell friends. The strapping young athlete who had been a "magnificent physical specimen" at 190 pounds when he had left Russell two years earlier had come back a shrunken invalid weighing only 120 pounds. To those who had known him as the fierce competitor, always running, he was a pathetic sight. And yet something about the young soldier's attitude did not jibe with his deplorable physical condition. He had a positive mental attitude, a cheery outlook that amazed practically everyone who saw him.

Back at Winter General Army Hospital, Dole faced long months of painful recovery. "That damn army almost killed him," Bub Dawson would later recall. Kenny added, "They kept him in that body cast, didn't even bother to move him at all, so the sulfa drugs they gave him crystallized in his kidney, and he lost the kidney."

Bob developed a severe infection in his kidney. The infection spread, and his temperature rose to 108.7 degrees. "I remember going to visit him in his hospital room," Kenny Dole recalls. "He was so badly infected, his arms hung out over the sides of his bed, and the pus dripped from under his fingernails and into buckets they had on the floor."

The doctors told Bob's mother he had only a few hours to live, and his life literally hung in the balance even more precariously than it had upon first being wounded two and a half months earlier. Bina rented an apartment near Winter Hospital to be near her son and visited him night and day, giving him encouragement as his life hung on by a string.

On July 11, 1945, doctors operated to remove Bob's right kidney, which had developed kidney stones as well as infection and crystallization of the sulfa drugs. Amazingly, Bob recovered from his surgery, but he never forgot nor forgave the army for its neglect and insouciance.

In the meantime, the army gave Dole what he later called a "bedpan promotion" to captain. He began to recover, and each day his mother helped him relearn to walk, though it was many months before he could stand up without assistance.

As has happened to so many wounded and crippled war veterans, the bedridden Dole found himself haunted by the question "Why me?" As he admitted more than forty years later, his faith was shaken as he found himself wondering "if anyone was looking out for me up there. With only three weeks left in the war, why did I have to get hit?"[5]

Bob himself later described this period as a time when he was "completely helpless . . . I couldn't feed myself for almost a year or do anything with my hands." He required assistance even to go to the bathroom and to dress, and when he got the first real look at himself in a mirror since he'd been wounded, he was shocked at his appearance. So intense was his traumatic reaction that even forty-three years later he says he still has trouble looking in the mirror. His brother Kenny quoted Bob as vowing to "get back the ten years he lost" because of his injury, by living extra hard and driv-

---

[5]Forty-three years later, when he looked back at his extraordinarily productive life, Dole felt that "someone up there maybe had a plan for me, had something else in mind for me." David Frost's interview with Dole on ABC-TV's "The Next President," January 3, 1988.

ing himself with all the more determination and by fighting the specter of "dependence."

In the army hospital, Bob's bitterness toward his doctors—"the experts," as he would derisively refer to them—was compounded when they told him he would remain a cripple for life. He rejected their professional opinion, and for years he refused to believe that he would never regain full use of his limbs. Still quite helpless as 1945 drew to a close, however, Bob was moved from the Topeka hospital to faraway Percy Jones Army Medical Center in Battle Creek, Michigan, in November. The hospital, bursting with 11,000 patients, was a major amputation, orthopedic, and neurosurgery center.[6]

Shipped in his plaster body cast, Bob arrived at Percy Jones, where he would remain for the next two and a half years. Whether this move from Topeka to Battle Creek was medically sound or necessary is dubious. Certainly, it could not have helped his morale, for it took him far away from his parents and friends in Kansas, particularly from his mother, Bina, who had practically moved in with him in Topeka's hospital.

Just before Christmas 1945, Bob developed a dangerous pulmonary infarct, leading to severe chest pains. Menacing blood clots, which easily could have killed him, developed, and dicumarol was administered to dissolve the clots. The doctors insisted on total inactivity and then inexplicably and abruptly terminated the dicumarol treatment.

The consequences of this decision were nearly fatal. Without dicumarol, Bob developed a severe infection, producing a 106-degree fever. Penicillin failed, and Dole would have died had it not been for a new, experimental antibiotic called *streptomycin*. Because the new wonder drug was considered dangerous and had been administered only to a tiny number of people up to that time, Dole's parents had to consent to its use. They did so, and the drug saved Dole's life.

While streptomycin saved Bob's life, there would be no medical miracle to restore strength to his atrophied, virtually useless limbs.

---

[6]Dole's ex-wife, Phyllis, says that Bob was also treated at Hines Army Hospital near Chicago during this time, but Dole has never mentioned this. Hines has since shut down.

For the next two years, Bob exerted the utmost willpower in a daily struggle to regain mastery of his body.

Initially put in traction, he advanced to a wheelchair and then tried to struggle to his feet. Falling often, he disdained assistance and tried to pick himself up—a discipline of extreme self-reliance that would carry through to his Senate years, when he tried to do everything by himself and kept aides at an arm's length.

When he wasn't struggling to walk, Dole occupied himself with tasks as diverse as reading everything from Plato to military history, selling cars to fellow patients (for a commission), and making up jokes for them as he was wheeled around to various wards to cheer them up. Dole's keen comedian's talent, impressive in Russell before the war, was now honed to a razor's edge. Humor became his antidote to the grim realities of his physical condition and a shield to camouflage his true feelings.

Dole's brother Kenny believes Bob's fierce drive also was further developed at this time, as the result of his struggle against falling back into helplessness. "He just can't stop; he can't slip back at anything in life," Kenny says. "He won't dare wear a clip-on tie or loafers, he won't let others do things for him, because he knows that if he ever stopped, it'd all be downhill, and he'd wind up where he started," in the grip of dependence and humiliation. Even while serving as U.S. senator or running for president, Dole would always act instinctively, shunning assistance and refusing to delegate tasks to his staff. This extreme self-reliance would become both his strength and his weakness. It would make him a "one-man band," reluctant to delegate and trust his aides.

In 1946, as the months of his convalescence dragged on, Dole spent the long, lonely days at the hospital exercising in a desperate campaign to strengthen his once-muscular track star's legs, learning to dress by himself, to eat, and to write with his left hand. At first, it took him half an hour to button a shirt and even longer to knot a necktie or tie a shoelace. Gradually, he shortened the time necessary to perform these tasks and challenged himself by playing a little game: each day, he would mark down the number of minutes it took to perform a task, then try to beat his own record by shortening the time, progressively. The game rekindled his competitive energies, and he pretended that he was "competing against another guy. If I hadn't tried," I heard him say thirty years later, "I'd still be in a wheelchair now, drawing disability."

While he regained the use of his legs and left arm and hand (though the fingers of his left are partially numb to this day), his shattered right arm and shoulder remained physically grotesque and useless. The muscles in his arm and shoulder had atrophied horrendously, and he was intensely uncomfortable about his appearance, with a useless fragment of an arm hanging from his shoulder.

A less determined or vain man might have been content to carry his arm in a sling for the rest of his life, but Dole demanded that the army operate on his right limb in the hope that it could be fully repaired, feeling that the country owed him at least that much after what he had been put through in the army hospitals. The same Dole who would later object to being photographed wearing eyeglasses (which he occasionally used for reading) now shuddered at the thought of going through life as a deformed, one-armed man.

When the army rejected his request, Dole refused to give up. With the characteristic thoroughness that would mark his later years, he began making the rounds among the patients, asking each one whether he'd heard of any doctors who might be able to perform an appropriate operation on the arm. He struck gold: a patient named Bill Eilert (injured in Okinawa) had heard of a Dr. Hampar Kelikian in Chicago, a surgeon who might be able to help.

Dole's uncle made contact with people who knew Kelikian, an Armenian immigrant who had risen from poverty to become one of the nation's top surgeons. Out of sympathy for Dole's condition and a sense of obligation to his adopted country, Kelikian volunteered to operate on Dole without charging any fee.

The Chicago hospital was less generous. It told Dole that he would have to pay a hospital fee of about $1,800, and Dole had no money. At this point, the people of Russell, Kansas, poured out their souls and their coins. The Russell VFW post started a "Bob Dole fund" drive to raise the hospital fee money from local citizens. A cigar box was placed on the counter of Dawson's Drug Store, and some people contributed $100, others a few dimes.

The cigar box drive raised the fee, enabling Dole to go to Chicago in 1947 for three operations, which left him with partial use of

---

*Phone*
OFFICE 404; RESIDENCE 1396

RICHARD M. DRISCOLL
ATTORNEY AT LAW

RUSSELL, KANSAS

July 18, 1947

BOB DOLE DONATIONS

| | |
|---|---|
| Dick Driscoll | $ 5.00 |
| Al Peterson | 1.00 |
| Earl McConigly | 1.00 |
| Ted Steinle | 5.00 |
| Bobbie Lyons | 1.00 |
| George Brandt | 1.00 |
| Gene Rouse | 1.00 |
| Margarett McGee | 1.00 |
| Rozella Fox | 1.00 |
| Ralph Ewing | 1.00 |
| Clem Werth | 1.00 |
| Mae Voltz | 1.00 |
| Judge J. D. Steinle | 1.00 |
| Art Dawson | 1.00 |
| Pearle L. Comer | 1.00 |
| Art Turner | 1.00 |
| Lester A. Brannum | 1.00 |
| Ralph Sellens | 1.00 |
| John Hildebrandt & Wife | 2.00 |
| N. Mills | 1.00 |
| Ford Deines | 1.00 |

*When Dole needed rehabilitative surgery in 1947, hundreds of donors in Russell contributed $1,800. Dole never forgot this hometown generosity. (Courtesy of Russell Townsley.)*

his right arm. He could now hold a piece of paper or a pencil in his right hand, but he would never be able to write with it. For many years, he had difficulty controlling his right arm; it would sink to his side, so he would have to reach over with his left hand and lift it back up. It now remains permanently frozen at his waist; he cannot lift it on its own power. His right hand is permanently gnarled.

The generosity of the people of his hometown affected Dole deeply, as was clear from his show of emotion that would interrupt his 1976 campaign-launching speech in Russell with President Ford at his side.

Dole would also be forever grateful to Kelikian for the "miracle" operation that enabled him to feel, at least, "sort of whole again." Kelikian, too, kept in touch. When Dole married the following year, the Armenian surgeon sent him a telegram: USE THAT ARM I FIXED LOVINGLY.

Later, Dole had to go back to the hospital for a repair job on his arm, and he experienced severe pain for years, but in terms of physical appearance the operation was a stunning success.

For many years, Dole remained self-conscious about his withered arm and studiously avoided discussing his feelings about it. But in 1983, when Kelikian died, those suppressed feelings came gushing forth in a mighty torrent. On the Senate floor he delivered a moving eulogy to the man who had fixed his arm. Midway through his speech, however, he was overcome with emotion and had to leave the Senate chamber, unable to continue.

According to his brother, Kenny, it turned out that Kelikian "took care of" all the hospital fees and Bob returned the $1,800 to the local VFW post. Kenny says that the citizens of Russell then decided to apply the money to a "Chevrolet especially made for Bob, with a gear stick on the left," which a local welder and car buff had pieced together. Townsley says he saw Dole driving around in a car but remembers it as an Oldsmobile, one of those that he sold.

This touching story was a fit ending to the most traumatic period of Dole's life. The young man abandoned by the army had come home to open arms in Russell. For the rest of his life, Dole would remain a man who could rightfully say, as he once did to me, "I live and work in Washington, but my home is in Russell."

# 4
# THE MAN WITH THE WITHERED ARM

After his three operations, Dole returned to the Percy Jones Army Medical Center in Battle Creek at the end of 1947 to finish his long convalescence. By this time, he had been presented with a second Purple Heart for his injury in combat and with a Bronze Star with Clusters for heroism and bravery under fire, and had been promoted to captain.

By a curious twist of fate, in the hospital Dole found himself in the company of two other wounded servicemen who would join him in the U.S. Senate twenty years later—Daniel K. Inouye of Hawaii (who lost an arm in the war) and Philip A. Hart of Michigan, for whom the Hart Senate Office Building, housing Dole's office, is named.

As he lay in his hospital bed, day after day, Dole pondered what kind of a future he had now, with one good arm and a precarious medical condition, a college education half completed, his early dream of becoming a doctor forever shattered.

"You think nobody could have it worse than you, why did God do it to me," he recalled many years later. "I didn't do anything, it's unfair. . . . You think, 'I'm never going to get married, never going to amount to anything. Might live off a pension.' You change the way you measure everything. Life becomes a matter of learning how to use what you have left."

"What he had left was his head," his brother Kenny recalls. In a phrase he often repeated to explain his seemingly impulsive actions, Bob said of this period, "You have to make a decision," and he made that decision with the savage intensity and tenacity that would mark his entire career. He resolved to compensate for his physical deficiencies by "running at 110 percent," to race by "at seventy-five miles per hour while everyone else was doing fifty-five."

From his hospital bed, the young man who had aspired to be a track star now watched some of his comrades from the Tenth Mountain Division competing in the 1948 Olympic Games. Men such as Devereaux Jennings, who had been his platoon sergeant, were now Olympic stars, while Dole was a semi-invalid. Now that Dole could no longer excel in sports, politics was a perfect outlet for his stifled but ferocious competitive drive.

Meanwhile, in the White House, another acerbic small-town midwesterner, "Give 'Em Hell" Harry Truman, standing his ground against the interests and running for reelection against overwhelming odds, served as a role model for Dole. Bina and Doran, staunch Democrats, admired the "Little Man" from Independence, Missouri, who talked like them and whose hometown was less than 300 miles from Russell. Truman was living proof that a small-town boy from the heartland could make it to the big time. Bob Dole watched him with admiration and was inspired by his example.

As his health improved and he faced discharge from the army and the hospital, Bob was uneasy about going back home, where he might be tempted to let others do things for him and where he would be pitied because of his handicap. Though he appreciated his family and townspeople, he wanted neither their pity nor their help. He wanted to make it on his own.

Early in 1948, Dole made two decisions that would help lift him out of the hospital bed: to look for a wife and to run off to faraway Arizona to complete his college education.

With characteristic determination, he started casting around for a wife, appearing at social functions at the Officers Club in Battle Creek while still at the hospital. One day, he spotted a young occupational therapist named Phyllis Holden and asked her to dance. A rather plump, modest-looking woman who held a bachelor's degree from the University of New Hampshire, Phyllis had been working in the psychiatric ward of the Percy Jones Medical Center (Bob was never a patient of hers). She hailed from a Concord, New Hampshire, upper-middle-class family and therefore was socially a cut above Bob.

Dole, who had shown hardly any interest in dating back in Russell, decided that marrying Phyllis would be a step up and would provide him companionship in his move to Arizona. Within a few weeks, he asked for her hand and she agreed. They were married June 12, 1948, a bare three months after meeting.

The wedding took place in Phyllis's hometown, at the Episcopal church attended by the bride's family. Phyllis recalls that the only member of Bob's family to attend was Bina. The newlyweds honeymooned at Lake Winnipesaukee, New Hampshire.

After his marriage, Bob arranged for his discharge with what the army called a "total and permanent disability." He began receiving a veteran's disability pension (which he still receives) and financial assistance on the GI Bill for his college work.

In the fall of 1948, Bob and his new bride took the train across the prairie and into the deserts of the Southwest. In Tucson, Arizona, he enrolled as a junior at the University of Arizona, prepared to finish the college work he had begun at Kansas University seven years earlier, and once again resolved to become the first member of his family to get a college degree.

Phyllis worked in occupational therapy (her specialty being psychiatry) and helped pay the rent. Contrary to subsequent myth, she did not regularly attend classes with Bob. "I attended classes only occasionally," she told me, "and only showed up to write his exams, as he dictated them to me, if the professor didn't allow him to take oral exams. But usually they let him take orals."

Exhibiting vehement self-reliance, Dole went to classes alone, armed with a so-called sound-scriber machine, a heavy box with two little plastic records, obtained from the Veterans Administration. He sat in a chair near a wall, plugged his sound-scriber into the socket, and recorded all of the professors' lectures. At night, he played the records and meticulously took notes on the lectures with his left hand. "It would take him hours to transcribe all the notes each night," Phyllis recalls, "because he couldn't write very fast, and he wasn't naturally left-handed." He was a fanatical student who studied every night into the wee hours.

"He set goals for himself in every class," Phyllis says. "He always had to get A's. Once, while he was studying German, I asked him, 'Why do you have to get all A's?' He answered, 'You tell me how to study a B or C's worth and I will. . . . I gotta study until I get it all.' " One is reminded of the little game Dole played in the army hospitals when he would try to beat his own record time in performing a set task ("indoor track competition," he later called this).

For Dole, then as later, winning meant beating the competition *on your own*. He bristled at the thought of leaning on his wife—or anyone else. Indeed, one of the reasons he had chosen to attend the University of Arizona was to be as far away as possible from anyone he might be tempted to lean on.

The other reason, according to Phyllis, was that he felt the warm desert climate of Tucson would be more comfortable for his left hand, which was still sporadically numb. He was also suffering from severe pain off and on.

Yet he drove himself to the limit and beyond, not only in studying but also in running. He ran for miles and miles in the afternoons, trying to beat his own records for the longest distance run in the shortest time, and as he had as a teenager, he ran alone. He showed no interest in student government or any of the social functions that preoccupied most other students. He generally kept to himself, a good student with a peculiar taste for running hard and alone.

According to Phyllis, Bob was hoping to enter law school in the Southwest, but the University of Arizona had no law school at the time. It did offer Arizona residents a reciprocal law school education at the University of New Mexico, but since Dole was not an Arizona resident, he was ineligible for this program. Once again, society had shut the door to success in his face, and he was furious.

By the spring of 1949, the young Kansan faced the prospect of returning home if he wanted to go to law school, just when he had grown accustomed to the haunting desert mountain scenery and the climate of Arizona. He had set himself the goal of going into politics and resented the bureaucratic mentality of the university, which banned him from law school and seemed as unreasonable and unfair as the army medical bureaucracy he had fought against during the previous three years.

Frustrated, he ran harder into the desert winds, which Phyllis believes to be the reason why blood clots began reappearing in his lungs. That spring he was forced to check into a Veterans Administration hospital in Tucson, where he was subjected to a battery of blood tests and given medication to thin his blood. The problem, a recurrence of the lung obstruction that had nearly killed him in the army hospital in Michigan, made his future all the more uncertain. This time, however, his hospital stay was relatively brief, and he emerged from Arizona feeling like a carpetbagger and returned to Kansas in the summer of 1949.

His lung and blood problems persisted, and he was obliged to bypass Kansas University because there was no medical lab in Lawrence sophisticated enough to give him the ongoing blood tests he needed. The only Kansas city that had both a lab and a college was Topeka, says Phyllis, so Dole headed there. He enrolled at Washburn Municipal University in the fall of 1949 and pursued a program aimed at securing a joint bachelor's and law degree by 1952.

Dole's forced move to Topeka turned out to be a blessing in disguise. Had he stayed in Tucson or gone to law school at Lawrence, Dole would have been an obscure student, struggling with hundreds of other would-be politicians in a crowded pool, further disadvantaged because of his modest social background and lack of money. But in Topeka, the state capital of Kansas, he stumbled into a political gold mine.

During Dole's first year at Washburn, 1949–50, America was embroiled in an anticommunist hysteria that swept the country like wildfire. Following Truman's upset reelection victory over Thomas Dewey in 1948, the president had found himself on the receiving end of a savage political assault by the right, which accused the Democratic Party of losing China to the Communists

and of giving away half of Europe to Joseph Stalin. The Soviet
Union had exploded its first atomic bomb and imposed the Berlin
Blockade, initiating the Cold War. Truman had countered by announcing the program of foreign aid called the Truman Doctrine,
and young right-wing Republicans like Richard Nixon were earning a name for themselves in Washington by blasting the "party of
treason" in sensational hearings of the House Un-American Activities Committee.

In the Midwest, anticommunist hysteria ran high, with Republican senator Joseph McCarthy of Wisconsin announcing to the
world that he had a list of hundreds of "card-carrying communists" working in the State Department and other government
agencies. As McCarthy ranted about communists in Washington, a
whole army of communists invaded South Korea, and the belea-
guered Truman ordered U.S. troops into action in that far corner
of the world in the summer of 1950.

The president's approval ratings in the polls plummeted to an
all-time low of 26 percent as the unpopular war raged on in stalemate and McCarthy-Nixon Republicans shouted "treason" in
Washington.

As Dole later put it, 1950 "was not a very good year to be a
Democrat," especially in a state like Kansas, where Republicans
held a two-to-one majority in voter registration and elected officials.

The ambitious law student who had his own ideas about the
incompetence of the government and the army listened excitedly in
Topeka and Russell to the seasoned Kansas politicians lambasting
the Democrats. He was neutral in the war of words—possibly
because of indecision, possibly because his parents were Democrats and supporters of Truman, and he feared offending them.

John Woelk, who was Russell county attorney from 1949 to 1953
and a Republican, was looking for a good man to challenge incumbent Democrat Elmo J. Mahoney for the seat in the Kansas House
of Representatives, representing Russell County in the Eighty-
First District. Since the Kansas legislature met in Topeka, and
since Dole was a law student there and a war hero with an interesting past, Woelk and several other Republicans tried to recruit him
as a candidate.

"I didn't know back then whether he [Dole] was a liberal or a conservative," Woelk would say thirty-seven years later, "and I still don't know, and I don't think he knows, either."[1] Nonetheless, because Dole, with his cigar box fund-raiser and his war record, had already become a Russell legend, it seemed logical to Woelk and his friends to back Bob. "Besides," Woelk noted, "he needed the money, and the legislature does pay something," although that salary was small.

The Republicans were not the only ones seeking to recruit Dole. A Democratic law librarian who had seen the young man studying often and hard suggested he run as a Democrat, and she was joined by several colleagues in what Dole later called a "tug of war" for his political soul.

Urged from both sides and figuring that politics had cost him his arm and ten years of his life, he resolved to go into politics in order to get back what had been taken from him. All those acrimonious statements that he would later utter—"All wars this century have been Democrat wars"; "the Democrats had a plan for curing unemployment . . . sending half a million young boys to South Vietnam"—would spring from his equating war with politics.

In making the most momentous political decision of his life—which party to join—Dole was ultimately swayed by the most pragmatic consideration: "As John Woelk told me," Dole later recalled, "there are a lot more Republicans than Democrats in Russell County." Then, as later, pragmatism and a desire to win determined his conduct.

Sensing that this was no time to run as a Democrat and knowing that Russell County and Kansas GOP voters outnumbered Democrats two to one, Dole agreed to run as a Republican. "It didn't take much persuasion to get Bob to run," Woelk recalls. "Whenever it came to running, he was more than willing. He enjoyed campaigning" and would launch into the task on a nonstop basis, working night and day.

Dole's immediate and wholehearted embrace of the Republican

---

[1]Woelk, who still lives in Russell, told me, "Bob doesn't have any strong philosophical beliefs; he's a practical politician." He added that Bob was "very good in dealing with people; he knew how to handle people."

Party served as a blueprint for his later instant conversions to a wide variety of positions in Washington. Though initially shy, he rapidly distinguished himself on the hustings as a fiery, partisan speaker. He energetically defended his newfound party in a manner that struck observers as fanatical. "I think he was so partisan because he was trying to prove his loyalty to the Republican Party, because his parents were Democrats, and everyone [in Russell] knew they were Democrats," Woelk told me in 1987.

Apart from needing to disown his parents' party affiliation, Dole felt compelled to campaign as hard as he did for the same reason he had to get all *A*s: he simply could not stomach the thought of losing and feared that any loss would be demoralizing and would take him back to where he had started, lying on a hospital bed with no future, drawing disability, "selling pencils on the street corner." Haunted by the specter of total helplessness, which he equated with any defeat, Dole campaigned like a man who *had* to win, a man for whom there would be no tomorrows and for whom the stakes were all or nothing.

His Democratic opponent, incumbent Elmo J. Mahoney, was a colorful homespun character with a great gift of gab. But Dole won the seat from the Eighty-First District by 2,576 to 1,803 votes and became one of 125 representatives in Kansas's lower house (105 Republicans and 20 Democrats).

In the official handbook of the Kansas legislature for Dole's first term, 1951–52, Dole appears strikingly boyish in his photograph. He is surrounded by pictures of his colleagues, virtually all of whom look old enough to be his father or grandfather. The youngest member of the legislature at age twenty-seven, he again found himself playing the role of outsider, the boy among older men.

Then, as later, Dole compiled an outstanding attendance record in the legislature as well as in the classroom, making certain he was present for all key votes and debates, no matter how obscure the bill or the issue. "The legislature was in session only three months of each year," Phyllis recalls, "and they met only in the mornings, when they met at all. . . . Bob arranged to take his classes at Washburn University in the afternoons so he could attend the legislature in the mornings."

He saw the legislature as a "do-nothing, part-time debating

club" and showed no interest in running for another term in 1952, when he graduated *magna cum laude* from Washburn with his bachelor's and law degrees.

Just as Dole graduated, another Kansan was being nominated by the GOP for president of the United States. Dwight D. Eisenhower of Abilene was now the top Republican in the country and virtually certain to win the election in November against the hapless Democratic candidate Adlai Stevenson. Like Dole, Ike had no prior affiliation with either political party and had been selected as an "instant Republican" because of his war record. Just as he had been inspired by the Little Man from Independence, Dole was inspired by the Kansas farm boy from Abilene, whose prominence was another good omen for his own political future.

Armed with his law degree, Dole returned home to Russell, where he hoped to promote his career. On his first day back in Russell, Dole rented a new office and hung up his shingle. "I remember it was a very modest office," recalled Eric "Doc" Smith, another young Russell lawyer, who formed a law partnership with Dole and then became a judge. "The first thing Dole did was to go out and buy a magnificent, very expensive chair that he put in his little office. I was struck by the fact that it looked like a hundred-dollar saddle on a ten-dollar horse."

What type of man would buy a hundred-dollar saddle for a ten-dollar horse? The type of man who wanted to impress people, the type of man who, as a penniless college student eleven years earlier, had worn a hat because he had been told that anyone who wanted to move up in the world had to wear a hat. "Dole ran his law office to *please people*," John Woelk recalls. "He wanted to be liked, to impress."

An obsession with making a good appearance extended to his clothing as well. He wanted to be the sharpest dresser of all, the man who would stand out far from the competition. The adulation he had once craved and received as a high school athlete he now eagerly sought as a sharply dressed attorney. He would stand for hours while a chubby German tailor at Banker's clothing store measured him, specially altered his suits with padding on the right shoulder to conceal his withered arm, and otherwise created a perfect fit. "The tailor would mumble, '*ja, ja*' " Dean Banker recalls, "and Bob would stand there for hours, insisting that every inch of the suit was a perfect fit."

Bob's vanity and sensitivity about his appearance extends to his face. In a photograph taken with several young lawyers and politicians on Russell's Main Street in 1952, he was caught wearing eyeglasses—for the first and last time. He avoids wearing glasses in public, slipping them into his pocket at the approach of a photographer.

Camouflaging his crippled right arm, about which he was acutely sensitive, probably was, and is, what lay behind his concern with physical appearance. In the same 1952 photograph, Dole can be seen with his right hand in his pocket, a ploy that worked only to a point. When a stranger offered to shake his right hand, Dole would wince uncomfortably as he held out his left hand, thumb down.

Eventually, he developed various other tactics, such as holding a pencil or paper or a very light briefcase in his right hand. Al Nencioni, his old army buddy who visited him in his congressional office in the early 1960s, recalls seeing Dole carrying a little briefcase or pencil even in his own office. And I cannot recall any time when I worked for him when he did not have something in the hand, even with his own staff. The camouflage tactics had become a habit.

Phyllis played an important part in helping Dole live with his handicap. She tried to help him feel human and whole, rather than like some Captain Hook figure. "Probably the most important thing I did," Phyllis said, "was not treating him as handicapped but treating him as normal. I knew when to ask if he needed help, when not to. . . . I think what it has to do with is not pressuring him to help him. To perhaps notice if he needs a little bit of assistance and do it quietly without making an issue of it."

Phyllis remembered most vividly how difficult it was for Dole to shake hands with his left hand. "That took courage," she noted, "to shake hands and have people notice that he couldn't shake hands with his right hand."

One of the most embarrassing moments came when Dole tried to cut steak one night at a restaurant. Because he could not hold a knife and fork at the same time, the task was impossible. "We learned early on to have it done in the kitchen," Phyllis said. He tended to drop glasses and spill drinks because his left hand was initially quite weak and had to be repaired in another operation after their marriage. But he learned and survived.

For Bob Dole, the struggle for survival was an ongoing war that had to be fought every day on many battlefields for the rest of his life. "I've got to confess," he said forty years later, "I think there was a time when, you know, you get depressed because you can't do things. I don't mean you go into a depression, but you're frustrated and you want to get angry with yourself. And you know when you've got to have somebody help you dress and undress when you go the bathroom, you go back to those years; now that gets pretty touchy sometimes. So, I think there probably was a time there when I just had not quite half recovered when I got maybe a little too independent for my own good."

Dole's insistence on doing everything himself was evident repeatedly in his Senate office. He insisted on reading every detail of a bill or an amendment and personally scrutinized every single letter mailed out to the most obscure constituents. He rebuffed offers from staffers to help him and obstinately refused to delegate authority. I believe that he habitually set difficult and time-consuming tasks for himself, thereby forcing himself to work fifteen-hour days that left him no time for hobbies and entertainment. His unwavering drive, in evidence before the war injury, was intensified by his constant fear of lapsing back into dependence.

# 5
# A LIGHT BURNING
# LATE AT NIGHT

T he strapping young lawyer with the withered arm who returned to Russell in the summer of 1952 was anything but
content to hang up his own shingle and scrounge around
for clients.

He was at a disadvantage in the competition for clients because,
unlike his competitors, he did not hail from a professional family
and could not rely on Daddy to feed him a steady menu of lit-
igants. "Just about every young lawyer in town had a dad who was
also a lawyer," says John Woelk, then Russell county attorney. "It
was hard for Bob to get started, because most of the people went to
the older lawyers, so the best way for a young attorney to get
known was by serving as county attorney."

Woelk, the man who had recruited Dole to run for the legislature
two years earlier, announced that, having served as county attorney since 1949, he would not seek reelection and thereby opened
the door for Dole. "The county attorney positions were always very
hotly contested in the elections," Woelk explains, "because they
were a stepping-stone for you if you wanted to get clients or if you
wanted to go into politics."

Bob Earnest, another young Russell attorney and a Democrat who would run against Bob six years later, says that Bob found the law too mundane and never really wanted to become a career lawyer, but instead yearned for the excitement of politics. As far as Dole was concerned, the law was just a means of earning an income and an entree into politics, a chance to meet Republican kingmakers, who were often lawyers and judges.

The county attorney made about $248 per month, had an office in the county courthouse in Russell, and was responsible for representing the state of Kansas and Russell County in criminal and civil matters. The salary was considered minimal—"less than the janitor made," Bob said—and the county attorney was expected to supplement his income by maintaining his own private law practice. Often, people Bob met in the county attorney's office recommended private clients or became private clients themselves, so the county attorney's time was divided between private and public duties.

For Bob Dole, who had always yearned for public recognition, the county attorney's election offered the chance of a lifetime. If he won the election, he would be looked up to by everyone and would gain the respect and security he had hoped to win as a doctor. People would become dependent on him as they sought his help with their problems, and he would earn their respect. On the other hand, if he lost the election, he would be condemned to an obscure and frustrating role as a pettifogger eking out a precarious existence. With no prospects for advancement in sight, he would have to wait at least two more years before he could run again, probably against a popular incumbent, and he would be wasting precious time. Once again, Bob faced a "must win" situation, and once again he campaigned like a man literally running for his life.

Unlike his state legislative race two years earlier, Bob did not find himself recruited to run for county attorney. There was no great popular demand for his candidacy, and the local Republican movers and shakers favored Dean Ostrum, another young lawyer and a son of a lawyer. Ostrum announced his candidacy, and Dole suspected that Woelk and the other GOP bigwigs were behind him—a charge Woelk denies today.

Struggling against the odds, Bob cast around for bright ideas on how to mount an effective campaign. "He was an unusually good listener, and he sounded out people for their advice," Dean Banker recalls. "Some people advised him to declare his candidacy in the city of Russell, but another fellow suggested he announce in Bunker Hill [a small town in Russell County] because that was the hometown of Ray Shaffer, who was Russell County Republican chairman. Bob said, 'I'm gonna announce in Bunker Hill. That'll impress Shaffer, and he'll endorse me.' So we went to Bunker Hill."

Banker introduced Bob at a meeting in the high school auditorium of Bunker Hill. Banker was a "warm-up man" well known for introducing a singing barbershop quartet before Rotary Club meetings, and his family was well known countywide for its clothing store. In his announcement speech, Bob dutifully paid homage to Shaffer and his wife and won their hearts. Through such gestures, Dole would ingratiate himself with the powers that be throughout his career.

Dole's gesture of respect toward party elders, aimed at winning their support, extended to the courtrooms. Judge C. E. "Ben" Birney, then a district judge in Graham County and a Republican party activist, would later recall Dole's unusual politeness when he came before the bench in a trial or hearing. And Russ Townsley, the *Russell Daily News* publisher who covered Dole's trials in court, recalled the deferential respect Bob would show to the judges.

John Woelk, commenting on Bob's zealous courting of political powerhouses, said, "He identifies with politicians, not with the common man." Bob's deference to his party elders was not, however, merely a cynical ploy for their support. He viewed the party as a quasi-family and the party elders as quasi-parents and sought from them the affection and approval he had been denied by his own stoic parents at home. Dole sought to fill a great gap in his life by means of his political career, then and later.

As the August 1952 primary approached, Dole campaigned hard against Dean Ostrum, and the race was very close. "Basically, the key factors in those early races [for county attorney] were (1) personality and (2) who needed the job most," says Woelk. And Dole was the man who needed the job most.

He simply outcampaigned Ostrum, barely managing to overcome the latter's advantage of wealth and status. Dole beat Ostrum by a scant fifty-two votes in the GOP primary.

After narrowly surviving the GOP primary, Dole coasted to an easy victory over his Democratic opponent. He defeated George Holland by a two-to-one margin, 4,207 to 2,065, on the same day that another Kansan, Dwight Eisenhower of nearby Abilene, was elected president of the United States.

Dole was sworn into office as Russell county attorney in January 1953 by a wizened old district judge named J. C. Ruppenthal, whose son Phil had been a high school pal of Bob's. Photographs depict a lean, unhappy-looking young man with an intense, serious expression on his face. Strikingly absent is the broad smile he had worn as a child and a young man, prior to his wartime injury. In the photos from the 1950s, Dole generally looked like an angry man, a man with a chip on his shoulder or, as Dr. William Roy, one of his later opponents, would later say, "a man with something burning deep inside his gut."

He launched into his job as Russell county attorney with relentless energy, prosecuting criminals and traffic violators, mediating family and business disputes, and explaining the law to myriad county workers and officers. He also began to build a small private practice, but his heart was never in it. His caseload consisted mainly of real property title work, divorces, and family law— pretty drab stuff for a volatile and energetic personality like Dole's.

One day, Bub Dawson recalls, Dole showed up saying he had a "case." Dawson rounded up Bob's brother and friends, saying, " 'Hey, Bob has a case.' Everyone thought it was a case of beer. But it actually was a real legal case."

When he appeared in court for a trial, Dole impressed with his fiery wit and agile mind. He was particularly effective when in combat against Norbert Dreiling, a Democrat and an attorney from nearby Hays.[1] "Whenever those two got together for a trial,"

---

[1]Dreiling, Kansas state Democratic Party chairman from 1966 to 1974, severely criticized Dole over Watergate. His hometown, Hays, has been one of a handful of Democratic strongholds in Kansas.

Russell Townsley recalls, "the whole town wanted to come out and see them go at it. It was the best show in town, better than watching a prizefight."

Dole would watch his opponent make an oral argument before the judge and then would typically brush past him and make some remark like "That was a stupid thing to say. Haven't you read the rules?" In Russell fashion, the two would engage in one-upmanship, "but they then went off and had coffee together right after their court appearance, with no hard feelings on either side," Townsley added with a chuckle.

Apart from jousting in court, Dole cast a hungry eye toward the political horizon and devoted his spare time to looking for a way to rise to statewide or national office. He knew that he needed two things: a financial base and support from the state GOP bosses who recruited and handpicked candidates and then let the largely Republican state newspapers know whom to endorse in editorials.

He knew that at least he was on the right side of the political tracks, for the Republican Party truly dominated Kansas, but he was still unknown outside of Russell County, and he had no real financial base of support.

Dole had seen the impact of the oil boom in Russell as he had grown up. Gradually, khakis had come to replace overalls, and oil came to rival wheat in value and importance in the county. The oil boom reached its peak in the 1950s, when Dole was county attorney. There were more than three thousand oil wells in Russell County alone, and Kansas was one of the biggest oil-producing states in the nation.[2] Over 60 percent of Russell County's valuation was now attributable to oil, while only 40 percent was based in farming and real estate. America was roaring into the age of the automobile, with interstate freeways crisscrossing the land and a booming economy, and oil was king in Kansas.

Dole ran unopposed for reelection as county attorney in 1954, and he defeated Democrat Clifford Holland (brother of George Holland) in 1956 by a vote of 3,175 to 2,319. Increasingly confident of his electoral base, he looked for a way to attract support from the prosperous oilmen. He hit upon a brilliant scheme in 1957.

---

[2]To the present day, Russell's official emblem is an oil rig. In the 1950s, Russell county alone produced about five million barrels of oil per year (today it produces about four million).

The state legislature, bent on reaping revenue from the oil boom, infuriated the oil industry by imposing an oil and gas severance tax of 1 percent in 1957. The tax also angered farmers who received royalties for oil produced by wells on their land. Dole organized a concerted effort with county attorneys from five other counties to file a *quo warranto* suit, asking the court to declare the law unconstitutional on several different grounds.

One of those grounds was a technicality, and Dole exploited it to the hilt. Article 2, Section 16, of the Kansas Constitution provided that in order for any bill or law to be valid, its "subject . . . shall be clearly expressed in its title." The Supreme Court of Kansas, in an opinion issued in January of 1958, agreed with Dole and declared the tax unconstitutional because its title was "fatally defective."

The oilmen and the royalty-earning farmers went wild upon learning of this opinion. Dole had single-handedly saved them millions of dollars and had used an extremely clever tactic to do so. Here was a man who knew how to get things done and who seemed to have their interests at heart. Pretty soon word began circulating all over western Kansas: support Dole.

"Bob attracted the financial support of the oil industry because of his role in nullifying the severance tax," according to John Woelk. Pretty soon, when he became a candidate for Congress, oil and farm money would flow to the man who had overturned the tax.

Dole's duties as county attorney were not limited to helping the oil industry, however. He took an active lead in prosecuting companies and individuals who had allowed salt water to escape into streams and then onto the soil, damaging farmers' land. He reached out to farmers, supported their interests in the courtroom and the courthouse, and appealed to their populist tendencies by speaking out against "the interests" who were "ruining your land and mine." Just as his father had done, Bob spent hours listening to farmers airing their gripes against the powers that be, agreeing with them, and promising to look after their interests.[3]

---

[3]One of the most disheartening tasks facing Dole as county attorney was that of approving monthly welfare benefits for his Dole grandparents, former tenant farmers who had been kicked off their land. This is a story Dole frequently tells in his stump speeches in order to emphasize his poor roots.

His popularity was not limited to rural Russell County. In the small cities of the county, Dole impressed common people as a brilliant and witty firebrand who deserved their votes because he was simply better than anything the competition offered.

The degree of Dole's appeal is revealed by an incident during his 1956 reelection campaign against Clifford Holland in what seemed a pretty close race. One day, Dole ran into Holland's mother, a woman he hadn't seen for eighteen months. He remembered her name, thereby startling and charming her at the same time.

Dole's memory for names and faces was, and still is, phenomenal. When I worked for him, he was able to recall and recite from memory the addresses and names of obscure constituents he hadn't heard of for fourteen years. And, after briefly scanning a complicated piece of legislation, he would be able to recite its key provisions from memory weeks later. In campaigns, he would excite local audiences by reciting a story of a local citizen last heard from years earlier, and this talent would earn him great admiration and support.

In his early days as an aspiring politician, Dole displayed an appetite for work was as impressive as his ability to pull old names and addresses out of his hat. "Every night," Dean Banker recalled, "I would walk by the county courthouse and see only one light still on—Dole's. Even the janitor left before he did." Often, Dole would appear at a party at seven o'clock and leave by eight so that he could return to his office, where he worked until midnight. "He'd come home at midnight, sleep in the basement, and then be off by five the next morning," Bub Dawson recalled. "It didn't make for much of a home life."

Dole stayed in his office such long hours in order to build his personal power base and organization, which he hoped to use in a congressional campaign. One night, he struck pay dirt. McDill "Huck" Boyd, publisher of the weekly *Phillips County Review* at Phillipsburg and one of the Republican power brokers in Kansas (he subsequently became state GOP chairman and a GOP national committeeman), drove through the streets of Russell near midnight and noticed that the lights of one office on the third floor of the county courthouse were still burning. Boyd decided that he wanted to meet the government official who worked that late, so he stopped his car, went up the stairs, and introduced himself to Dole. Thus began a thirty-year relationship that would help propel Dole to the pinnacle of national politics.

Through Boyd, Dole finally gained entry into the old-boy network that ran the state GOP, the old "Alf Landon machine,"[4] which had originated in the twenties and thirties and secured voter support by dispensing political patronage. The fifties were a transition period between machine and "independent" political processes in Kansas. With the advent of television and the decline of political parties, especially after 1960, the bosses' clout declined as candidates quit relying on political patronage and fended for themselves.[5]

But in the 1950s the machine was still alive, if weakened. If you wanted to get elected anywhere in Kansas, you still had to have the endorsement of the old Landon machine quasi bosses—men such as Boyd, Dane Hansen, Lacy Haynes (editor of the *Kansas City Star*), Harry Darby, and Landon himself. (In his seventies, Landon was the elder statesman of the Kansas Republican Party.) They operated by word of mouth: if they liked you, they would call their friends at the newspapers and the financial powerhouses. Boyd would tell people throughout west-central Kansas what a great guy Bob Dole was and tell them to endorse him and tell all their friends. The voters and moneymen would fall into line.

Dole knew how to make the machine work for him. He buttered up Boyd, again playing the role of dutiful son toward an older and more powerful man. He made known his strong interest in running for Congress, and Boyd encouraged him. He became increasingly active in Republican party organizational and promotional activities all over western Kansas, collecting political IOUs and building a personal network of supporters. He made a personal pilgrimage to see boss Dane Hansen to secure his support.[6]

[4]Landon was governor of Kansas and the GOP presidential nominee in 1936. Landon reached his 100th birthday in September 1987, and died in October 1987. His daughter, Nancy Landon Kassebaum, has been a U.S. senator from Kansas since 1979.

[5]In the mid-1960s, for example, the Kansas Republican Party lacked coherent leadership and became badly factionalized. Dole steered an independent course during this split and acted as his own political mentor, according to Russell Townsley.

[6]Hansen's niece, Polly Bales, is still an avid Dole supporter. Among other things, she helped write and disseminate a Dole for President 1988 campaign song.

While acting the role of respectful, unassuming son toward his powerful party elders, Dole also displayed brash, aggressive tendencies among his peers that would later surface on a national scale. According to Norbert Dreiling, Dole "just took over" the local Russell County Republican political machine in the mid-1950s. He "pushed out" John Woelk, who was part of the liberal wing of the Kansas Republican Party and a rising state senator. "He just cut the support from under Woelk and took it over himself. That was the end of Woelk's political future," notes Dreiling.

Bob won his last election as Russell county attorney in 1958, beating Democrat Bob Earnest, 2,807 to 2,195. Earnest, who later took over Dole's private practice caseload after his election to Congress, says that "Bob channeled his competitive energies from athletics into politics. He made his brain act as his arms and legs." The two men became lifelong friends.

Harry Morgenstern, who was Russell County sheriff when Dole was county attorney, recalled Dole as "kind and personable, but if a person was wrong, he was wrong—no matter who he was. Bob hated to see children abused; that was one thing he didn't tolerate, if he knew about it. He had a good personality, was very neat, and always got everything done. He was businesslike, but had time for everybody. He had a good sense of humor, yet could be real stern when he had to be."

Dole's concern for children was reflected in many ways during his eight-year stint as Russell county attorney. He took a leading role in advising the legislature to draft a new juvenile code that dictated the treatment of juvenile offenders. In addition, he made sure that juvenile offenders were strictly segregated from adult criminals in prison, he got the first juvenile probation officer assigned to Russell, and he arranged for youthful offenders to receive foster care as an alternative to incarceration. He also played an aggressive, emotional role in taking abused and neglected children away from their parents.

Dole's notable interest in the welfare of youth came at a time when he had just become a father. On October 18, 1954, Phyllis gave birth to a daughter, named Robin (a name derived from his own).

As the fifties came to a close, the aging President Eisenhower prepared to leave office after serving two terms, and the incumbent congressman serving in Dole's district was getting tired. Wint Smith, a huge and gregarious man, had represented Kansas's Sixth District in Congress since 1947. Nicknamed "The General" because of his imperious take-charge personality and his military background, Smith had always been a man of action, serving as a Kansas Highway Patrol commander before embarking on a frustrating congressional odyssey. He defeated the hapless Elmo J. Mahoney, Dole's first opponent back in 1950, in the 1958 congressional election, in which Dole worked for Smith. Smith became frustrated with what he called a "do-nothing stalemate Congress"—and had lost the taste for any more electoral battles.

Traveling around the state in his khakis and huge cowboy hat, Smith quietly put out the word among Landon's old boys that he would gladly retire in 1960 if the right man could be found to come in after him.

That man was sitting in the courthouse at Russell, Kansas, with his office light burning late into the night, every night.

# 6

# "SOMEWHERE TO THE RIGHT OF GENGHIS KHAN"

B oy," droned the corn-pone hulk of a man known as The General, "I want you to come on in and take over my seat in Congress. I don't know what you want it for, but it's all yours." Thus spoke Congressman Wint Smith as he slapped his huge hand on Bob Dole's back one spring day in 1960.

A provincial conservative who seemed the epitome of the largely rural Sixth District he had represented in Congress for fourteen years, Wint Smith handpicked Bob Dole as his successor and made it clear that he was willing to retire only because he had finally found the right man to succeed him.

Dole became known as "Wint's Golden Boy" among the old-boy network of the Alf Landon machine, which went busily to work endorsing him, lining up oil money for his campaign, and otherwise spreading the word among the largely conservative, Republican newspaper editors to endorse Dole.

It was 1960, the year of Francis Gary Powers's ill-fated U-2 flight over Russia, an abortive summit meeting between Ike and Khrushchev, and the rise of a young Catholic Democratic presidential candidate named John F. Kennedy. The Cold War was raging anew, Nixon was about to be nominated by the GOP as Ike's successor, and the nation's voters were trying to decide whether they wanted four more years of staid Republican rule or the fresh "new frontier" offered by the young Catholic from Massachusetts.

The Sixth Congressional District of west-central Kansas was a huge, largely rural area with considerable anti-Communist as well as anti-Kennedy sentiment. Dole kicked off his campaign at Topeka's Jayhawk Hotel (the political hub of both political parties in Kansas at the time) on Kansas Day, January 29, 1960, with a flair. On March 2, 1960, Mary Humes (a clerk in the Russell County courthouse) wrote a letter to the editor of the *Salina Journal* endorsing Dole for Congress. Humes praised his "integrity, character, intelligence, and capacity for public service." Humes's letter gave Dole a populist hue, which he exploited cleverly by presenting himself to poor farmers as "one of you."

In photos from this election campaign, Dole is never smiling, but instead wears a sneer. Perhaps he deliberately cultivated a tough image in an effort to show that he was not a weak cripple. Also, some perceived a certain ruthless quality about him, particularly in light of the way Woelk was pushed aside.

Nevertheless, with common citizens like Mrs. Humes and the old-boy network and The General backing him to the hilt, Dole might have been a shoo-in had it not been for a charismatic young Republican state senator named Keith Sebelius, who denounced Dole as "the candidate of the special interests."

Sebelius, who hailed from Norton, in northwestern Kansas, displayed considerable gumption in taking on the still-powerful remnants of the Landon machine. He had unsuccessfully challenged Wint Smith himself in the 1958 GOP congressional primary election and was something of an iconoclast. Sensing that there was something negative about Dole that bothered a lot of voters, Sebelius tried to exploit latent populist sentiment by painting Dole as a puppet of "the interests," while presenting himself as the independent and conscientious champion of the common man.

Dole, who felt he had earned the right to represent the Sixth District in Congress because of his hard work for Smith in his 1958 campaign and his endorsement by the old-boy network, was infuriated by Sebelius's audacity. As the August Republican primary election approached, he was particularly incensed when a third candidate named Phillip J. Doyle of Beloit, Kansas, appeared on the ballot. He was convinced that Doyle had been put up by Sebelius as a ploy to take away Dole votes by confusing voters with the similar-sounding names of Dole and Doyle.

"In those rural areas," Dole's then-wife Phyllis told me recently, "people often pronounced 'Dole' and 'Doyle' the same way, so they were confused as to which one Bob was. In addition, Doyle's first name was Phillip, which was similar to mine, and he had the middle initial J, which was also Bob's middle initial."

In an effort to eliminate the confusion between himself and Doyle, Bob Dole hit upon the brilliant idea of stocking his campaign rallies with cans of Dole pineapple juice. Dole publicized his rallies and meetings by announcing that Dole pineapple juice would be handed out to anyone who showed up. "We had to get special clearance from the Dole Pineapple Juice Company to use their name and their product," Bob's brother Kenny recalls. "They said to us, 'Fine. Anything that promotes the sale of Dole Pineapple Juice is fine with us. Go ahead and use all you want.' And we sure did." The pure, wholesome image of pineapple juice had great voter appeal in Kansas, which was still a dry state at the time.

The pineapple juice campaign served to project another message, darker and subtler. According to several sources, rumors were spreading that Keith Sebelius had a drinking problem. This stemmed from the fact that Sebelius was allegedly seen one day entering a church, armed with a box filled with groceries for the needy. Unfortunately for Sebelius, the box happened to have a whiskey company label and insignia, and a photographer managed to snap his picture as he entered the church. Soon there were rumors that Sebelius was bringing booze into a church.

There is no proof that Dole authorized or approved of any of these rumors.[1] Quite possibly, some of his more fanatical supporters took it upon themselves to exploit the issue. Some speculated that Smith himself was behind this incident. But Sebelius's widow

[1]Similarly, Dole denied that he had anything to do with actions of his more fanatical supporters in his 1974 Senate reelection campaign against Dr. William Roy. Just two days before the election, right-to-life groups papered Kansas churches with leaflets depicting dead fetuses in garbage cans and distorting Roy's position on abortion.

evidently maintained a lifelong resentment toward Dole. When her husband died in 1982, she pointedly refused to invite Dole to a reception at her house.

But booze was by no means an official issue in the 1960 GOP primary, and Dole never publicly accused Sebelius of being an alcoholic or of hauling crates of booze into a church. Booze, as abortion would fourteen years later, seems to have excited some of the more zealous, fundamentalist Christians who saw red whenever they heard about a bottle of liquor being sold. Though the federal Prohibition constitutional amendment had been repealed in 1933, Kansas state laws had essentially maintained prohibition until 1948 and still restricted liquor sales in 1960. Liquor was permitted by law only by the drink at certain "private clubs" and could be sold only in specially licensed liquor stores; not even beer could be bought off the shelf. It is easy to understand why even the mention of booze in association with a political candidate's name would cause many fundamentalist voters to turn their thumbs down at the polls.

Dole, to his credit, maintained a clean, wholesome campaign and hit upon many clever gimmicks and slogans. Always on the lookout for bright ideas, he had a peculiar talent for coming up with original slogans and techniques aimed at winning name recognition and voter support. His two campaign slogans were "Young Man on the Move" and "Roll with Dole"—which accurately captured his incessant activity and indefatigability.

He designed a wheel-shaped campaign business card that he and his aides handed out on every street corner and on every farm they could reach. The card was three inches in diameter. On one side was the candidate's photograph, surrounded by the words R. J. 'BOB' DOLE● REPUBLICAN● CONGRESS. On the other side was a colorful blue-and-red wheel with twelve spokes. At the hub was the name BOB DOLE; on the rim were the words PUT YOUR SHOULDER TO THE WHEEL AND ROLL WITH DOLE IN '60. And on each of the twelve spokes were the candidate's achievements: BORN 7-22-23 . . . KU & WASHBURN . . . METHODIST . . . RUSSELL NATIVE . . . LEGIS-LATURE 1951 . . . WON 7 ELECTIONS . . . BOY & GIRL SCOUTS . . . SEC. 4-H FAIR ASSOCIATION . . . SER. OFF. VFW & AM. LEG . . . ELKS-MASON-KIWANIAN . . . CO. ATTY. 4 TERMS . . . TWICE WOUNDED VET.

As the last item indicates, Dole continued to use his handicap— a major factor that led both parties to urge him to enter politics in 1950—to his political advantage. And today he is not shy about discussing his wounds and subsequent struggles during the many interviews he gives to the media, and the subject often constitutes a large portion of feature stories about him.

*"Roll With Dole" campaign material from 1960. Wheel spokes listed Dole's qualifications as "Co. Atty. 4 terms," "Russell Native," and "Twice Wounded Vet." (Courtesy of Polly Bales.)*

The campaign wheel and Dole pineapple juice gimmick were the static elements of Dole's unique campaign in 1960. The active elements consisted of groups of attractive young women, in identical uniforms, who sang in barbershop quartets. These girls were later dubbed "Dolls for Dole," but originally they were called the Bobolinks.

The Bobolinks began when Mary Humes was working at the Russell County courthouse and mentioned to Dole that her daughter, Nancy, and friends, students at nearby Fort Hays State University, sang in a barbershop quartet. Dole eagerly seized on the idea and formed the Bobolinks. The original group consisted of four girls from the Russell area: a pair of twins from Lucas, Dorothy and Delores Voss; Nancy Humes, who played the ukulele; and Bonnie Langdon, who went with Dole to Washington as his secretary after he won his election.

"We traveled around with him from town to town," Dorothy Voss recalls. "We would go door to door and sing a song for the voters. We would go into stores and meetings, too"[2]

Dole organized several other groups of singing girls in many different towns. When he showed up, they would greet him with a campaign song. One song rang: "Knick, knack, paddywack, Roll along with Dole. . . ."

Phyllis and Bina Dole sewed special dresses and skirts for the Bobolinks and for many other young women and girls who appeared with Bob at campaign rallies and posed with him for photos. In one such photo, dated July 23, 1960, Dole is crouching down, surrounded by twenty-four females, wearing identical dresses and huge buttons in the shape of a sunflower sporting Bob's face and name.

Dole also extensively used his own daughter, Robin, and his nieces during his campaign. Robin wore a dress with the message I'M FOR MY DADDY. ARE YOU? sewn at the hemline and a huge sunflower-shaped button with the same words. Her cousin wore clothes and a button with the message I'M FOR MY UNCLE BOB.

Dole's use of young "cheerleader" types of girls was a subtle and extremely clever use of sex appeal to sell his candidacy. The sweet young things also served to counter the negative aspects of his image by presenting him as a lovable family man. In addition, the attractive girls tended to divert attention from his withered arm. Dole continued to use the Bobolinks and Dolls for Dole in his campaigns as late as his 1974 Senate campaign. They were an integral part of his message, an original and clever tactic that worked wonders for him at the polls.

It should also be pointed out that the Bobolinks–Dolls for Dole, by sporting identical costumes, probably appealed to Dole's love of regimentation. The wearing of standard uniforms symbolized

[2]Dorothy was so devoted to singing on Dole's campaign that she stood up her future husband on their first date in order to show up for a Dole campaign rally with the Bobolinks. This was a last-minute call-in, and Dorothy went eagerly.

absolute loyalty to Dole and the acceptance he craved. Had the girls worn a variety of different clothes with different colors, they would not have been as effective or as symbolic. In their uniforms, they appeared as Bob's soldiers, marching to war for their hero— an image immensely satisfying to a man for whom politics was sublimation of his combative and competitive drive.

Finally, Dole's use of young women and his own daughter probably appealed to many young couples who had recently become parents during the peak of the baby boom. As in his championing of juvenile rights as Russell county attorney, Dole shrewdly realized that the bulk of the voters were preoccupied with raising their children and grandchildren. He aimed to be, in their minds, a man who cared about youth, who paraded young people in the front lines of his campaigns, and who was deeply concerned about their children's future.

Dole defeated Sebelius[3] and Phillip Doyle at the GOP primary, but just as in his first primary victory for county attorney eight years earlier, he barely managed to scrape up enough votes to win. Dole got approximately 16,000 votes, Sebelius 15,000, and Doyle only 4,400.

In the heavily Republican Sixth District, winning the primary election against Sebelius virtually guaranteed Dole a victory in the November general election. He handily defeated Democrat William Davis, of the far-western Kansas town of Goodland, to win a seat in the Congress that convened in January 1961. He won by a three-to-two margin.

Bob went to Washington at the same time that John F. Kennedy entered the White House. Dole shared the anti-Kennedy views of his constituents, though not their prejudice against the new president's Catholicism. What irritated Dole most about Kennedy was the latter's genteel breeding and wealth, which stood in stark contrast to Bob's own background. Just as he would later come to despise George Bush, another patrician Ivy Leaguer from New England, Dole disliked Kennedy at a gut level. With his rural Kansas twang and his country bumpkin upbringing, Dole realized he had no place in Kennedy's Camelot.

In Washington, he felt like a true outsider, a backbencher who

[3]Sebelius later won this same congressional seat when Dole moved up to the Senate in 1968.

occupied himself primarily with agricultural issues. He won a seat on the House Agriculture Committee, where he excoriated Kennedy's farm policy in strikingly strong-worded attacks and questioned the wisdom of selling American wheat to the USSR.

Garner Shriver,[4] also a congressman from Kansas in the 1960s, remembers Dole as a loner and a workaholic, who would attend "only those social functions where there would be people who had come a long way from Kansas to see him. . . . He used to work the phones a lot, and we used to call him a workaholic back then. Because of that, he was a loner; he didn't have many close friends. When he wanted something accomplished, he was relentless and aggressive in hanging on until he got what he wanted." In addition, like so many others who knew him, Shriver recalled that Dole "used his handicap politically, to an advantage."

Another Kansas congressman, Larry Winn, who represented the Third District in the 1960s, recalled Dole as "the hardest-working person I ever met in my life" and noted that "his humor often gave the impression that he was a smart aleck, but he was so good that he could be a stand-up comic if he weren't in politics."

Winn was particularly struck by Dole's stupendous memory for "faces, names, and the ability to tie people up with certain events." He would, says Winn, recognize a person he'd seen years before and say something like "And how is your grandma's quilting coming along?"

While displaying his incredible memory, humor, and fervor for work, Dole championed the causes of anti-Communism, the handicapped, veterans, and agriculture during his years in the House. He compiled an impressive overall attendance record of over 90 percent, one of the highest in Congress. Even later, when I worked for him in the Senate, he was obsessed with being present for every roll-call vote, not merely because he wanted to impress voters, but because he wanted to be in on every little detail, to feel a sense of control over legislation, to be a part of history in the making. He was meticulous about preparing his floor speeches and remarks for publication in the *Congressional Record* and had little respect for colleagues who treated Congress as a playground—another reason

---

[4]Shriver represented the Fourth Congressional District from Kansas, including Wichita and Abilene.

for his disdain for people such as JFK, who had had an atrocious attendance record while in Congress from 1947 to 1961.

In 1962, Kansas lost one of its six congressional districts through reapportionment, a sign of its population decline. As a result, Dole's Sixth District was merged with the old Fifth into a new First District that now included fifty-eight counties. Spanning the entire western half of the state, the new First was geographically one of the largest districts in the country, presenting Dole with quite a challenge as he sought reelection.

In the 1962 election, he faced a tough opponent in incumbent Democrat J. Floyd Breeding, a popular congressman from the old Fifth District. Dole realized he needed a big issue to attract votes and earn name recognition in this still largely rural, conservative, and anti-Kennedy area. He hit upon a gold mine in the person of Billie Sol Estes.

On March 29, 1962, the FBI arrested the thirty-seven-year-old Estes, a Texas wheeler-dealer reputed to be a crony of Vice President Lyndon Johnson, on fraud charges involving forged mortgages. In a series of financial shennanigans, Estes had bilked farmers out of their land through a Byzantine web of shady dealings involving the lease of grain storage bins to the Kennedy government.

Dole, ever on the lookout for a target on which to vent his ferocious indignation, seized on the Estes case in February 1962, when it was exposed by a Pecos newspaper, and called for a congressional investigation into the Department of Agriculture's handling of Estes's cotton allotments and other matters. Dole accused the Kennedy Administration of suppressing evidence linking Estes to Lyndon Johnson. On June 8, 1962, the Republican congressional committee, echoing Dole, charged that a counsel on a House subcommittee had been fired when he found out Estes had had chummy contacts with LBJ, and the whole affair led to Senate and House investigations.

Dole gained considerable publicity, making the *New York Times* and earning kudos back home. His call for an investigation[5] revealed a gut instinct for publicity and gained him many votes

[5]Dole introduced a resolution in the House in April 1962 calling for an investigation of the Stabilization Service by the House Agriculture Committee or a subcommittee.

among the Republican farmers in the new First District. He defeated Breeding in the election, having shrewdly sent his wife and daughter home to Kansas to campaign for him while he stayed in Washington to lead the charge. Dole defeated Breeding in November 1962 by 21,000 votes.

Dole's popularity at home was not universal, however. Jim Parrish, who was then a high school student interested in politics, recalls attending a Dole congressional campaign rally. "I was really interested in meeting him," Parrish said. "I went up to him and offered my hand. He looked at me with a demeaning glance, then quickly moved away to mingle with the more 'important' voters. At that instant, I became a Democrat." Parrish went on to become Kansas state Democratic chairman and one of Dole's severest critics.

Following the October 1962 Cuban Missile Crisis, JFK made dramatic strides toward rapprochement with the Soviet Union, starting with his famous American University speech in June 1963, in which he called for peaceful coexistence. The landmark Nuclear Test Ban Treaty was ratified by the Senate a few months later. Kennedy further hinted that he was about to withdraw American troops from South Vietnam, dropped his support of the corrupt anti-communist Diem government there, and proposed selling wheat to the Soviet Union.

Kennedy's outreach to the Soviets did not play well in conservative western Kansas, and Dole reflected his constituency perfectly. On September 30, 1963, Dole and nine other conservative congressmen wrote Kennedy a letter asking for clarification of this proposal, and hinting that they would oppose it. On October 8, JFK approved the wheat sale. Although Dole represented the largest wheat-producing district in the country, on November 6, 1963, he stated on the House floor, "It is hard to justify fighting communism with the one hand and feeding it with the other," and railed, "We are dealing with an international communist conspiracy."

Two weeks after Dole's speech, on November 22, 1963, Kennedy was assassinated in Dallas. Dole, who makes no mention of this momentous event in his 1988 autobiography, nonetheless did make a speech on the House floor on December 5, 1963. This speech affords an insight into the qualities of JFK which Dole admired.

While most other public figures praised JFK's vision, states-manship, and humanity, Dole chose instead to laud the assassi-nated man's *ability to win.* "Kennedy was a politician in the finest sense," Dole told his colleagues. "He laid *careful plans for win-ning*—and serving in—the presidency." After quoting laudatory editorials from western Kansas newspapers, Dole concluded his speech by praising Kennedy as a successful *professional politician.*

Dole went on to remark that "strangely," Kennedy, like the three previously slain presidents (Lincoln, Garfield, and McKinley), "was slain during a period in his administration when there was peace, prosperity, and happiness. Furthermore, on the day the crime was committed, each was *unusually happy. . . .*" Dole's reflections on the irony of fate are indicative of his general world-view that life is unfair, and that one may be most vulnerable even at the very peak of success and happiness. Hence, one must be ever vigilant, never contented or satisfied. One must be forever on guard and ready to strike out at whatever or whomever is waiting to sabotage one's own good fortune.

Kennedy's assassination put into the White House Lyndon B. Johnson, a man whom Dole loathed but admired, and to whom he himself would later be compared for his adeptness at wielding power as Senate majority leader. Although he had never cared for the Kennedy brothers, LBJ benefited enormously from the massive public grief and nostalgia for JFK. As the nation headed into the fall 1964 campaign, the Republicans, fighting against the ghost of Kennedy now personified in the Democratic Party, faced very tough races all over the country.

In the congressional 1964 campaign, Dole faced Bill Bork, a Democrat who felt the full force of Bob's tongue lashing. Dole organizers ran radio and TV ads stating, "Bork is a jerk," as Bob fought for his political life—and won. Richard Nixon campaigned for Dole in Kansas, sizing up the congressman for a future Senate seat, and Dole supported Barry Goldwater for president.

During the campaign and throughout the sixties, Dole con-tinued to capitalize on the reactionary views of his constituency—and to please Nixon and Goldwater—with his fair share of red-baiting. According to Kansas Democrat Norbert Dreiling, "Dole out-Nixoned Nixon. He was always looking for Commies under every rock—especially every Democratic rock."

Lyndon Johnson made a special effort to have Dole defeated, not only because of his role in the Estes matter and his vociferous partisanship and criticism of the Democratic administration, but also because of Dole's vehement opposition to Johnson's Great Society programs in 1964 and 1965. Bob voted for the landmark Civil Rights Bill of 1964 and for the Voting Rights Act of 1965 but voted against an Open Housing Bill of 1966 and virtually all of the Great Society programs, including the bills establishing food stamps, Medicare, Judicare, federal educational assistance, and other programs aimed at helping the needy. Ironically, Dole would champion many of these causes in the 1970s and 1980s. But, as one colleague accurately noted at the time, "Dole is somewhere to the right of Genghis Khan in his philosophy." According to former aide Richard Norton Smith, Dole even refused to watch the television series "Bonanza" because the principal actors were Democrats.

Because of his staunch conservative voting record in the House, Dole was presented with a plaque given annually to the most conservative congressmen by the Americans for Constitutional Action. He received this award every year it was given and became the darling of the right wing. Meanwhile, liberal and progressive lobbying groups consistently gave him a zero rating.

Dole's right-wing reputation from his House years contrasts sharply with his later reputation as a mealy-mouthed pragmatic opportunist. Was he truly a conservative in the 1960s? Norbert Dreiling remarked recently, "Dole will do what it takes to get elected. He has always accurately reflected the constituency he happens to represent. In the sixties, when he represented the First District in Congress, he reflected their views: anti–Great Society, anti-Johnson, anti-Kennedy. Then, after he expanded his base to cover all of Kansas [when he became senator in 1968], he moderated his views. Then, when he began running for president [in 1980], he modified and moderated them again."

The real question, impossible ever to fully answer, as we look at Dole's "right of Genghis Khan" record in Congress, is: to what extent did Dole actually *believe* in what he was voting for or against, and to what extent did he merely play along in order to win votes?

Dole's image as a political chameleon, which would later haunt him, may not be entirely fair or accurate. However, it does seem to have some truth to it when we contrast his later voting record with his reactionary votes in the House. The man who would later call himself the "candidate of compassion" was busy compiling an anticompassionate record in the sixties.

He easily won reelection to the House again in 1966, this time using a more low-key approach in this race against the only woman opponent he has ever faced, Berniece Henkle of Great Bend, Kansas. Although his foe was not particularly formidable, Dole went about campaigning with characteristic thoroughness, visiting virtually every small town and making sure he met the voters. Unlike many candidates, who settled for meeting company bosses alone, Dole insisted on greeting every worker, explaining, "It's a sad mistake to overlook anyone. . . . I want to see them all."

He seemed to be more available in body than in spirit, however. Reporters traveling with Dole sensed, then as later, that he didn't feel very comfortable meeting and communicating with voters. When he met a voter, he said little beyond, "Hello. I'm Congressman Dole. What's your name?" With his phenomenal memory for names and faces, he would startle the voters in later encounters by remembering their names. He usually had a young state legislative or county attorney candidate in tow and deflected attention from himself by introducing the voters to his sidekick.

In the 1966 campaign, as always, Dole boasted of his near-perfect attendance record in Congress, reminding voters that he had answered 192 of the 193 roll calls in the House and explaining, "I'd have been back in the district sooner, but [President Johnson] wouldn't turn us loose. . . . I stayed to the bitter end, trying to do what I was sent to the capital to do: represent you."

Dole's essential loner quality was as evident during his congressional days as it is today. The young man from Russell never seemed to have completely overcome his youthful shyness and has always found it hard to mix with strangers socially. A man who inspires more respect than affection, he has never been a backslapping, gregarious politician. Indeed, in 1966, he seemed the anti-politician running a one-man show. He became famous as a lone sniper who became well-known as an outspoken and ceaseless critic of the Johnson Administration and the Democratic Congress.

Dole served on a U.S. congressional delegation to survey the food crisis in India in 1966 and on another delegation to study the Arab refugee problem in the Middle East in 1967.[6] He favored sending wheat to the starving masses in India and elsewhere but other than that showed little interest in U.S. foreign policy and bypassed a chance to serve on congressional committees specializing in foreign policy. His lack of interest in this subject would also be apparent in the Senate.

While compiling an impressive conservative record in the House, Dole remained in close contact with Frank Carlson, the senior Republican U.S. senator from Kansas and one of the elder statesmen and powers of the Alf Landon old-boy network. Carlson, who had been governor of Kansas from 1947 to 1950 and U.S. senator since 1951, treated Dole as his fair-haired boy, much as Wint Smith had done eight years earlier. Dole, eagerly stepping into the role of dutiful son, ingratiated himself with Carlson during his eight years in Washington. Not surprisingly, Carlson chose him as his successor when he retired from the Senate in 1968.

On October 10, 1968, a month before the general election, Dole was treated to an effusive outpouring of praise from his Republican colleagues. One by one, the congressmen rose in the great well of the House chamber to shower kudos on the man who had stood in their ranks for eight years. There is something presumptuous about their comments. Virtually every congressman who spoke announced with seeming certainty, even before the election, that Dole would be "promoted" to the Senate. As Representative Burt Talcott of California said, "I am pleased to participate with the friends and colleagues of my colleague from Kansas in wishing him *bon voyage* into the political maelstrom of the other body [the

---

[6]In his House years, Dole also served on the Republican Task Force on Urban Affairs and as an adviser to the U.S. Delegation to the United Nations Food and Agriculture Organization at Rome in 1965. His interests in foreign affairs seemed limited to agriculture.

Senate]." "I know his [Dole's] arrival in the Senate will brighten, enliven, and enrich that body," Representative Paul Findley echoed. "I am confident he will continue this same splendid record in the other body," Representative Alex Pirnie chimed in.

His House colleagues were right. In an overwhelmingly Republican state where Carlson was king, Dole bounced into the Senate three weeks later with a resounding election victory over Democrat William I. Robinson.

Nixon, another Republican phoenix, had been resurrected from his close loss to JFK in 1960 and his trouncing by Pat Brown in his 1962 bid to become the governor of California. Now he capitalized on anti-war and anti-LBJ sentiment to barely defeat Vice President Hubert Humphrey and become president in 1968. While Dole and Nixon campaigned for each other that fall, there was no particular reason to expect that the new president would take Dole under his wing. But Bob had a history of cozying up to powerful party elders and the new senator was about to transfer his allegiance to the new man in the White House—just as his long odyssey to becoming a truly national political force was about to begin.

# 7

# "NIXON'S DOBERMAN PINSCHER"

Flushed from his landslide victory, Bob Dole entered the world's most exclusive gentlemen's club, the United States Senate, in January 1969. After eight rather lackluster years as a backbencher in the House of Representatives, where he had never had much of an audience outside of western Kansas, Dole suddenly found himself in the stratosphere of American politics.

Dole's deep-rooted resentment at being an outsider had been exacerbated by his fringe status in the House, where, as he told me, he had been "lucky just to get a good seat," in an era when the Democratic Party dominated Congress and controlled the White House.

The 1968 election had changed all that. Besides sending Nixon to the White House, the Republican Party made stunning gains in the House and Senate. Ten years later, reflecting on the significance of the 1968 election, Dole said that for the first time in his career he then felt that he belonged in the government.

Though the Democrats still held a majority in the Senate and therefore still controlled its agenda and ruled its committees, the practical reality was that the forceful President Nixon initiated much of the legislation it considered and that, more often than not, the Senate reacted to what Nixon was doing. Lacking any coherent leadership, the Democratic Senate princes lacked a foil for Nixon—save perhaps Ted Kennedy, who in those pre-Chappaquid-dick days was still regarded as a political deity by much of the country.

Dole considered the Democrats anemic gutless wonders, and he hated Kennedy, the limousine liberal rich kid. Like Nixon, Dole was a poor kid who had been snubbed by the likes of Kennedy all his life and who particularly resented the hagiographic portrayal of the Kennedy brothers by what he considered the liberal press. Well aware that Nixon bore an equally intense loathing for Kennedy, for personal as well as political reasons, Dole saw a vacuum to be filled in the Senate: point man for Nixon and foil to Ted Kennedy and any other critic of Nixon. Thus he surprised his colleagues by immediately setting about patrolling the Senate floor and acting as a one-man "Dole Patrol," as many called it, to attack and contra-dict Kennedy and any other critic of Nixon.

Bristling with venom, cocky and aggressive, Dole was always ready and willing to pick a floor fight and violated virtually every unwritten rule of the Senate, which held that freshman senators should be seen and not heard in their first few years, that they should refrain from making personal attacks on their colleagues on either side of the aisle. When Arkansas senator William Fulbright objected to Dole's unorthodox rupture of normal Senate proce-dure, the Kansan shot back acidly, "Is it a rule of the Senate that one must clear everything with the senator from Arkansas?"

Feeling that politics is war and that the Senate floor is a battle-field, and realizing that Nixon shared his view, Dole launched into fanatical defenses of Nixon and attacks on Kennedy and Nixon's other opponents with a zeal that infuriated his colleagues. The Republican minority leader, Senator Hugh Scott of Pennsylvania, a "moderate" who was lukewarm on Nixon, was particularly in-censed at what he considered to be Dole's brash, iconoclastic as-saults into his own personal territory. Scott, who epitomized the despised Eastern Establishment—or as Dole called it, the "Rocke-feller wing" of the GOP—was deeply irritated that Dole constantly ran end runs around him and defied his authority. But to Dole,

Scott was just a figurehead who had no business standing between him and the president. Dole's loyalty was to Nixon and Nixon alone, and it did not go unnoticed by the angry and gloomy man in the Oval Office.

In contrast to most of his Republican Senate colleagues, Dole developed a one-on-one relationship with Nixon, frequently visited the White House, and unofficially became Nixon's "direct line" to the Senate floor. Not surprisingly, rumors began floating around that Nixon would like to see Dole challenge Scott for Senate minority leader in 1970. Meanwhile, in the Senate, Dole was referred to as "Nixon's pet" and "Nixon's Doberman pinscher."

The cement binding Nixon and Dole was highly personal. As a matter of chemistry, the moody president got along extremely well with Dole, who gave him 100 percent loyalty and shared his general view of the world. In their personal relations, Nixon behaved with consummate tact, always shaking hands with *his* left hand, thereby sparing Dole embarrassment and awkwardness. Ten years later, Dole still recalled Nixon's left-handed handshake, wistfully reflecting that nobody else had ever done that.

Notwithstanding the human bond between the two men, there was something chillingly mechanical about the *way* in which Dole defended Nixon in the Senate. He acted like a true myrmidon, a robot who was Nixon's alter ego and enforcer, never questioning any of the president's policies in the slightest, furiously defensive and bitter toward anyone who dared to oppose the commander in chief. Indeed, there was something almost *military* about Dole's allegiance to Nixon. "You don't question the orders of your commanding officer in combat," Dole said later in explaining his role. It seemed as if Dole were back in the Po Valley leading his platoon into combat, but this time using ballots instead of bullets and with Nixon as his commanding officer.

During Nixon's first term, his handling of the Vietnam War was a source of bitter controversy. Having campaigned in 1968 by claiming he had a "secret plan" to end that war, Nixon disappointed virtually everyone except Dole when, in 1969, he revealed that plan to be "Vietnamization," a painfully slow process of gradually replacing half a million U.S. combat troops in Vietnam with South Vietnamese ARVN forces. Under this murky plan the U.S.

would train the ARVN troops to handle combat effectively so that they would eventually be able to assume the duties of the massive contingent of U.S. troops deployed in the meat grinder.

The bogus nature of Vietnamization was soon evident when Nixon announced in June 1969 that he was withdrawing a token force of 25,000 U.S. troops, less than 5 percent of the American force there. By early fall 1969, massive antiwar and anti-Nixon demonstrations were occurring all across the country, and these so-called Vietnam moratoriums, days set aside for everyone to go on strike against the war, became a staple of the nightly TV news.

In the press, Nixon was lashed severely, while in Congress and the Senate he was attacked by hawks for withdrawing any troops at all and by doves for deliberately prolonging the war in order to save face. Nixon, always defensive and bitter, unleashed Vice President Spiro Agnew to take on the press, while Dole performed a comparable job in the Senate. Agnew, in a now-legendary address in November 1969 in Des Moines, Iowa, glorified the "silent majority" and castigated the press and the war critics as "an effete bunch of intellectual snobs," "nattering nabobs of negativity," and "ideological eunuchs . . . who take their tactics from Castro and their money from Daddy."[1]

In the Senate, Dole sang much the same tune, in a harsh, bull-horn voice that seemed to outrage and shock many of his colleagues, who ostracized him. Dole attacked his colleagues in harsh terms, both on and off the Senate floor. Often, he would chase departing senators off the Senate floor and into the cloakroom or hallway, where he would continue the acrimonious colloquy that had just been cut short on the floor. The buttonholed colleague would receive a tongue lashing for opposing Nixon. Republican senator William Saxbe of Ohio coined the nickname "hatchet man" and stuck it to Dole with the glue of his own words. "Dole is so unpopular here," Saxbe said, "that he couldn't even sell beer on a troop ship."

These remarkable words, delivered by a fellow Republican, shocked Dole and reinforced his bitterness and sense of exclusion from the club. He began criticizing the inner circles of the Senate.

---

[1] As of January, 1975, Nixon had finally withdrawn all U.S. combat troops.

Personally, he resented Saxbe's "hatchet man" label, fearing he would carry its weight for the rest of his life. Ten years later, Dole was still complaining privately that the label was "unfair" and that it boxed him in and limited his freedom of action, for fear of provoking a "chorus of 'hatchet man' jeers from the press." Fear of being called a hatchet man would later stifle his individuality and expression, often making him a Caspar Milquetoast, for when he wanted to swing freely and "let Dole be Dole," the hatchet man label would reappear like a noxious weed.

Though Dole was a solitary, unpopular figure in his early Senate years, he was certainly not a Joe McCarthy. He maintained a level of credibility as a brash and angry, but smart, Nixon clone. Once describing himself as a "missionary " whose job was to spread the gospel of Nixonism, he was also known to say, "If you liked Richard Nixon, you'll love Bob Dole."

It is noteworthy that Dole, a lifetime maverick who always resented outside direction, came to identify so closely with Nixon, a man whose identity he seemed to assume on the Senate floor. Personally, he seemed to find in Nixon something he had been looking for all his life, a clear sense of identity. Later criticisms of Dole as an eclectic pragmatist and a nonideological opportunist contrast startlingly with his self-appointed role as the fanatical minion of Richard Milhous Nixon.

Although in the House, Dole had been a silent supporter of U.S. involvement in the Vietnam War, his defense of Nixon was at its most vehement during floor debates on the war. Generally, whenever senators rose to criticize Nixon's handling of the war, Dole popped up and reminded them that Nixon had inherited the Vietnam War and that they should be directing their criticism at the Democratic administrations of John Kennedy and Lyndon Johnson. Dole saw the Vietnam War as a Democrat mess that Nixon was trying to clean up and for which he was being unjustly blamed. Typically, Dole's oratorical thrust against a Nixon critic began with something like "I cannot leave unchallenged the charges that the president and his administration" and ended with a reminder of "the president's record of accomplishment."

Politics aside, Dole reacted to the Vietnam War in an intensely personal, emotional way, perhaps because it reminded him of his own tragic injuries in World War II, another "Democrat war." Though he never publicly admitted it, Dole was, in a sense, opposed to the Vietnam War from the start, because of the tragic loss of life it brought about and because of the painfully slow manner in which it was being pursued by Johnson. He once publicly referred to "the Vietnam tragedy" and said many years later that if he had ever had to lead the country into war as a president, he would do so "as quickly and as painlessly as possible." Being a highly impatient man in general, and a man whose life has been unalterably affected by wartime injuries, Dole's attitude of "all or nothing" in war is not surprising.

What is genuinely surprising is the vehemence with which he defended Nixon's continuation of Johnson's futile war. To millions of critics in 1969, Nixon seemed to be carrying out Johnson's masochistically slow policy of limited war by attrition, condemning hundreds of thousands of troops to the meat grinder for murky ends. Seemingly oblivious to this needless suffering, Dole defended Nixon as if he were the Almighty, all the while hurling insults and blame at Nixon's predecessors for having started the whole mess.

In his early days in the Senate, Dole's insensitivity toward hurting and offending people was evident even in his relations with members of his own and the Senate's staff. Many rumors have prevailed over the years that Dole was a difficult man to work for. Indeed, Dole's staff turnover has been high throughout his Senate tenure. For several years I was a member of Dole's staff and found it an exciting, challenging experience, but thin-skinned staffers did not last long. Dole often turns his ire on a particular staffer, but he is not uniformly harsh or overly demanding. He has little tolerance for mistakes and is quick to fix the blame for any defeat on a staffer. He wants staffers who are intensely loyal to him personally, and he probably felt uncomfortable with his first personal secretary, who quit shortly after beginning to work for him, because she was a holdover from his predecessor, Senator Frank Carlson.

As Dole's star rose in the Senate, his marriage was disintegrating. With his new prominence and responsibilities, and with his workaholic temperament, he literally had no time for a full-time marriage. "He sat with us for a family dinner only four times during 1971," Phyllis recalls. "He was always away, flying around the country or doing something else."

One issue that galvanized Dole in his early Senate days was the cause of the handicapped, a group of Americans with whom Dole deeply identified and whose cause he was intent on championing in the Senate. The intensely personal, emotional nature of this identification is seen in the fact that his first major address on the Senate floor was about aid for the handicapped and that he chose to give it on the anniversary of the date on which he was wounded in World War II.

Rising to his feet on April 14, 1969, Dole revealed much of his true self in his maiden speech. Calling handicapped people an "exceptional group which I joined on another April 14, twenty-four years ago," Dole described the handicapped as "a minority group whose existence affects every person in our society and the very fiber of our nation. . . . As a minority, it has always known exclusion. Maybe not exclusion from the front of the bus, but perhaps from even climbing aboard it; maybe not exclusion from pursuing advanced education, but perhaps from experiencing any formal education; maybe not exclusion from day-to-day life itself, but perhaps from an adequate opportunity to develop and contribute to his or her fullest capacity."

Asserting that "at least one out of every five Americans" belongs to this minority group of the handicapped, Dole spoke eloquently and movingly of the unique problems facing them and demanded the creation of a presidential task force or commission to "review what the public and private sectors are doing and to recommend how we can do better." The goal of all handicapped people, he said, was to "achieve maximum independence, security, and dignity for the individual."

Dole's loyalty to, and identification with, the handicapped would color his performance in the Senate for the rest of his life. He would always seek ways to channel federal funds toward helping this minority, and his sympathy extended to other minority groups, such as blacks, Hispanics, and farmers. It constituted the basis for his compassionate streak that set him worlds apart from Nixon.

Dole saw the handicapped and farmers as his two key constituent groups in his early Senate days. He won a seat on the Senate Agriculture Committee, where he pursued pro-farmer strategies. He also sat on the Senate Select Committee on Nutrition and

Human Needs, the Small Business Committee, and the Public Works Committee.

Dole's fanatical, unquestioning defense of Richard Nixon extended beyond the Vietnam War to include tax bills, economic policy, and Nixon's two doomed Supreme Court nominees, Clement Haynesworth and G. Harrold Carswell.[2] He opposed Nixon on nothing.

The overwhelming impression of Dole in his early Senate days is that of a self-appointed gladiator, a scrapper always thirsting for a fight, "one of the toughest men I've ever met, the kind of guy I'd like to stand back to back with in a knife fight," according to Senator Bob Packwood, and "the first man we've had around here in a long time who will grab the other side by the hair and drag them down the hill," according to Senator Barry Goldwater.

With his lean six-foot, two-inch frame and his jet-black hair and sideburns that reached his earlobe, Dole actually looked the part of gunslinger as he patrolled the Senate floor in search of Nixon critics to gun down. He was a menacing presence, always lurking on the floor.

Dole's biting criticism of GOP Senate minority leader Hugh Scott intensified. He was quoted as saying that Scott should be replaced by "younger and more aggressive leadership" and left little doubt as to his own choice for that new leadership.

Nixon, nervous that Dole might split the party by challenging Scott for the post, decided to offer him the position of Republican National Committee chairman in January 1971, replacing Rogers Morton, a heavy-set, joyful person who had been nicknamed "Nixon's St. Bernard." Dole's impending selection created a storm of protest among the Senate's forty-three Republicans, half of whom protested to Nixon. Some of the senators claimed Dole was too conservative, while others objected to his abrasive personality. Hugh Scott opposed Dole's selection on the ground that the job required a full-time chairman, not someone who already had a job as senator.

[2]In his 1988 autobiography, Dole wrote, "I voted for both men. In retrospect, I was right on Haynesworth, wrong on Carswell." Bob and Elizabeth Dole with Richard Norton Smith, *The Doles: Unlimited Partners* (New York: Simon and Schuster, 1988), 115.

Becoming ever more defensive and bitter, Dole scoffed at these criticisms, taking his opponents' attacks as personal affronts, and he assured Nixon that he could handle two jobs with one hand. Nixon, who saw the challenge to Dole as an attack on him by the hated "Rockefeller establishment" wing of the party, stood by his man, and Dole was confirmed by the party.

For his part, Dole was interested in the new post not only because he wanted a more visible pulpit from which to spread his own message, but also because he felt that Nixon wanted to groom him for possible selection as his running mate in 1972, as a replacement for Spiro Agnew.[3] With an incipient "dump Agnew" movement gathering steam, and the ever-practical Nixon already casting around for a new running mate, Dole saw a Nixon-Dole ticket in 1972 as "a real possibility."

Dole took on his new role as RNC chairman with a vengeance. Flying around the country three or four times a week, then rushing back to Washington to cast key Senate votes, he became a human whirlwind, putting in eighteen- to twenty-hour days on a regular basis.

With a presidential election coming up the following year, Dole tried to generate enthusiasm among party kingpins all across the country for his own vice presidential candidacy. Over the past two decades, he had run up a string of political victories—indeed, had been undefeated—and he began to view himself as destined for the top.

[3]Agnew had gotten himself into numerous legal problems as governor of Maryland in the 1960s. Following press revelations of these matters, he was forced to resign the vice presidency in 1973. Eventually, he pleaded *nolo contendere* to criminal charges.

# 8

# A SUGAR-COATED STEEL MAGNOLIA

The new year of 1972 found Bob Dole riding high, waiting in the wings to be tagged as Nixon's running mate. But, as if he secretly felt undeserving of such success, he did something to sabotage himself.

In 1972 divorce was still a serious handicap for a politician. No president had ever been divorced, and Nelson Rockefeller's divorce had been a large factor in his defeat in the GOP presidential sweepstakes eight years earlier. In Richard Nixon's puritanical, old-fashioned morality, divorce was an unpardonable sin. Nixon, like Dole's own Methodist parents, believed that marriage was supposed to last forever. Such was the message that had been drummed into Dole's head not only by his parents and his mentor, but also by his conservative constituency back home in rural Kansas, where he would be facing a tough reelection campaign in two years.

Because of these political realities, Dole had kept up the pretense of having a good marriage for years. The reality, as he later admitted, was that he had outgrown Phyllis many years before 1972. He spent so much time in the office and on the road that he

93

was seldom at home. Long before 1972, according to their daughter, Robin, he and Phyllis had simply stopped communicating.

Suddenly, in September 1971, Dole demanded a quick divorce from Phyllis. He simply came home one night and announced, "I want out," surprising her with the suddenness of his decision. He refused to discuss the details, presenting her instead with a *fait accompli.*

By means that remain a mystery to this day, Dole somehow persuaded Phyllis to file the divorce petition herself, to make it appear as if *she* wanted out of the marriage, when in reality she was deeply hurt and opposed to this divorce. This tactic was apparently intended to minimize political damage to Dole by making him appear the victim.

Phyllis showed up with her lawyers—Bob did not come—in Shawnee County (Kansas) Court on January 11, 1972 (the day after her birthday), and filed her petition for an emergency divorce decree, expecting that there would be a sixty-day waiting period, as is customary. But instead she found the divorce was granted on the spot—the very same day.

The divorce was granted on grounds of incompatibility, and Phyllis was given custody of their seventeen-year-old daughter. Phyllis returned to Kansas, and Robin remained on the East Coast, enrolling in the Virginia Polytechnic Institute, where she would be near her father.

On January 15, 1972, the *Topeka Capital* quoted Phyllis as saying, "I'm still in shock. It [the divorce] was at his urgent request . . . I'm still trying to find a reason why he feels the way he does . . . I didn't want to do it. I tried to stall. Since spring there has been a change in him. I think he has been working too hard."

There seems to have been no pressing reason for the "urgent request" divorce. Dole has not explained it, commenting only that "I think you have to make a decision sooner or later."

Being by nature an indecisive person in many ways, Dole may have agonized for many years before bringing himself to swing the ax. Evidently, he never even discussed it with Phyllis, and he may have opted for an instant divorce so that he would not be faced with the burden of having to think it over for sixty days after filing, perhaps wallowing in indecision as he had been doing for years. This way, it was done, with no turning back.

As soon as the divorce was granted, Dole went to Nixon and tendered his resignation as Republican National Committee chairman. Though Nixon did not accept the offer at the time, rumors were rampant that Dole was in the doghouse with Nixon. He found himself ostracized from Nixon's inner circle and "cut off at the knees" as he was repeatedly bypassed in the Nixon 1972 reelection campaign. Nixon created his own committee to run his campaign, the Committee to Reelect the President, which acted independently of Dole's Republican National Committee.

Why did Dole do it? Why, at a critical juncture in his career, did he knowingly throw away a chance to be Nixon's running mate and risk losing his RNC chairmanship and his Senate seat?

Many rumors circulated around Washington and Kansas to explain his behavior. It was said that he wanted to marry another woman, but these rumors proved to be unfounded, and Dole went out of his way to deny them, insisting, "I have no plans to remarry." Once, when he went to Chicago, a local gossip columnist phoned him and said she wanted to be "in on the ground floor about the blonde" he had come to visit. Dole quipped that the blonde was three thousand Lithuanian-American women he had come to address.

The *Kansas City Star*, which followed such rumors closely, reported that "because he is Republican National Chairman, there is more than passing interest in the senator and his personal life." On May 18, 1972, the *Star* published a gossip column story on Dole's alleged relationship with a former model who worked on his Senate staff—a story that returned to dog him during his vice presidential campaign four years later, even though that story was reported four months *after* his divorce.

Though Dole had a sharp eye for female pulchritude, and though Phyllis was a rather plump, plain woman toward whom he appeared to be rather apathetic, there is no evidence that his first marriage broke up because of another woman.

Dole himself later explained the reasons for his divorce in a typically vague way. "We weren't programmed for fights," he has said. "We didn't have time. Instead I was either on a plane or at the office. I often wondered what would have happened had I not been a politician. The marriage probably wouldn't have been a failure . . . but then I couldn't have been a judge and sat in that black robe all day, say. That really isn't exciting."

His view of the marriage was echoed by his daughter, who described a relationship of apathy between her parents. "I never saw any personality clashes between them," Robin said. "I think maybe because he worked all day, and when he would come home at night he was distant. The biggest thing they lacked was communication. He didn't take her places, places she could have gone. I can't speak for her, but for myself, my first reaction would be rejection. There wasn't tension, but to me, it wasn't a perfect marriage for quite a while. I don't know anything about their private life together. He was home rarely, and when he was home he was tired."

The portrait painted by Robin is that of a cold, distant father who simply was not there, physically or emotionally. Dole himself said of his daughter, "I don't think I really knew her well. I was there for ceremonial things in school. But mostly they [Phyllis and Robin] were here and I was not. Sooner or later you have to make a decision—is the child going to be fatherless? . . . If you become married to politics, something else is going to suffer."

When I asked Phyllis why Bob had decided to divorce her, she replied tersely, "communications gap." When questioned further, she explained, "He didn't get home until 10:30 or 11:30 at night, and then he was gone again at sunrise. . . . After he became Republican National chairman [in 1971], he was gone all the time."

In 1976, Phyllis acknowledged that, although it was not clear at the time, the divorce was "the best thing that ever happened to me. . . . Once free, I found out just how numbly unhappy I had been all those lonely years." She admitted that during the last year of their marriage, Dole had been home for supper "only four times," and that he had always said he "didn't have time to talk about it."

"I was devastated by the divorce at first," Phyllis recalled in 1987. "I had thought I had been happy [married to Dole], but how can you tell, when you don't know what real happiness is?" She was glad, finally, to "be able to get on with my life."

"Phyllis was just too domestic for Bob," explained Bub Dawson, Dole's old Russell chum. "She wasn't politically oriented, that's all. She was more into home life, cooking, baking, that sort of thing. . . . But Bob didn't have time for a domestic life. He'd get home in a limousine at midnight, then be off again at five o'clock in the morning." Pointing to the contrast between Phyllis and Dole's second wife, Dawson added, "That's why Elizabeth is so good for him. She's politically oriented, too."

The communications gap mentioned by Phyllis has been confirmed by numerous persons close to Dole during his first marriage. Russell Townsley, the *Russell Daily News* publisher who lived near the Doles during the 1950s, told me that when Bob and Phyllis visited him and his wife, the two men sat in the living room reading their newspapers while the wives sat together in another room, sewing or watching TV. The silence was deafening. "So," Townsley would say. "So," Dole would echo.

"There wasn't a lot of idle chatter," Townsley recalled. "Bob was in too much of a hurry to waste time chitchatting."

"He doesn't like to argue or talk much in personal relationships," Phyllis told me.

Dole's communications gap was not limited to his home and social life. It has always been evident in his relations with his office staff. When I worked for him, he had a "will o' the wisp" quality about him, an elusiveness that made it difficult to establish a strong rapport. He preferred communication by one-page memos rather than *tête-à-tête*. Staffers were expected to simply submit a brief written description of issues and leave a check box for him to mark "yes" or "no." Ninety percent of the time, there would be no discussion. When there was, Dole would flit in and out and would expect instant analysis rather than lengthy discussion.

His contempt for genuine family life was illustrated in an incident in his office that I recall. A Kansas constituent showed up with his wife and five kids. After greeting them perfunctorily, Dole snarled, "How can that guy ever get anywhere, laden down like that? He's just a beast of burden." That acid remark said a lot about Dole's own values and attitude toward marriage and family life. He had to be a racehorse, as I often heard him say: "You can't saddle down a thoroughbred and then expect him to run in the Kentucky Derby." Apparently, Phyllis had weighed him down, made him feel like a beast of burden. And he had to be running in the Kentucky Derby, all the time, every day, every minute.

Nonetheless, Phyllis has remained loyal to Bob and his family through the years. She returned to Russell regularly, often visited Bob's parents after the divorce, and kept up her ties to Russellians. Phyllis married a Kansas rancher named Buzick in 1973. She was widowed and married again, this time to a New Hampshire man named Ben Macey, in 1987. They now live in Topeka.

Phyllis has become a Bob Dole admirer again in recent years. In November 1986, she began handcrafting little wooden "Dole for President '88" pins that she sells by mail to Dole supporters across the country. (The proceeds from the sales go to Phyllis, not to Bob's campaign.) "I just think that he'd make a fine president," she now says warmly. "He's a perfectionist and a workaholic. He is thorough and never gives up till he gets what he wants."

In 1972, however, Dole's divorce left a foul taste in the mouths of many Kansas voters—in large part because it had come about so suddenly, but also because Bob and Phyllis's marriage had become something of a legend spanning over two decades. The myth of the altruistic therapist nursing Bob back to strength after meeting and falling in love with him in the hospital had grown to epic proportions in the Sunflower State. Everyone had heard about Phyllis's attending classes with Bob, taking notes for him and writing his exams, sacrificing her own career for him. And now it appeared that she was being callously cast aside by the man to whom she had given so much.

Kansas newspapers blared in banner headlines, JUDGE REFUSES TO REVEAL "EMERGENCY" IN DOLE DIVORCE, and quoted Phyllis as being "in shock" over the heavy-handed trashing of their marriage. All in all, it wasn't a very pretty portrait of a man who aspired to become president. In one throw of the dice, he had managed to end his twenty-three-year-old marriage, tarnish his image among Kansas voters, and alienate his puritanical mentor in the White House.

After his divorce, Dole moved into an apartment in Washington's Watergate complex, the same cluster of residential, office, and retail buildings in which the famous Watergate burglary occurred on June 17, 1972. He still lives in that apartment today, with his second wife, whom he married in 1975. ("We haven't had the time to buy a house," he says, "but we've picked one out at 1600 Pennsylvania Avenue.") Having dropped the pretense of a good marriage and cut his losses decisively, Dole felt relieved, but not for long. Living alone in his bachelor pad, Dole found himself bored on those days with no work. Such occasions were rare, however, because he would almost always find something to do in the office. "Maybe I convinced myself I was overwhelmed with all this work because I didn't want to face going home," he says.

By offering to resign as RNC chairman, Bob was reacting to problems in a way that was to become his trademark. His offer was probably a way of seeking sanction and affirmation from Nixon. For the time being, Nixon declined Dole's offer to resign. But the divorce weakened the hitherto solid bond between the two men. Nixon would never again fully trust or favor Dole; he dismissed him as a possible running mate, complained that he wasn't a team player, and ultimately excluded him from his inner circle.

As 1972 wore on, Dole felt an increasingly "cold Arctic wind" blowing his way from the direction of 1600 Pennsylvania Avenue. Even though still nominally RNC chairman, he found himself on the periphery of power, shut off from access to Nixon by what he called "the faceless few of CREEP," the sarcastic acronym he coined for the Committee to Reelect the President.

In the summer of 1972, just after the Watergate burglary that would ultimately undo Nixon, Dole found himself in a peripheral job as a member of the committee working on Nixon's platform for the fall campaign. He was assigned the lowly task of helping draft the consumer rights plank, one of Nixon's pet projects, when he met a woman who would play a resurrecting role in his life.

Her name was Mary Elizabeth Alexander Hanford, and she was something of a *wunderkind* with a sugar-coated personality that obscured a deep-rooted and fierce personal ambition. She was thirty-six years old, a stunningly attractive brunette in a southern belle mode, and went by the name of Liddy. (Today she insists on being called Elizabeth.) In spite of her beauty queen looks and her roots in the South, where early marriage was the norm for girls, she had never been married.

When she first saw Dole, Hanford said to herself, "My goodness, he's an attractive man," and he jotted down her name on a blotter. He struck her as a shy person, and indeed his shyness made him wait several months before seeking a date.

Despite her liberal political views, Dole was awestruck by Hanford at first sight. He is fascinated by coincidences in dates, and he seemed particularly impressed that her birthday fell only seven days after his own.

Dole was both intrigued and frightened by Liddy Hanford. She was the very opposite of Phyllis in almost every way. Born on July 29, 1936, in Salisbury, North Carolina (four times the size of Russell), she had always enjoyed the advantages denied Dole in early life. Her father, John Hanford, was a politically conservative and wealthy wholesale florist, and her mother Mary, was active in the town's social life. She and her brother, John Jr., knew from an early age that they were protected from the winds of want. With brains, money, charm, and social contacts at her disposal, Hanford cruised through an easy four years at Duke University in nearby Durham, North Carolina. At Duke, where coeds were segregated from men and had their own mini-campus, Hanford excelled both scholastically and socially. She was student body president, May Queen, and a member of the Delta Delta Delta Sorority and Phi Beta Kappa.

By the time Elizabeth Hanford graduated from Duke in 1958 with a bachelor's degree in political science, Bob Dole had been through a lot of suffering and was still in Russell, Kansas, sweating it out as a low-paid and obscure county attorney. The two seemed worlds apart.

After her smooth ride through Duke, Hanford journeyed north to Cambridge, Massachusetts, where she got a job at the Harvard Law School library and then enrolled in a joint education and government program and later in the law school. In the summer of 1959, she studied at England's Oxford University and visited the Soviet Union. The following summer, she worked as a secretary in the Washington office of North Carolina's Democratic Senator, B.

Everett Jordan, and then joined Democratic vice-presidental candidate Lyndon B. Johnson on a tour of the South.

She was one of only twenty-five females in the 550-student Harvard law class of 1965 and smarted with resentment at being snubbed by egotistical professors who called on her rarely, only on "Ladies' Days." Hanford's law school classmates included Patricia Schroeder, who became a congresswoman from Colorado, and Elizabeth Holtzman, who became a congresswoman and district attorney in Brooklyn, New York.

After graduating with a law degree and a master's degree in education, Hanford moved to Washington and immersed herself in the Great Society programs of the Johnson Administration. Feeling that in government she could do more to help the poor, she obtained a job in the Department of Health, Education and Welfare. She then set up her own law practice representing mostly indigents as a court-appointed attorney for a year. In April of 1968, she then moved into the White House as an assistant to Johnson on consumer affairs. Hanford, as Dole would later quip, had "already made it to the White House by the age of thirty-two."

In the sixties, Hanford's politics were as different from Dole's as her social background. A limousine liberal who identified with the underdogs of society because she viewed herself as one of them (being a woman competing in an all-male power structure), Hanford worked for the very social programs that Dole was voting against in Congress. She had heard that his political views were to the far right and that Johnson was trying to get Dole defeated.

When Nixon replaced Johnson in the White House in 1969, Elizabeth stayed on, changing her affiliation on her voter registration from Democrat to Independent. Like Dole, she demonstrated great skill as a political chameleon. One of a few White House aides to survive the changing of the guard after the 1968 election, she showed remarkable powers of adaptability and a great instinct for bureaucratic survival.

She became a member of Nixon's team, working under Virginia Knauer, and in a sense was in a position superior to Dole's when they met in 1972, as she had the president's ear and commanded his favor.

Like Dole, she was a workaholic who didn't have time for romance or family life. She too had always put in grueling twelve-to-eighteen hour days at the office, six or seven days a week. She rarely dated and had little time for anything besides her career.

In Dole, Hanford recognized a man whose towering ambitions matched her own, which, according to the senator, included a lifelong desire to become the first woman president of the United States.

To Bob Dole, the supercompetitive human machine, Elizabeth represented a tempting challenge. He would seek to surpass her in accomplishments and in racing to the presidency, even as she purported to be his helpmate. In daily competition to work the longest hours each day and to write more laws and regulations and to get more press, they constituted a symbiotic and synergistic duo that would fascinate and tantalize the nation as none had ever done before.

In addition to her challenging competitiveness, her alluring good looks, and her insatiable appetite for work, Hanford appealed to Dole for another reason. She represented something Phyllis had never come close to symbolizing: the American dream. So desirable among the movers and shakers in the nation's capital ("She was the most desirable eligible woman in Washington," said John LeBoutillier, a GOP congressman from New York 1981-82, "and everyone wanted to marry her"), Elizabeth Hanford was, for Dole, an incarnation of success, prosperity, the upper crust of American life. She was a real prize—a trophy—and his passport to a part of society that he had always resented and envied because it had been closed to him. His ego, always looking for new sources of self-affirmation, would soar to new heights. And, with his star already plummeting in the eyes of both Nixon and Kansas voters, he needed all the self-confidence he could muster.

So that Nixon could retain the image of party unity, Dole was confirmed as GOP national chairman at the party's August convention. As the 1972 presidential campaign wound down, however, Dole found himself calling Hanford and asking *her* for inside tips. By election day in November, when Nixon coasted to a landslide victory over the hapless George McGovern, word was already out that Nixon wanted Dole out completely.

In contrast, Elizabeth's star was rising. By year's end, Nixon had decided to appoint her as a federal trade commissioner, a powerful seven-year position that enabled her to act in a quasi-judicial and quasi-legislative role as she decided cases, wrote opinions, and issued regulations affecting consumer rights, antitrust, and unfair trade practices.

Dole wistfully watched her career soar in inverse proportion to his own. To him, she was a "sugar-coated steel magnolia," the likes of which he had never known, for "they don't grow 'em like that in Kansas."

# 9
# THE MAN IN THE WATERGATE-PROOF VEST

Richard Nixon's 1972 reelection stampede rode roughshod over the incipient Watergate scandal that had erupted on June 17, 1972, when a group of men in the employ of James McCord's McCord Associates Security Consultants were caught red-handed while burglarizing the Democratic National Committee headquarters in the Watergate complex. It turned out that McCord was in the employ of the Committee to Reelect the President (the so-called CREEP), which was technically a separate entity, distinct from the Republican National Committee (RNC), of which Dole was chairman throughout 1972.

The distinction between CREEP and the RNC turned out to be immensely important to Dole's political survival, for it enabled him to dodge Watergate bullets by insisting that he knew nothing about the burglary or its subsequent cover-up by Nixon. When the world learned that Nixon had secretly bugged all conversations in the Oval Office, Dole joked, "Thank goodness I only nodded when I was in there." Later he wise-cracked that because of Watergate the GOP "got the burglar vote."

Kidding aside, Dole was able to survive Watergate because he could later point to his own fall from grace with Nixon, his assignment to a peripheral role in the campaign, and his ultimate firing by Nixon as head of the RNC. In one of the great ironies of this phoenix's life, Dole's divorce—which doomed him as a Nixon protégé—ultimately saved him from going down on Nixon's sinking ship.

For the moment, however, Dole plunged into the Nixon reelection campaign like a battering ram. He attacked George McGovern as "an opportunistic politician who has engaged in one of the dirtiest political campaigns ever to cover up a record of questionable conduct," and accused the *Washington Post* of being McGovern's partner in the campaign.

In December 1972, flushed with victory and now finding it safe to drop the pretense of party unity that had allowed Dole to be the nominal RNC chairman, Nixon summoned Dole to Camp David and unceremoniously told him he was finished in that position. Vindictive and cocky in victory, Nixon told the Kansan that he wanted a new team and criticized him for not being a team player. (Nixon's preference was for that consummate team player George Bush.) The president then asked for Dole's resignation, thus dismissing him from the mountaintop.

A much-shaken Dole, who had trusted Nixon like a father, held a press conference and announced that he was resigning as RNC chairman. As in the case of his divorce, he did not reveal that Nixon had fired him, and he pretended that he had volunteered to step down.

Only eight years later would the full story come out, when Dole discussed this incident with the press: "Having been pushed out of the RNC chairmanship to make room for Bush, I got the shower bath. . . . My reward for being a good chairman was execution at Camp David. . . . I was willing to carry water for the White House, but I didn't want the bucket dumped over me."

To add insult to injury, Nixon ordered Dole to fly to New York to ask Bush to resign his position as United Nations ambassador. Dole was unaware at the time that Nixon had secretly offered Bush his own position as RNC chairman and I later heard him complain that he had been misled into begging his own executioner to swing the ax. He never forgave Bush for this humiliation and always referred to him privately in the harshest of terms—"a guy who screws with his socks on," "the Rockefeller puppet," "the invisible man," or "a Mister Magoo in a blazer."

Dole exploded when Nixon assigned him to ride near the end of his inaugural parade on January 20, 1973. It was a slight that fueled Dole's fury toward the man he had defended so staunchly. Out of political necessity, however, Dole managed to maintain a public facade of being on good terms with the president. Years later, Dole would refer to ex-presidents Ford, Carter, and Nixon as "See No Evil, Hear No Evil . . . and Evil."

For the time being, Dole returned to his mundane Senate duties, pursued a romantic interest in Elizabeth Hanford, and looked worriedly toward his upcoming Senate reelection campaign in Kansas the following year.

Nineteen seventy-three was the watershed year for the Nixon presidency. The *Washington Post*, which kept up a steady drumbeat of attack as the Watergate scandal unraveled, and which Dole had condemned in 1972 as "George McGovern's partner," pushed top Nixon aides H. R. Haldeman and John D. Ehrlichman into early retirement in April and produced an almost daily barrage of damaging news reports relating to a criminal cover-up and the obstruction of justice. In the summer, the Senate Select Watergate Committee, under the chairmanship of the folksy Sam Ervin, held televised hearings that daily produced shocking revelations implicating Nixon and his top lieutenants in a massive conspiracy to break laws, engage in illegal espionage against domestic political opponents, and obstruct justice.

Dole watched the gathering developments with mounting apprehension. Reports surfaced that James McCord, the head Watergate burglar, had been on the payroll of the RNC during Dole's reign. McCord, facing a stiff prison sentence at the hands of federal judge John J. Sirica, decided to "sing" in hopes of leniency and implicated key figures in CREEP and the White House. Nixon lieutenants began falling like dominos, particularly after ex-White House counsel John Dean testified to Nixon's personal involvement in the cover-up, and the embattled president himself squirmed nervously and declared defiantly, "I am not a crook."

One particularly dangerous revelation for Dole was the testimony of Hugh Sloan, treasurer of CREEP, given in the Senate Watergate hearings in August 1973. Sloan reported that he had given Dole $3,000 for a trip to South Vietnam: "Internally, within the staff, we could not understand why we were paying for Mr. Dole's trip." Watergate Committee investigators found a memorandum from Bart Porter to Jeb Magruder, both CREEP officials, stating that Dole had been selected by Nixon as a spokesman for the administration's Vietnam policy in the summer of 1971. The memorandum noted that Senator William Fulbright, the severest critic of Nixon's war policies, had never been to Vietnam and implied that Dole should go in order to observe the war firsthand and thereby enhance his own credibility as a defender of the policy. The memorandum estimated that the trip would cost $2,000 or so and stated that Dole had rejected payment for his expenses from both Republican party or Senate committee funds. If the trip were paid for with party funds, the memo said, then Dole might be criticized for playing politics, while if Senate funds were used, he might be criticized for misappropriating government money.

According to the *New York Times*, "the memo suggested that [CREEP] would secretly supply the funds and that if Senator Dole were asked, he would reply, 'a private source supplied his travel funds.'" On August 5, 1972, the *Congressional Quarterly* routinely published Dole's report on his 1971 travels. The report noted, "August 17–22: Japan, South Vietnam, Cambodia, Thailand, to observe the progress of the Vietnamization program, treatment of POWs, and drug abuse problems among servicemen, personal expense."

The significance of the money for the trip to South Vietnam is that the $3,000 came from the same secret cache of money that was later used to finance the Watergate burglary. Though there is no evidence that Dole had any role in the Watergate break-in—he later joked that the burglary had occurred "on my night off"—the mere fact that he had received money from CREEP's secret cache was potentially very damaging.

However, he managed to dodge that bullet. Dole was never called as a witness before the Senate Watergate Committee, and there is no record that the committee investigators ever interviewed or investigated him on this matter.

Dole managed to sidestep another scandal involving the Nixon Administration that resulted in Senate Judiciary Committee investigations. The scandal concerned ITT (International Telephone & Telegraph) Corporation's 1971 alleged attempt to influence Nixon's Justice Department in its handling of an antitrust case involving ITT. In mid-1971, according to the *New York Times*, while Dole was still chairman of the Republican National Committee, the ITT–Sheraton Corporation "offered the committee a $400,000 'guarantee,' ostensibly as part of an effort to attract the 1972 Republican National Convention to San Diego, where the corporation was building a hotel. At the same time, the Justice Department was considering whether to require the conglomerate to divest itself of several of its major, profitable holdings" because of possible antitrust violation. John Mitchell, who was Nixon's key political adviser (and in 1972 his campaign manager), was U.S. attorney general at the time.

According to the *Times*, Ed Reinecke, then the Republican lieutenant governor of California, received the ITT offer in May 1971 and transmitted it by telephone to John Mitchell. Reinecke testified about his role to the Senate committee and was later tried and convicted of perjury. The conviction was overturned on the grounds that no quorum was present at the Judiciary Committee when he gave his testimony.

ITT's offer was made public in February 1972 by columnist Jack Anderson, who published a memorandum written by Dita Beard, a consultant for ITT, which suggested that the $400,000 was offered in order to induce the Nixon Administration to pressure the Justice Department to make a decision favorable to ITT on the antitrust divestiture issue.

At this time, the Senate Judiciary Committee was considering Nixon's nomination of Richard G. Kleindienst to succeed John Mitchell as attorney general. It reopened its hearings to investigate the ITT matter. Incredibly, Dole was not called as a witness here either, although he had been chairman of the Republican National Committee when the ITT offer was made in 1971.

There is a question about whether or not Dole was informed of the ITT offer at the time that Reinecke and Mitchell handled it. According to the *New York Times*, Reinecke later told the grand jury in Washington that he had informed Dole and Dole's assistant at the RNC, Daniel Evans, about the offer. Josephine L. Good, another of Dole's RNC assistants, testified that she gave Dole a memorandum on July 2, 1971, that completely outlined ITT's offer, but said she was not certain that Dole had read the memo or spoken to Mitchell about it.

In fairness to Dole, it must be pointed out that even if he had seen the memorandum, he would not necessarily have known whether or not ITT was making an attempt to manipulate the Justice Department's handling of the antitrust case, and there is no proof that he saw or read the memorandum.

In March of 1972, Dole held a news conference in which he said that the Republican Party had received ITT's offer but that this offer had no connection with the antitrust case. He insisted that he had rebuffed an effort by Dita Beard to meet with him in 1971. However, in 1974, when he was running for reelection to the Senate in Kansas and the ITT affair had become a campaign issue, the *New York Times* quoted him as saying he had never known about any ITT offer at all.

But this issue and others were overshadowed by the question of where Dole stood on the impeachment of President Nixon.

Nixon's viability and credibility as president collapsed rapidly after he fired Watergate special prosecutor Archibald Cox in the Saturday Night Massacre on October 20, 1973. Cox had insisted that Nixon turn over tape recordings of Oval Office conversations; Nixon refused and then ordered Attorney General Elliot Richardson to fire Cox. When Richardson refused and resigned, Solicitor General Robert Bork then followed Nixon's orders and fired Cox.[1] By early 1974, Congress had initiated impeachment proceedings, and the president's fate was considered a toss-up.

As more and more leaders from both parties called for Nixon's impeachment, Dole found himself in the awkward but familiar position of straddling the fence and remained officially noncommittal on the issue of Nixon's fate. His natural indecisiveness and reluctance to stick his neck out on controversial issues dictated his

[1]In 1987, Dole supported Reagan's nomination of Bork for the Supreme Court, introducing him to the Judiciary Committee. Bork was rejected by the Senate.

**Well, he'll still get his feet wet!**

course of action as he played a bewilderingly ambiguous role on Capitol Hill.

Dole was one of the last Republican senators to abandon Nixon, hesitating until the last minute. He still felt some loyalty toward his erstwhile benefactor and feared a backlash from pro-Nixon forces and constituents if he jumped ship.

Dole faced a tough reelection campaign for the Senate in Kansas in 1974 when a strong contender, Congressman William Roy, announced his intention to challenge Dole for the seat. Roy was a two-term Congressman from Topeka who held both a medical and a law degree and had specialized in obstetrics and gynecology from 1955 to 1970.

Life was breathed into Dole's campaign in June 1974 when the Senate Watergate Committee gave him a clean bill of health and stated categorically in its final report that the Watergate affair had

not been the workings of the Republican National Committee or of
its then-chairman. Nonetheless, back home in Kansas, Dole's
Democratic opponents began smearing him with Watergate mud.
Norbert Dreiling, Kansas state Democratic Chairman, challenged
Dole to confirm or deny that James McCord was on the payroll of
the RNC on June 17, 1972, the date of the Watergate break-in.

Two former top officials of the RNC, Tom Evans and Barry
Mountain, stated that Dole had not been involved in the RNC's
hiring of McCord, however, and this helped to clear Dole's name.
Evans stated that the RNC, not Dole, had hired McCord Associates and that Dole had called him after the Watergate break-in
and asked him about McCord's status on the committee. "I told
him, 'Senator, there is no status to report. He's been terminated,' "
Evans maintained.

In 1974, when Dole returned to Kansas, everywhere he went he
was asked whether or not he favored the impeachment of Nixon.
"It's an impossible dilemma," Dole complained. "One guy gives
me hell for betraying Nixon. The next guy comes up to me and
says, 'I'm for you, Bob, but you've got to get Nixon off our backs.'
There's no way to stay on that tightrope." In February 1974, Dole
stated publicly that "a legal case against the president has not been
made." Later he retreated slightly from that position but maintained until the bitter end that he hoped that Nixon would be
proven innocent. At one point, he toyed with the idea of calling
together all the Republican senators to draft a "statement of independence" from Nixon but gave that up as impractical. Then he
tried telling an audience that Nixon wanted him reelected to the
Senate but found himself whipsawed by angry pro- and anti-Nixon
voters. He even tried humor. When asked whether he would like
Nixon to campaign for him in Kansas, he replied that he "wouldn't
mind it if Nixon flew over the state." That joke produced widespread chuckles but also a batch of angry letters from Nixon supporters.

By refusing to abandon Nixon, Dole came disastrously close to
ending his own career. He thought increasingly of one of his distant predecessors, Senator Edmund G. Ross of Kansas, who in
1868 cast the deciding Senate vote against the conviction of then-
president Andrew Johnson. Johnson had been impeached by the

House and then stood for trial in the Senate after being hounded by radical Republicans protesting his benevolent post–Civil War policies toward the defeated South. Ross exhibited great courage and said, "I looked down into my open grave" as he resisted tremendous pressure brought on him and voted to acquit Johnson. His career was ruined.

Dole, seeing himself in the role of Ross, said in 1974, "I wouldn't mind losing my [Senate] seat if the man [Nixon] is innocent and I've voted to clear him. But I hate to be deceived. And I don't know, I don't know." He seems to have displayed a martyr's mentality, an almost poignant yearning to dangle over the edge of an abyss.

He was bailed out of his dilemma by Nixon's surprise resignation effective August 9, 1974, which obviated the need for a Senate trial and thus relieved Dole of a major burden. In September, however, President Gerald Ford pardoned Nixon for any crimes he may have committed and thereby angered a large number of voters, who suspected a "fix" and who now considered Dole, a surviving Republican, guilty by association. Polls showed Kansas public opinion running three to two against the pardon.

Dole went home to Kansas to face the toughest Senate reelection campaign of his life. The polls showed his Democratic challenger, Dr. William Roy, leading by as much as thirteen points, but once again luck played a role in saving Dole's career: he happened to be on the winning side of a divisive and inflammatory issue that became disproportionately important in the campaign.

Roy tried not to dwell excessively on Dole's alleged tie-in to Watergate. According to Robert Brock, a key adviser and financier for Roy's campaign, "We had things we could have used on Dole, but Dr. Roy held back. He didn't want to conduct that kind of campaign." (Brock also claimed that he had gotten on Nixon's "enemies list" by "local recommendation.") In his speeches, Roy said that "Dole knew or should have known about the Watergate affair in his capacity as [Republican] Party Chairman. . . . We need a candidate who will represent the state and the nation rather than his party and the head of his party." This was rather mild criticism, and Roy didn't go much further than that.

Dole launched a strong counteroffensive in September. He

shook up his campaign staff and fired his campaign manager, replacing him with David Owen.[2] Challenged by the uphill fight, he revived the Dolls for Dole and went all out for victory, aiming for the jugular and gung ho for combat.

What turned his campaign around was a clever television commercial that he came up with. In this classic ad, Dole's face was depicted on a billboard. A voice whined, "Bill Roy says Bob Dole is against old people," and mud was splattered on Dole's face simultaneously. Then the voice groaned, "Bill Roy says Bob Dole is against the farmer," and more mud splattered on Dole's face. Then, another voice cheerfully proclaimed, "Bob Dole voted thirty times for Social Security," and mud came off; the voice then announced, "Bob Dole served the Kansas farmer on the Agriculture Committee," and the rest of the mud disappeared revealing Dole's famous face.

Although Roy had declined to throw mud at Dole, that's what the ad accused Roy of doing. "Dole's a great crier," Roy told me recently. "He's very good at complaining about how poor Bob Dole is being whipped by the opposition." The ads illustrated the merit of Dole's general strategy of turning a weapon around and using it against his attacker, for, by all accounts, they were extremely effective.

Dole's standing in the polls began to improve. Going into the weekend before the election, most polls showed Dole and Roy running neck and neck. In some polls, Roy was slightly ahead, but the election was considered a toss-up. Then, with just a few days to go, something happened that proved to be the decisive factor in giving Dole a razor-thin victory, though it would eventually come back to haunt him.

In 1974, abortion was a very heated topic in Kansas. It was of interest to only about 15 percent of registered voters, most of them Catholics and fundamentalist Protestants, according to the polls, but to those people it was crucial. The year before, the Supreme Court had issued its controversial *Roe v. Wade* opinion, which

[2]Owen, a banker from Stanley, Kansas, went on to become Dole's protégé and close adviser for the next thirteen years, until his abrupt resignation from Dole's presidential campaign staff in January of 1988.

essentially stated that it was unconstitutional for any state to ban abortions outright during the first trimester of pregnancy. Dole bitterly criticized that opinion and said that he would support a pro-life constitutional amendment—"whatever that is," he told a reporter. "Who knows what they will settle on?" Roy, by contrast, appeared somewhat ambiguous on the issue. Soon the pro-lifers put out the word: "Vote for Dole." With that word came an ugly whispering campaign against Roy.

The right-to-life people opposed Roy because as a physician he had actually performed about ten abortions (done legally under Kansas's restrictive laws, which required independent second medical opinions for an abortion to be performed); and because he believed that the decision to end pregnancy before twenty weeks should not be covered by criminal law, as long as it is performed by a licensed physician in a licensed hospital. This position favoring this very restricted form of abortion was seriously distorted by Roy's enemies in the campaign, however, and he was painted as favoring abortion on demand.

On the Sunday before the election, leaflets depicting dead fetuses in garbage cans—clearly implying that Roy favored abortion on demand—appeared on automobile windshields outside Catholic churches and on hotel room doorknobs. In addition, voters were assaulted with a barrage of hand-delivered pamphlets and direct-mail, radio, and newspaper ads attacking Roy's position on abortion. Ads placed in major Kansas newspapers at this time depicted a skull and crossbones: one crossbone held the word *abortion* and the other the word *euthanasia*, and the ad read VOTE FOR LIFE— BOB DOLE WILL SUPPORT A HUMAN LIFE AMENDMENT. VOTE FOR DOLE. In addition, Roy was picketed and harassed by hecklers at virtually every campaign stop. "Sometimes there were so many pickets that you couldn't even get into or out of the building," says Roy today.

On November 5, 1974, Kansans went to the polls and gave Dole a victory by a bare margin of 13,000 votes; the final tally showed that Dole received about 393,000 votes (50.8 percent) compared to Roy's 380,000 (49.2 percent).

Dole later said that the turning point in his campaign had come in late September or early October, when he said he had regained confidence in his ability to win. But the real turning point may have been two days before the election.

Roy blamed his defeat on an unfair, last-minute campaign against him by the state's antiabortion forces, which cost him the election. During his concession speech, Roy said, "I was flat out beat on the abortion issue." It was unfortunate, he said, that the people of Kansas, "not many of them, but some of them," took that negative and harsh position on the abortion issue. He decried the distribution of antiabortion literature by the right-to-life organizations in such Catholic Democratic areas as Atchison and Leavenworth, Kansas, which depicted him as being "pro-abortion" and urged support for Dole. He also said that the right-to-life group was unusually well financed.

Roy contends today that Dole somehow managed to obtain the mailing lists of voters receiving veterans' and social security benefits, and that he targeted them for some very effective direct-mail ads during the last days of the campaign. This, combined with the surge of anti-abortion literature from the pro-life activists managed to barely save Dole's career.

Did Dole have any hand in the smear campaign against Roy, and, if not, were any of his supporters involved? It must be pointed out that no one has ever proved that he directly ordered or had any foreknowledge of the distribution of the leaflets showing the dead fetuses. However, at a news conference covered by the Associated Press the day before the senatorial election in November 1974, Dole did *not* specifically disavow any ads.

*The New York Times* reported in 1976 that, according to the federal election records filed after the 1974 campaign was over, Dole accepted in-kind contributions worth $288.56 from a Shawnee Mission, Kansas, woman for five insertions of an ad in separate newspapers. She was the signer of an ad placed by the Eastern Kansas Right to Life Organization that carried the skull and crossbones. In addition, Dole accepted an in-kind political contribution for "postage" from a Shawnee Mission man who was also affiliated with the Kansas right-to-life organizations.

The *Times* also reported that, according to the Right to Life Affiliates of Kansas, an umbrella group over the antiabortion forces in that state, Dole had assigned a full-time staff member to coordinate with them. "On October 5, 1974, less than a month before the election, Mr. Dole appeared before the right to life state convention in Hays, Kansas. He is quoted as telling an audience of 150: 'If you want a human life amendment [to the Constitution], then elect those who will support your position. The people must be asked to speak. We must ask the American people what they want.' He also reportedly told the group, 'I say I am against the interruption of human life and the law ought to oppose this interruption.' He also said, 'That's what right to life is all about—the interruption of human life.' " Although Dole had not officially pledged to join Senator Jesse Helms of North Carolina in coauthoring a bill calling for a constitutional amendment to ban abortion, he was basically on record as opposing abortion.

In *Lifetime*, a pamphlet of the Right to Life Affiliates, which was published after the Hays convention, its members were urged to place newspaper ads. According to the *Times*, the pamphlet stated, "The last week before the election is the right time for ads. Run six small ads (one each day) and a larger one on November 5 [1974]." A sample copy of the skull-and-crossbones ad was shown as an example, along with others that read DOLE FIGHTS ABORTION, ROY PERFORMED ABORTIONS. The pamphlet urged its readers to "get some sponsors (don't be shy, it's not for yourself), then with money and ad in hand, go place your ads."

According to federal election law regulations enforced in 1974, it was perfectly legal for individuals to place ads opposing a candidate without having to set up a political action committee or report the cost. Any ads placed or contributions made or services performed on behalf of a candidate, however, had to be authorized by the candidate and deducted from the amount allowed for media expenses. Dole insisted that he had never authorized ads and therefore had never deducted their cost from his expenses.

It must be pointed out that Dole's brother Kenny says that he received a call from Topeka on the Sunday before the election saying that "someone" had been placing the abortion flyers on motel doorknobs and auto windshields outside Catholic churches. Kenny went out and removed the flyers and threw them away because he felt they would embarrass Bob and feared Bob might be blamed for them.

Even Norbert Dreiling, the Kansas state Democratic chairman and one of Bob Dole's harshest critics,[3] later said that Dole had made special efforts to restrain his more zealous supporters. Dreiling, whose mother, Molly, had grown up with Dole's mother, Bina, in Russell, recalls that during the 1974 campaign Dole used to tell an amusing little story to his supporters to restrain them: "My mom just heard what Norbert Dreiling said about me," Dole would say. " 'That can't be Molly's boy,' my mom said the other day. . . . Well, I don't want folks saying, 'That can't be Bina's boy.' " Whether he succeeded in restraining his more fanatical followers or not, he did make the effort.

Dole understood "hayseed humor" very well and often managed to get his point across by reciting a yarn or an anecdote. According to Kenny Dole, Bob used to tell people in western Kansas towns, "There's a shortage of doctors in this area, and you need to keep all the doctors you can get. If Dr. Roy goes to the Senate, you'll lose a much-needed doctor." His audience rocked with laughter.

Although one can never completely rule out someone of his stupendous drive and determination, it seems clear that if Dole had lost this particular election, his career would have probably ended there and then, and Dole would have probably gone down as a footnote to history and as a casualty of the Watergate disaster. Instead he surged into a second Senate term with a sense of personal destiny. As was the case with his war injuries, Dole barely managed to sidestep catastrophe, and his narrow brush with disaster made him all the more cocky and aggressive.

Shortly after securing his victory over Roy, Dole was heard to joke, "They said that since my opponent has a medical degree and a law degree that he was one in a million. Now he's one in ten million—he's unemployed."

Back in Washington, Dole continued to court Elizabeth Hanford. During the 1974 campaign, he had called her frequently, often late at night or early in the morning, and asked her advice. "I told him fine, go ahead and call anytime," she later recalled. He had been dating her for three years. He may also have put off

[3]Dreiling attacked Dole for being RNC chairman during Watergate and insisted Dole knew or should have known about what had been going on.

marriage because of his fear of losing his reelection campaign. Now that his seat was secure, Dole finally asked Elizabeth for her hand and got it.

During the year-long engagement, Dole launched into a pro-consumer crusade from the floor of the Senate, picking this as his pet project for the time being, perhaps influenced by his future bride's deep commitment to consumers' rights. On February 24, 1975, Bob rose to his feet on the Senate floor and praised Virginia Knauer, who had been Elizabeth's boss in the Nixon White House, as "a lady with heart" for her role as the "top consumer advocate in the [Ford] administration." Knauer, he said, "is a woman who understands and deals with human problems, not statistics." Three months later, on May 7, 1975, Dole spoke in the Senate on the need for "legislation to increase consumer representation in the federal government" and discussed his work on a consumer protection bill which, he claimed, had irritated "many in private industry and government."

Bob and Elizabeth's wedding took place on Saturday, December 6, 1975, and was a private fifteen-minute service performed by longtime Senate chaplain Reverend Edward Elson in the austere, molded stone and wood Bethlehem Chapel of the Washington Cathedral. The best man was Assistant Defense Secretary Robert Ellsworth,[4] Bob's longtime Kansas friend, and the matron of honor was Elizabeth's sister-in-law, Burnell "Bunny" Hanford. About seventy relatives, friends, and cabinet officers attended the wedding breakfast at the fashionable F Street Club.

Among the guests were Julie and David Eisenhower and Secretary of Agriculture Earl Butz. Richard Nixon telephoned his congratulations to Dole the day before and invited the new couple to come to his exile in San Clemente "for a cup of tea."

Dole's parents arrived from Russell on Thursday, December 4, and stayed at his Watergate apartment when the couple took off for a honeymoon in the Virgin Islands. Tragedy marred the Doles' honeymoon when, only two days after the marriage, on December 8, Bob's father suffered a severe heart attack in the apartment. He

---

[4]Ellsworth is a former Kansas congressman and was Dole's initial campaign chairman in the 1988 presidential campaign.

underwent surgery and died the next day. Shaken, Dole cut short his vacation and returned to Washington.

Doran Dole, who had "missed only one day of work in forty years," had collapsed suddenly. Upset about Doran's demise and once again feeling victimized by fate, which had intervened to deprive him of what should have been a joyous occasion, Bob stoically suppressed his feelings. They were revealed indirectly, however, in subtle personal comments made in later years and in his gesture of hanging a large portrait of Doran above his desk in his Senate office. There Doran would always be watching over Bob, making sure he worked as hard as possible.

# 10
# 1976:
# GOP HATCHET MAN

B ob Dole seemed even more cocky and aggressively acerbic following Doran's untimely demise. Entering Senate committee hearing rooms in early 1976, he seemed like a jack-in-the-box, ready to pop up and cut down the liberals who inevitably called for "full funding" of one social program after another. Dole was particularly harsh toward Walter Mondale, the pallid Minnesota Democrat who had always gotten every position by appointment only.[1]

Once, when Hubert Humphrey walked in late to an Agriculture Committee hearing while a milk bill was being discussed, the ever-punctual Dole was waiting for him with a glass of milk, which he raised high in the air in a mock toast.

His hard-hitting tactics were earning him praise among Washington Republicans while the hapless President Ford sat in the eye of a political hurricane of recession and stagflation. The economy

---

[1] A protégé of Hubert Humphrey, Mondale had been appointed to the Senate by Minnesota Governor Karl Rolvaag in 1964, when Humphrey left to be Johnson's vice president. In 1960, Mondale had been appointed Minnesota attorney general by Governor Orville Freeman, in whose law office he had worked.

was in a deep recession, unemployment lines were lengthening, and inflation was soaring toward double digits, but Ford played the role of a mini-Hoover by vetoing bill after bill passed by the Democratically controlled Congress that was aimed at giving the economy a shot in the arm. In 1974, Dole had privately worried that the clumsy Ford would "kick the ball away in the first quarter. He's already fumbled a couple of times."

And now the presidential race was on, and Dole watched eagerly from the sidelines as the charismatic right-wing ideologue, Ronald Reagan, mounted an impressive challenge to Ford for the 1976 GOP nomination. Reagan beat the president in a string of primary states, dividing the party right down the middle and leading the GOP into a showdown at its August convention in Kansas City.

Meanwhile, on the Democratic side, Jimmy Carter was busily chalking up presidential primary victories by attacking Ford over the recession and the "Misery Index"—a combined figure of the unemployment and inflation rates. By July, when the Democratic convention met in New York, Carter had won the nomination easily, had selected Mondale as his running mate, and held a commanding thirty-point lead over Ford in the polls.

Among the Republicans, Ford's nomination was by no means assured. Though the party establishment backed him overwhelmingly over the insurgent Reagan, both men went into Kansas City claiming they had enough delegates to win the presidential nomination on the first ballot.

Dole, whose main goal, as always, was to win, and who had kept up his contacts with the Alf Landon old-boy machine,[2] shrewdly concluded that Ford would win the nomination because he had the GOP establishment behind him and seemed to be slightly ahead of Reagan in the delegate count. Dole jumped on the bandwagon, and he went to the convention as a Kansas delegate pledged to vote for Ford.

Selected to act as temporary chairman of the convention, Dole, on the rostrum banging the gavel on Monday, August 16, impressed delegates and a national television audience with his no-

---

[2]Huck Boyd, Dole's fatherly patron who had helped him into Congress via the Alf Landon old-boy machine, had also been a national GOP committeeman, and he tooted Dole's horn when Ford began casting about for a running mate.

nonsense, take-charge demeanor. The tall, dark, lean Kansan bearing a striking resemblance to actors Humphrey Bogart and John Forsythe seemed to breathe fire from his nostrils as he touted the Grand Old Party and excoriated the Democrats and their nominees. (In later campaign speeches, he referred to Carter as "chicken-fried McGovern" but subsequently said, "I take that back—I've learned to respect McGovern.")

Dole was involved in an early convention floor fight and helped Ford's forces secure a decisive victory over Reagan's. Meanwhile, the convention listened to speaker after speaker extol Republicanism. John Connally, the former LBJ protégé and Democrat turned Republican, spoke eloquently about the GOP's standing up for "the uncommon man"—and Dole listened eagerly, perhaps thinking the reference applied to him.

On Wednesday night, on the first ballot, Ford won the nomination with 1,187 votes to Reagan's 1,070. It took 1,130 to win. Dole voted for Ford.

A few hours earlier, Dole had been walking through the lobby of his hotel when he spotted Dorothy Voss Beecher, one of the original Bobolinks barber shop quartet from his first congressional campaign of 1960. "He came up to me and told his friends, 'Hey, there's one of my Bobolinks!' " Dorothy recalls. "I couldn't believe he still recognized me. My hair was up and I looked so different; my friends were stunned."

Running into a ghost from his first race turned out to be a good omen for Dole. Within twelve hours, he became the GOP vice presidential nominee. Dole's selection was not exactly a bolt out of the blue, however. Ford had made it clear in 1975 that Nelson Rockefeller, his sitting vice president, would not be his running mate in 1976. And for weeks, Dole's name had been mentioned to Ford by members of the Landon old-boy network. David Owen, who had run the last few months of Dole's successful 1974 Senate reelection campaign against Bill Roy and who was closely allied with Huck Boyd and the network, had written to Ford a few days before the convention recommending Dole for vice president. "Senator Dole takes a back seat to no one in his ability to communicate with people," Owen wrote. "He is capable of taking the attack to the Carter-Mondale ticket." "Dole is a real cage-rattler,"

Ford was told, and just what was needed—a conservative with a strong base in farm states, with a southern wife who could challenge Carter in his own backyard.

Dole's talents as a fence straddler and a compromiser were on full display in Kansas City. He was in contact with Reagan and let his aides then know that he agreed with their hero's ideology and that he was interested in the position of vice president.

On Thursday, August 19, at 3:15 A.M., Ford gathered with his aides in his Crown Center suite after returning from paying homage to his vanquished challenger at Reagan's suite in the Alameda Plaza Hotel. They met to deliberate on Ford's running mate, and the list was soon narrowed to four names: Anne Armstrong, ambassador to Britain; former deputy attorney general William Ruckelshaus; Senator Howard Baker of Tennessee, who had sat on the Senate Watergate Committee; and Bob Dole.

It was generally felt that American voters just weren't ready for a woman on a national ticket, so Armstrong was ruled out. Nelson Rockefeller spoke strongly in favor of Ruckelshaus, but Ruckelshaus was known to be a moderate Republican, and concern was expressed that it might be difficult to persuade the conservatively-minded convention to nominate him. Ruckelshaus had crossed swords with Nixon over Watergate and thereby alienated the Nixon loyalists, who still had power in the party.

Baker's name had dominated public speculation throughout the convention because of his major role in the Watergate probe; he was seen as a foil to Ford's possibly ill-advised pardoning of Richard Nixon. However, this role had also antagonized the pro-Nixon loyalists, and Baker's wife had acknowledged her own past drinking problems. Moreover, Ford was deeply worried about his ability to beat Jimmy Carter in the South and was eager to pick a running mate acceptable to southerners, and Ford considered Dole even more popular than Baker among southern Republican leaders because of his supposed conservatism and his southern wife.

In addition, because Dole was a more aggressive, slashing campaigner than Baker, as revealed in his 1974 campaign against Dr. Bill Roy, he was better suited for the campaign strategy that was being urged on Ford by his aides. According to this plan, Ford would spend much of the fall in the White House Rose Garden looking presidential, while his running mate would vigorously stump the nation and heave spears at Carter and Mondale. What it seemed to come down to was that Dole's name brought the most enthusiastic reaction from the widest range of party people, that he was a good campaigner, and that he would help in the farm belt, where the president had a real problem.

But the final, decisive factor in Ford's selection of Dole seems to be that the Kansan met with Reagan's approval. As a *quid pro quo* for his endorsement of the Ford ticket, Reagan had insisted that Ford pick someone with Reagan's own ideology, and he found Dole acceptable.

Whatever Ford's ultimate reasons may have been, he gave the nod to Dole early in the morning of August 19, and Dole accepted eagerly, later joking that "When I got the call, this morning, I thought Ford had the wrong number." Dole welcomed the nomination, quipping, "The vice presidency is a great job—it's all indoor work and no heavy lifting."

On August 19, only 1,921 of 2,259 convention delegates voted for Dole's nomination: 103 delegates abstained, mostly as a protest against Dole. Another 235 delegates voted for 31 seemingly random choices instead of Dole.

In his acceptance speech to the convention, he stated that Ford had successfully and properly resisted the argument that "the best medicine for a crippled economy was to cripple it further." Taking on the challenge of explaining away a deep recession in the U.S. economy, he backed Ford for knowing that "the way back to prosperity is through persistence and perseverance—yes, and through sacrifice." He said that Ford had refused to resign the country to "the seductive panaceas of more government spending." "Until we get the government out of the business sector," he said, "we are going to have difficulty getting people back into jobs that are real and productive."

"My fellow Americans," Dole declared, "President Ford has begun the great work of building peace, renewing prosperity, and restoring the confidence in the basic institutions of freedom in America. But there is more to be done. We have heard much about offering the American people a choice this year. I believe we should. I believe we do. America has weathered the storm of the recession." Dole then castigated Congress, "which lurches along in search of more and more ways to gain control not merely over the way we live but over the purposes for which we live—which ought to be left to the decisions of the hearts and minds of each single individual.

"Until we break the stranglehold of the party of big government over the Congress of the United States," Dole insisted, "we are going to have more federal spending, more federal control over our lives, and more empty promises that leave our people disillusioned and frustrated."

Dole's choice of words is significant, for it illustrates how he personalized party policy. In referring to a "crippled" economy and to the Democrats as the party that sought to "control our lives," he was relating them to two of the biggest issues in his own personal life.

Dole went on to attack Jimmy Carter, claiming that "the Democratic candidate for 1976 has shown that the arrogance of power is nothing compared to the power of arrogance." Dole considered Carter as a particularly weak and incompetent "Boy Scout."

Just after the conclusion of the national convention in Kansas City, Dole approached Ford, telling the president, "If you want to start the campaign in the heartland, I know of a little town in heartland America where we can start it." The next day, August 20, giving the town less than twenty-four hours' notice, Dole dragged Ford home for the first presidential visit to Russell since 1905, when Theodore Roosevelt spoke for a few minutes from the rear platform of a Union Pacific train.

The small town went wild with the news of the big day, putting up a huge homemade banner that proclaimed in red letters: WEL-COME HOME, BOB: GLAD YOU COULD COME ALONG, JERRY. The *Russell Daily News* printed a banner headline declaring BOMB-SHELL HITS RUSSELL.

They brought out the old town grandstand, set up bleachers, and installed communication systems on the shady courthouse lawn. After Ford and Dole's arrival by chartered helicopter from Salina, Kansas, the president and his entourage had to wait outside for several minutes while Dole's mother searched for her misplaced house keys and found them in the bushes.

Dole, smiling broadly, rode with Ford in a motorcade through a crowd of several thousand on Main Street and then onto the lawn of the courthouse, where he had once worked as a county attorney earning less than the building's janitor. Dole mounted the platform and made his speech. As he began to express his appreciation to the town, recalling "the time I needed help, and the people of Russell helped," his words suddenly stopped, tears welled in his eyes, and he lifted his left hand to cover his face as he paused for fifteen seconds to regain control of himself. Dole's rare show of emotion was brought on by his recalling how the citizens of Russell had taken up a collection to pay for surgery to repair his arm after World War II.

A news photograph taken at the moment catches Dole wiping the tears from his eyes. In an age when a politician's crying in public can be seen as a sign of weakness, and in some cases may be fatal to his career (witness Ed Muskie's public tears during the Democratic New Hampshire primary campaign in 1972), it is a testimony to the strength of Dole's public image that his momentary loss of control was considered by the media and voters not a sign of weakness but a touching display of gratitude and strength.

Since Dole was now a candidate for major national office, his wife's employment status raised questions about conflict of interest. Elizabeth took a leave of absence from her position with the Federal Trade Commission until after the November election in order to campaign actively for her husband. She was criticized nevertheless by John Moss, a Democrat from California and the chairman of the House subcommittee that oversees regulatory agencies, who alleged that there was still a possible conflict of interest because, with her husband running for vice president, she was in the position of directly or indirectly asking for votes and financial support from persons and corporations over whom she would later sit in judgment as a federal trade commissioner. The quasi-judicial role of an FTC commissioner was inherently incompatible with the partisan role of a campaigner, the chairman alleged. But Elizabeth ignored such criticism and hit the hustings with a vengeance.

Perhaps in an effort to maintain the illusion of impartiality,

Elizabeth remained registered an Independent voter, stating that she was "not quite ready yet" to register as a Republican.

During the vice presidential campaign, the issue of Dole's role in his nasty race for the Senate in 1974 resurfaced, and he found himself on the defensive. On "Face the Nation" in 1976, Dole acknowledged that he had been "accused of that and all sorts of things; and frankly we ended the last two days of our campaign [in 1974] disavowing ads that some right-to-lifers were running in the papers." On the program he maintained that the skull-and-cross-bones ad was one of those he had disavowed. Also in 1976, William Wolford, then Dole's administrative assistant, claimed that "these ads were placed without our knowledge. They were not authorized in advance."[4]

Soon after his selection as a vice presidential candidate, Dole was bombarded with press stories dredging up other old allegations as well—relating to Watergate, the ITT scandal, and Gulf Oil Corporation lobbyist Claude Wild.

The most damaging charge was Claude Wild's statement in early September 1976 that he had given $2,000 to Dole in 1970 to pass on to other Republican Senate candidates. After Dole vehemently denied the charge, Wild recanted his statement a few days later, saying he had been "in error," but the damage had already been done. Questions were being raised about Dole's past and his potential liability as Ford's running mate.

From 1960 until 1974, Claude Wild had been a Gulf Oil Corporation lobbyist in charge of dispensing about $4 million in political contributions. Many of these contributions were considered illegal. In January 1976, the Watergate special prosecutor's office gave Wild a grant of immunity and compelled him to testify about $170,000 in Gulf funds that he had dispensed in 1973. The *New York Times* reported on September 6, 1976, that Wild had told a federal grand jury that he had made a Gulf corporate contribution to Dole of $5,000 in 1973. Wild refused to comment publicly about this alleged contribution.

[4]A man named Sterling E. Lacy, of St. Marys, Kansas, held a news conference reported in the *New York Times*, August 25, 1976, and stated that he had distributed about fifty thousand anti-abortion, anti-Roy pamphlets during the 1974 campaign. He denied receiving any help or direct contact from Dole but refused to disclose his backers.

On March 8, 1976, Dole had voluntarily testified before a federal grand jury investigating Gulf. "They were concerned about whether I had received any money from Gulf Oil, and the answer was no," Dole said in September. "They were concerned about whether I had received any money from Senator Scott [Hugh Scott, Republican Senate minority leader in 1973], and the answer was no." Dole said he had voluntarily offered to turn over his records to the special prosecutor, but insisted that "they've never asked for them" except for "one little book."

The *Washington Post* printed stories in September 1976 alleging that the first ten pages of that "little book," Dole's cash ledger in which monies received were recorded,[5] were mysteriously missing and that the ledger book "has drawn renewed interest from the Watergate special prosecutor, who is investigating the alleged 1973 $5,000 Gulf Oil cash contribution to the reelection campaign of Senator Bob Dole." The ledger, purported to record all cash received and spent during 1973 and 1974 in Dole's Senate reelection campaign, had been kept by Jo-Anne Coe,[6] Dole's office manager.

The *Post* reported that Wild had testified to the grand jury that he had given $5,000 in cash to Dole's then-administrative assistant, William Kats.[7] The cash book showed no listing of a contribution from Wild to Dole, however, and Dole cited the book as proof that no such contribution ever took place. Questioned several times by the special prosecutor about receiving the Gulf money, Kats said, "I just don't recall."

The ledger book was significant because its first ten pages were missing when it had been made available to the special prosecutor in March 1976. The ledger pages were all numbered, a list of cash contributions began on page 11, and the first date listed was April 17, 1973. If the Wild contribution was made, it would have been

[5]Under the federal election laws in effect in 1973, an organization spending cash was required to file with the secretary of the Senate's public records any expenditures above $50.

[6]Coe has held several positions with Dole since 1967, including chief assistant and political operative, as well as administrative director in his Senate office. In 1985, when he became majority leader, Dole made her the first woman secretary of the Senate. She returned to his Senate office in 1987.

[7]Kats served as Dole's administrative assistant in the Senate from 1969 to 1974. His son, also named Bill Kats, served as Dole's press assistant in the Senate from 1978 to 1981.

made before that date. On the inside cover of the ledger book, Coe had written that the record of cash receipts began "on page 9." Page 9, however, was one of the missing pages. On September 30, 1976, Dole said that the ten pages were "always missing. They were never there. Nothing was taken out. . . . I didn't keep the records." Coe explained that she had made some "mistakes" on page 9 and, after tearing it out, had begun recording the contributions on page 11.

The allegations hurled at Dole proved to have some effect, but the Ford-Dole ticket gradually made inroads into Carter's huge lead nonetheless. In late August, Carter had led Ford in the polls, 49 to 39 percent. By the end of September his lead had narrowed, 50 to 42 percent.

Irritated by the rehashing of these Watergate-era accusations, Dole became increasingly testy during the campaign and began slashing at Carter with reckless abandon. He lashed Carter for being fuzzy on the issues and ridiculed his status as a "peanut farmer." Lyn Nofziger, a top aide to the Ford-Dole ticket who had been assigned to Dole, complained later that Dole had acted as an "unguided missile." Richard Nixon himself criticized Ford's selection of Dole as a running mate. "They're going to have trouble with that guy," Nixon growled. "He's able, but his personality's abrasive as hell, and he's going to cause a helluva lot of problems with the press. They better get somebody good to handle him, someone who can control him, limit his appearances to select audiences, or this guy's going to alienate a helluva lot of people." Nixon was right.[8]

As disillusioned with Dole as Nixon were some civil rights leaders, one of whom, Roy Wilkins, denounced him as an enemy of blacks, an unfair charge in light of Dole's voting record on civil rights.

With Ford sitting quietly in the White House, Dole roared

[8]The press attacked Dole with a vengeance during this campaign. A *New York Times* editorial called him "Ford's Doleful Choice," and political cartoonists ridiculed him as a snarling dog, a mudslinger armed with cans of black tar, and the like. Dole never forgot or forgave the press for what he called its "smear campaign" against him. He spoke to me of being "ambushed" by the press. As late as 1987, he voiced a fear that the press would "dismantle" any "vision" he might declare as a presidential candidate, so he deliberately avoided articulating any clear, specific policy proposals.

through the country like a loose cannon, alienating a helluva lot of people indeed and mounting a major side show that threatened to upstage the main attraction. He acted very much as a candidate independent of Ford. He could not stand to be controlled in any way. "We're not on a leash; we're sort of on our own. If we do something wrong, I suppose Ford will rein us in," he said at this time, characteristically referring to himself in the plural. Dole's campaign speeches were written by his own aides, not by the Ford organization.[9]

In the early part of the campaign, Dole showed little evidence of having a coordinated strategy. "The trouble with this campaign is that no one is in charge and Dole does not know how to delegate responsibility," one insider told the *Washington Post*. Ford campaign aide Jim Baker referred to the Dole campaign as a "rough spot." He pointed out that virtually none of Dole's staff had national campaign experience, a result of Dole's tendency to hire young staffers because they were not a threat to him.

One of Dole's speechwriters in the campaign was a man named George Gilder, who in 1987 wrote in *Life* magazine about an incident early in the fall in which Dole hurled the pages of a speech Gilder had drafted across the room and onto the carpet. "Bad . . . bad . . . bad," Dole snarled as he pointed to the scattered pages as if they were an especially disobedient dog's excrement. Then, turning to Gilder, he thundered, "Pick up the papers and get out!"

Although Gilder considered quitting right there and then, he hung on and learned that he was by no means the only one to receive such abuse. Other staffers told him similar tales.

Dole made "little effort to control his temper, relate to his staff, research his positions, or uplift his rhetoric," Gilder recalled. He struck Gilder as a Lone Ranger, a dark, pessimistic, and cynical Tartar with a "gloomy view of the world" and a startling "hostility to ideas and affirmative visions." Candidate Dole "did not like to read speeches," Gilder recalled.[10]

[9]Later, particularly during his 1988 presidential campaign, Dole claimed to have just been doing what he was told in the 1976 campaign, fulfilling the role of hatchet man that he had been assigned by the Ford organization. This is his standard response when queried by the press about his hatchet-man image.

[10]In 1987, Gilder also recalled that Dole had once criticized Elizabeth Dole, saying, "She reads everything, to a point where I think she overdoes it sometimes."

In general, on the stump Dole spoke rather stiffly from a prepared text and was at his best when he went off the cuff, sprinkling his impromptu comments with spontaneous put-down humor delivered with the timing of a professional comedian. Gradually, he found his stride, slashing mercilessly at Carter and Mondale. "It took Jimmy Carter a long time to decide how many debates to have," he snapped. "He finally decided to have three so he can tell each of his positions on each issue." When asked at a press conference if he would play the role of a "one-man truth squad" following Carter around the country, Dole quipped, "It would take more than one." He attacked Carter as a "hypocrite," a "waffler," a "man of contradictions and false promises" who "gets his orders from George Meany," then president of the AFL-CIO. "Would you buy a used peanut from Jimmy Carter?" Dole asked his audiences. When Carter admitted to *Playboy* magazine that he had occasionally "lusted in [his] heart," Dole said, "We'll give him the bunny vote." Dole referred to George Meany as "Walter Mondale's makeup man." When asked why he was savaging his opponents, Dole replied, "You want to leave a little raw meat in the audience."

In what turned out to be one of the turning points of the campaign, Dole was scheduled to debate the Democratic vice presidential nominee, Walter Mondale, on October 15 in the first such debate between vice presidential candidates in history. About to appear before a national television audience estimated at more than eighty million, Dole arrived in Houston on a cold and rainy night suffering from a cold and grumbling about the upcoming debate. During the debate, he leaned noticeably against the podium on his left arm and appeared most unpresidential and graceless. He seemed uncomfortable, irritable, flippant, and particularly harsh-tempered as he roasted his opponent.

Ford, who made a fool of himself by declaring in the second presidential debate on October 7, "There is no Soviet domination of Eastern Europe," watched with mounting concern as the GOP "Punch and Jerry Show" turned into a comedy of errors. "If we added up all the killed and wounded in Democrat wars in this century," Dole taunted Mondale before the viewers, "it would be about 1.6 million Americans, enough to fill the city of Detroit." That remark, more than any other, remains embedded in the national consciousness as evidence of Dole's harsh and slashing personality. At the time it also called his judgment into question.

At one point during the debate, Mondale looked solemnly at Dole and declared, "I think Senator Dole has richly earned his reputation as a hatchet man tonight." And the nation seemed to agree.

The "Democrat wars" comment came right from the heart, however. Dole was voicing his own bitterness at having been crippled in a war that he blamed on a Democrat, Franklin D. Roosevelt. But that wisecrack, coupled with several other smart-aleck potshots and delivered with a facial sneer and a most unpresidential posture, raised questions about Dole's will to win and the possibility that, in some subtle way, he actually *wanted* to lose.

After the debate, Dole criticized himself: "I thought of all the things I could have said." (Ten years later he joked about the 1976 debate, "I went for the jugular all right—my own.") Explaining why he had charged Democrats with warmongering, Dole said, "We did want to make it clear that if they wanted to keep on dredging up Watergate and the pardon of Nixon, we will dredge up a few wars. If it's fair to judge us by something that's happened in the past, we can judge them. He [Mondale] didn't like that very well, but we resent the implication of Watergate every time he stands up." Dole was also hurt by Mondale's calling him a hatchet man on national television. He said he had great respect for his opponent and added, "I thought I said several nice things about Mondale at the debate. He ended up calling me the hatchet man. I can't understand that."

Dole's dismal performance in the debate may have turned the tide inexorably against the Ford-Dole ticket. It also seemed to cement in the public consciousness the image of Dole as hatchet man.

During the campaign, Dole found himself answering questions about his wife's having her own campaign plane for the remainder of the race. He had started using two planes, he explained, because of the increased number of reporters who wanted to travel with him. However, Elizabeth did do some campaigning of her own during October and required a chartered airplane for some of her trips.

Then, as later, Elizabeth reveled in making speeches. Flashing her smile and campaigning with Bob or as a surrogate candidate, she was a natural—gregarious and attractive. She urged him to mention his war injury.

"I'm not used to it [the withered arm] yet. I'm still embarrassed about it. I'm reminded about it every morning, trying to button the shirt collar with only one hand," he told the nation in 1976, taking his wife's advice at least partially.

Meanwhile, seventy-three-year-old Bina Dole spent many tiring hours campaigning for her son throughout Kansas in 1976. When asked whether her son had always wanted to be a politician, Bina said she never expected him to be one. "I thought he had a potential for something," she said, "but I certainly never thought of politics. However, I worked every one of his campaigns and imported a lot of Dole pineapple juice. . . . If Bob loses, it won't be the first time he's lost something. If he can adjust to the loss of his right arm, I guess he can adjust to losing an election."

On election day, Bob voted in Russell before flying off to Washington to watch the election returns with Jerry Ford in the White House. He was mobbed by local well-wishers in Russell and didn't have time to have lunch with his mother. But Bina rushed after him, handing an aide a bag filled with fried chicken, saying she couldn't let her son leave home without her cooking.

Bob flew across the eastern half of America that November afternoon wondering whether or not he would wake up the next morning as vice president–elect, a heartbeat away from the presidency.

Watching the election returns on television that night with Ford in the upstairs family quarters of the White House, Dole sadly watched the slow tally of votes projecting defeat. He became increasingly testy as Carter and Mondale rolled up a narrow but decisive victory.

In the final tally, the Democrats had 40,827,394 votes, compared to the Republicans' 39,145,977. Carter won 297 electoral votes, while Ford picked up 240 (one elector cast a vote for Reagan, who was not even a candidate).

After racking up fourteen straight victories since 1950, Dole suffered the first electoral defeat of his life. And he was a sore loser. He lashed out mercilessly at his staff, blaming them for his defeat. "He was like a snake," said a friend who was with him.

The day after the election, Dole received a phone call from another sore loser, Richard Nixon, who commiserated with him over the defeat. Nixon, who also had a phoenixlike career, encouraged his former disciple to rise from the ashes. Nixon also warned Dole that some people would be looking for a scapegoat and encouraged him to ignore such anticipated attacks.[11]

Dole later said that for months after the November 1976 defeat, he would order his driver to coast past the White House each day so that he could stare at the massive white portico and pillars and dream about what might have been.

But Dole was a man obsessed with becoming president and occupying, not just working in, the mansion at 1600 Pennsylvania Avenue. The vice presidency has never really interested him, and he would probably have been bored playing second fiddle to Jerry Ford. Indeed, his take-charge temperament would have been severely frustrated had he been elected to the vice presidency, a job traditionally lacking in any real duties or responsibilities.

"Besides," he once told me, "no vice president has ever become president since Van Buren, except through assassination or resignation."

---

[11]One such attack came as late as January 1988, when a leaflet from the George Bush presidential campaign blamed Dole for "single-handedly" bringing down the Ford-Dole ticket.

# 11
# A QUIXOTIC QUEST FOR THE WHITE HOUSE

M uch later, when it was all over and he had had time to reflect on its futility, Bob Dole would say of his quixotic campaign for the 1980 GOP presidential nomination, "Nobody noticed I was running . . . whenever I spoke, the three empty chairs got up and walked away."

During the campaign itself, he would say that a successful candidate needed the "five *M*s" in order to win: money, management, manpower, momentum, and media. On all five counts, he came up woefully short. The real question is: Why did he run, and why did he keep running when it was clearly futile?

The story of Dole's race for the 1980 presidential nomination is a tragicomedy. It is the story of a man who nearly wrecked his political career in search of something he desperately wanted for reasons he could never fully explain to himself or to anyone else who might have supported him. And it is the story of a man with a communications gap, an inability to establish an emotional rapport with followers, crowds, even his own staffers; it is a tale of a one-man band playing to tiny audiences that couldn't hear the music. The campaign illustrated Dole's major shortcomings as a national candidate and highlighted the intensely personal nature of his political outlook and *raison d'être*.

I was on Dole's Senate staff during the height of his 1980 presidential campaign, when he brought himself to the edge of the precipice and came within an inch of throwing away his entire political career. I had the opportunity to observe him in action as he mounted his quest for the Impossible Dream.

Dole rebounded from his 1976 vice presidential campaign debacle like a boxer who has been knocked down but not out, ready to go after his opponents with renewed zest even before the bell sounded. Within weeks after the disaster, he was back on his feet, crisscrossing the country and making speeches to anyone who would listen, seeking to solidify a broad base of support for his own 1980 presidential candidacy.

In 1977 and 1978, he hired and fired consultants and managers, sounded out every conceivable source of support within the party, and tried to co-opt the conservative supporters of Reagan, who was playing coy about running for president again.

In the Senate, Dole played a major role in opposing the Panama Canal Treaty negotiated by President Jimmy Carter and bitterly opposed by Reagan and other conservatives. Dole was against the treaty, which provided for the relinquishment of U.S. control over the canal to the Panamanian government in the year 2000, was ratified by the Senate on April 18, 1978, but with an amendment Dole offered that would give the United States navigation priority rights in time of war.

Dole's vehement stand on the Panama Canal Treaty came straight from the heart, I believe, and derived from his innate personal sensitivity to being pushed around by anyone, but it was also a shrewd ploy to attract the right-wing supporters of the aging Reagan, who had also opposed the treaty vociferously in the 1976 campaign.

Dole made yet another pitch for right-wing votes by filing a lawsuit in federal court challenging President Carter's intent to return a thousand-year-old crown to Hungary's communist government. The crown, which had been attained by the U.S. Army in Europe in 1945 (at the very time Dole was being shot at by Nazi troops), had originally been given to Hungary's King Stephen by Pope Sylvester in approximately 1000 A.D. As a gesture of detente, Carter planned to return the crown, which had been in the U.S. for over thirty years, to Hungary.

Extreme right-wingers were infuriated by Carter's giveaway, and Dole sought to lead their charge by filing his lawsuit in December 1977. A preposterous, naive attempt to enjoin the president from giving away a petty symbol, the lawsuit was dismissed by the federal court judge on the grounds that Carter's action was not a treaty and therefore not in the Senate's jurisdiction. Two appeals, one to a federal appeals court and one to the U.S. Supreme Court, were denied. Although Dole received much publicity, the spectacle of a senator going to court to force the president's hand only highlighted Dole's powerlessness within Congress and therefore did little to enhance his appeal to the right-wingers. Dole's action illustrated the essentially solitary quality of his leadership: rather than winning over a majority of his colleagues in the Senate and then passing a bill banning Carter from returning the crown, he filed a lawsuit as a solitary citizen.

Dole's delving into the arcane issue of the Hungarian crown was only one result of his casting around for sensational issues on which to hitch his star and attract media attention during the period between his vice presidential and presidential campaigns.

He found another issue in the bizarre world of religious cults. In November 1978, 913 followers of the reverend Jim Jones's People's Temple committed mass suicide in the jungle of Jonestown, Guyana. The group, whose leader had attacked Americanism and capitalism and who admired Russia and Cuba, drank poisoned Kool-Aid and went down in a horrendous orgy of self-destruction, killing California congressman Leo Ryan and some members of his entourage in the process.

The People's Temple had been one of numerous quasireligious cults that had sprouted up like weeds all across the U.S. in the 1970s. The cults recruited young people off the streets of America and allegedly programmed them into mindless zombies who joined a tightly knit group and gave up all their money and possessions to a diabolical cult leader.

Dole became fascinated with the cult phenomenon. It was something disturbingly alien and un-American, about as far removed from the mentality of Russell, Kansas, as possible. He genuinely saw the cults as a menace, and when a constituent whose child had been recruited by a cult appealed to Dole to do something, he found a vacuum of leadership in Congress, so he decided to take action himself. In February 1979, he chaired a sensational day of hearings of a temporary, ad-hoc Senate committee formed to look into the cult problem. The hearing attracted considerable publicity—but of the wrong type. Dole was accused of staging a witchhunt on Capitol Hill and received threats against his life. He was besieged by all kinds of people accusing him of trampling on freedom of religion.

He found himself leading a one-man band on the cult problem, for he had failed to adequately communicate his concerns and proposals to his colleagues or the press. Upon encountering serious opposition, Dole withdrew from the spotlight and dropped the whole issue, never again chairing such a hearing. In the Senate Judiciary Committee nine months later, however, he quietly introduced an amendment to the comprehensive Criminal Code Reform Act, S. 1722, which made it a crime for one to harass people in airports and on federal property, an amendment directed against cults. Dole's amendment never even reached the Senate floor.

The cult issue is one example of Dole's tendency, throughout his career, to give up on an issue or project if he sees it's not going anywhere. If he thinks he can get what he wants through hard work and compromise, he'll do all he can; but, unlike some more ideological legislators, he is not one to propose measures simply to make a point or crusade for an issue close to his heart.

While playing for the right-wing vote with his stand on the Panama Canal Treaty and the Hungarian crown, Dole was also joining ultraliberal Democratic senator George McGovern in sponsoring a bill calling for increased eligibility for food stamps. Although Dole had originally voted against creation of the federal food stamp program when he was in the House in 1966, he was now supporting food stamps, consumer rights issues, Great Society programs, and civil rights measures that placed him at odds with the right wing.

Dole's support for poor people, blacks, and underdogs derived not from a cynical attempt to broaden his base of support among these relatively powerless groups, but from a deep-seated personal empathy for such outsiders. As he had maintained in his maiden speech to the Senate ten years before, he considered himself a member of a minority because of his handicap. However, the question remains: Why did he significantly change his voting pattern on many Great Society programs after 1976?

The answer to this question lies partly in his failure to win the vice presidency in 1976 and partly in the influence of his new wife. Immediately after the 1976 debacle, Dole received a barrage of criticism from all quarters, charging that he had lost the election because he had been too harsh in his campaigning and in his savage attacks on liberal Democrats. His wife echoed such criticisms and urged him to mellow his style.

The Kansas boy who had grown up in a stoic, emotionless family, learning by the example of his parents' conduct, now turned to his wife for example. In many ways, he began to mimic her style, aiming to emerge from the shadows as a compassionate candidate, a man with a heart of gold toward society's underdogs. The word *compassion* was a Liddy trademark and now became Bob's own. He wore it as proudly as he wore the Purple Heart in his lapel. He hoped that by exuding compassion in his voting record, he could broaden the base of his appeal, bringing blacks and other underdogs into the party and into supporting his candidacy.

There was something incongruous about a reputed hatchet man now spouting homilies on compassion. Clearly, something didn't jibe, and Dole's credibility was open to serious question. More than changing the way he voted in the Senate, what was needed was a wholesale revamping of his personality—nothing less than personality surgery.

Whether a man in his fifties could dramatically change his personality, formed over the decades on life's rough road, seems doubtful. But altering his public image was another matter.

Dole enrolled in a course called "Speech Dynamics," run by a woman named Dorothy Sarnoff in New York. Speech Dynamics was a personal training program to restructure the presence, image, and style of politicians, corporate executives, and other public figures. It cost $3,500 and involved extensive training before cameras, lengthy discussions, and other techniques. "We change behavior very, very fast," Sarnoff boasted, noting that "My father was a surgeon, and I like to think of the camera as a surgeon's knife."

Of Dole she said, "He was a wonderful student. We discussed his sense of humor. We changed that. We took the snideness away from him. We changed the way he dressed to more of a classy look."

Dole set about overcoming his personality handicaps with the same determination that he had shown in surmounting his physical handicaps after the war, once again aided by a supportive wife. Out went the old Dole with the hatchet, and in came the new Dole with the halo.

But the transformation was not always comfortable. To me, Dole seemed like a man constantly struggling to contain his old, tough self, a man angry at having had to deny his true personality in order to please the cameras and the voters. He was still ill at ease around strangers, a man fundamentally solitary and genuinely accustomed to "telling it like it is" and often uneasy in his new role as a kind of ersatz Man of Compassion.

Something was missing in the equation, and no one knew that better than Dole himself. You could see it in his eyes, as he strained to contain the reservoir of anger welling deep inside and crying for release. And you could see it in his occasional bursts of fury, his wholesale chewing out of aides, and his attacks on opponents—in absentia. Among his favorite whipping boys were George Bush, a man he genuinely loathed, and his own campaign managers and top Senate assistants. He seemed like a tightly wound coil that might unwind at any minute.

Clearly he was confused as to how far he could go in venting anger and being negative in public. Those on his staff prayed that he would let Dole be Dole and were disturbed by the contradictory signals they were getting.

Near the end of 1978, he played cat-and-mouse with the Kansas press, coyly refusing to reveal whether he would really be a presidential candidate for 1980. At one point he blurted out that he would run, but the next day he reversed himself.

Originally, in 1977, he had maintained that he would not be a presidential candidate in 1980 if either Reagan or Ford chose to run. Ever fearful of being embarrassed, at the polls or elsewhere, he had not wanted to run a futile campaign against a powerful front-runner. He knew that his Senate seat was up in 1980, and he didn't want to risk losing that in order to pursue an impossible dream.

But Elizabeth urged him onward, telling him that he could win the presidency by projecting his new compassionate image. Her own seven-year term as federal trade commissioner was due to expire in 1980, and she wanted to move right into the White House. Dole, who had always believed that affection must be earned, wanted to win the big prize in order to please his wife. Perhaps from fear that she would not be impressed if he remained "only" a senator, he felt compelled to serve up a menu of steadily rising accomplishments in order to hold his place in their partnership.

In the early weeks of 1979, Dole made several tactical moves in the Senate aimed at buttressing his unannounced presidential candidacy. He dropped his position as ranking Republican on the Agriculture Committee in order to become ranking member on the more publicly visible Finance Committee, a move that antagonized many Kansans, who charged he was shortchanging his home state in order to seek national office.

He also took a newly available seat on the Judiciary Committee, hoping that he could attract media attention by publicly needling its popular Democratic chairman, Ted Kennedy. "Wherever Kennedy is, there goes the press," Dole would say to me, complaining bitterly that the media flocked to the Kennedy family in droves "just because of the name." "I know I'll never be a Kennedy," he whined to the *Kansas City Star,* just before launching into a thorough denunciation of the man whom he then considered his arch-foe.

In 1979 he was certain that Kennedy would run for president against Carter, now unpopular with the public and the media, and he was equally sure that Kennedy would win the nomination. Because Kennedy was a man who had always had what he had lacked, Dole took his rival's success as a personal challenge. If he could "beat Kennedy," as he liked to say, he would accomplish a lifelong dream by proving himself "the best."

So concerned was Dole about his role as a Kennedy foil, and the media attention that he hoped to generate, that he delayed hiring a Judiciary Committee staff for *six months*, from January to July 1979, endlessly debating with himself who would be best suited to pinpoint his attacks on the "rich boy" and also who would present him in the best light.

For his Finance Committee chief of staff, Dole hired a surprisingly young lawyer, just five years out of Georgetown Law School, a golden-haired man named Bob Lighthizer, whom he also entrusted with interviewing and recommending Judiciary Committee staff to him. Lighthizer, who looked barely twenty, was one of the few staffers whom Dole felt he could trust. The man's youthful appearance and lack of any ties to other politicians made him an ideal candidate to be taken under Dole's wing.

Another young-looking operative Dole hired was Tom Bell, a former Senate aide to Senator Bill Brock of Tennessee[1] and head of his own political consulting firm, Response Marketing. Bell was hired to serve as Dole's presidential campaign manager in May, when the candidate finally broke the worst-kept secret in Washington—that he was truly running for the White House.

Dole realized from the start that his fund-raising capacity was far less than that of Reagan, John Connally, George Bush, and other GOP rivals—in contrast to his subsequent presidential campaign, when he had raised over $14 million by the beginning of 1988. Though his resources were limited, he hoped that he could use his highly visible Senate position to gain media attention and thus attract supporters.

At the start of the Ninety-Sixth Congress in January 1979, he introduced several bills aimed at impressing key constituent groups. With George McGovern, he coauthored the very first bill of the year, a farm bill that was a pitch for the farm vote in the crucial Iowa presidential caucuses. Under this bill, farmers would get 100 percent of parity (about $5 per bushel of wheat, compared with the then-current market price of $3 per bushel) for "setting aside" and letting lie fallow the maximum amount of acreage available under the law.

[1]Brock became Dole's presidential campaign manager in 1987.

In proposing his bill, Dole said, "Without new farm legislation, American farmers could spend all of 1979 with their backs against the wall. We cannot refuse to raise farm prices under the banner of fighting inflation when farmers are losing money." He didn't use the term *flexible parity*, anathema to budget-conscious conservatives, calling it instead a variable target price program, or VTPP.

This farm bill clearly had a detrimental impact on the federal budget deficit, but in typical fashion, Dole introduced another bill calling for a constitutional amendment to balance the budget and a third bill limiting federal spending to 18 percent of the gross national product.

The balanced budget amendment, on which I worked for him on the Judiciary Committee, was wholly impracticable and politically unviable. It had no chance whatever for passage in the Democrat-controlled Senate and House, and Dole knew it. He never took it seriously and rarely attended Judiciary Committee hearings, except to vote on bills and amendments to bills. Instead he devoted the majority of his time to attending Finance Committee hearings, where he hoped to gain more media attention by playing a key role in the oil company windfall profit tax bill, which Jimmy Carter had proposed as a means of taking some of the windfall profits oil companies had made as a result of his decision to deregulate oil and gas prices and which Kennedy had denounced as "a fig leaf."

In the Finance Committee, Dole pushed yet another futile proposal—one to index federal income taxes by tying tax rates to inflation rates, so that taxes would not rise artificially faster due to rampaging inflation, which was then in the double-digit range. Dole's indexing scheme attracted very little media attention. In a desperate ploy for press coverage, he staged a little demonstration outside the IRS building in downtown Washington, showing up armed with charts and graphs pointing out the need for indexing. He actually did get a few reporters to snap his picture and put him in the newspaper—but at an obscure position on the back pages.

Dole also introduced legislation declaring the birthday of Martin Luther King, Jr., a national holiday, thereby expressing his genuine support for civil rights but also hoping to attract black supporters. In numerous appearances before black groups around the nation, he spoke about the need to bring blacks into the Republican Party and of broadening the base of the party.

I worked on several pro-civil rights proposals for Dole in the Judiciary Committee and am convinced that his support for blacks and other minorities is genuine and emotional. The biggest joke around the office was that Dole was far more liberal on civil rights than his staff, some of whom said King was a communist and covertly supported Reagan because of his supposed opposition to further civil rights gains. I recall having to make end runs around some of these staffers in order to get to Dole and inform him of the actual issues at stake in committee votes on civil rights bills. I felt confident he would support such bills, even while his own staffers and GOP colleagues scorned them. But Bob was so alienated from his own staff that he wasn't aware of their true sentiments or motives.

The general consensus among political observers was that Dole didn't have a prayer of a chance in his quixotic quest for the White House. But Elizabeth egged him on, resigned her seat on the Federal Trade Commission on March 9, 1979, in order to campaign full-time for him, and sold her Exxon stock in order to avoid any appearance of conflict of interest while her husband voted on oil industry tax bills. Elizabeth also lent Bob $50,000 borrowed from Dave Owen's bank and secured by $250,000 of her own certificates of deposit—prompting a Federal Election Commission investigation into whether or not the loan was an illegal campaign contribution because it exceeded the legal individual limit of $1,000. Bob claimed that the $50,000 was as much his as his wife's. (The investigation was quietly dropped in 1981.)

Now Bob, ambitious himself and feeling obligated to his wife, had little choice but to sign up for the long haul, and he became a man on a treadmill.

"I think you'll see a different Bob Dole from the one who was assigned the bad-guy role in 1976," Elizabeth told reporters in May 1979. "He's really a nice guy," she added. After her talk, one of the handful of reporters present quipped, "Methinks the lady doth protest too much."

Elizabeth strongly supported the Equal Rights Amendment, and, in contrast to his more conservative rivals, Bob shared her view. He also tended to support her strong commitment to consumer rights, but not all the way. Consumer rights was a touchy issue that was bitterly opposed by big business, a linchpin in the GOP and a key source of support Dole hoped to secure. Dole's Senate staff was composed mostly of pro-business right-wingers, who pulled him in a direction opposite that urged by his wife.

"The senator's wife is too liberal," complained Lighthizer when he was interviewing a staff applicant. "We need some good conservatives here to convince him to vote the right way."[2]

It seemed to me that Dole often seesawed on controversial issues in response to the pressures applied by Elizabeth and his right-wing staff. On one highly controversial bill affecting consumer rights in the antitrust field, the bill to overturn the Supreme Court's pro-business and anticonsumer ruling on the Illinois Brick case,[3] Dole remained undecided for months. The bill was a brainchild of Ted Kennedy, which would have made it *ipso facto* loathsome to conservatives. But to Dole, who was being influenced by opposing forces, the issue was not cut and dried.

Regarding another bill to prohibit large oil companies from using their vast resources to merge with or acquire other non-energy companies—another brainchild of Kennedy, who chided big oil for using windfall profits to buy up department stores—Dole told me that he would vote for the bill if the committee accepted his compromise amendment, which would have created an exception to this rule. He expressed bitterness at having played "bat boy" for the oil companies for so long in the Senate, only to see them "bankrolling George Bush" in the campaign.

Dole's campaign strategy seemed to rely on the hope that front-runner Ronald Reagan, the darling of Republican conservatives and money men, would bow out or be blown out of the 1980 campaign due to old age. Reagan at sixty-nine would be the oldest man ever inaugurated as president, and Dole thought he could inherit "Old Methuselah's" conservative support to become the party's standard bearer. As he traveled about the country, however, he found complete apathy toward his candidacy. Though he

[2]Bob Lighthizer worked for Dole in 1979-83, then joined his presidential campaign in 1987.
[3]The Supreme Court decision had restricted the consumer's right to sue a manufacturer for violations of antitrust laws. Kennedy's bill sought to amend the Statute to permit such suits. The bill never came to a vote on the Senate floor.

labeled himself a conservative and "a Ronald Reagan who's ten years younger," he lacked both the charisma and the sound conservative credentials of the front-runner. Besides being a secretive, solitary man with a rough-edged and awkward speaking style, he had an erratic voting record in Congress that bespoke no particular ideology. As a result, he had no political or personal power base in the Republican Party.

Wherever Dole went, if he was greeted at all, it was with little applause and much disdain. Forever conscious of being an outsider, Dole sometimes blamed his plight on Ford, who had "abandoned" him. (Ford refused to endorse any candidate and toyed with the idea of running himself.) Whereas GOP kingpins dismissed Dole's candidacy as something of a joke and viewed him as an unelectable hatchet man, Dole viewed himself as the victim of what he called the Establishment or the Rockefeller wing of the party. "I'm just a scapegoat," he complained bitterly while vainly searching for an oasis in a political desert.

His fund-raising activities were as futile as his search for votes and endorsements. With virtually no support outside Kansas, and with an eroding political base even there (some were saying he had sold Kansans down the creek in order to pursue his national ambitions), Dole set out to combat his six opponents running for the Republican presidential nomination: Reagan, Senator Howard Baker, George Bush, John Connally, and Congressmen Phillip Crane and John Anderson. Referring to himself as "jousting with a toothpick" and backed by a pauper's pence, he complained about his wealthier and more popular rivals. He said to me, "Connally can zoom into town with a vacuum cleaner and suck up all the money, while I come by later with a whisk broom."

As the 1980 primary campaign approached, the polls showed Dole to be the choice of fewer than 6 percent of Republican voters nationwide. But he persisted in running a campaign, though his heart never seemed to be in it. He seemed undecided about the seriousness of his candidacy, pointedly staying away from key primary states, such as Iowa and New Hampshire, except on weekends, until the last minute.

The pragmatic Dole realized that by running for president, he was jeopardizing his chances for reelection to the Senate in 1980.

Because he was not allowed by Kansas state law to run for both offices, he had to choose between one and the other. He hoped to use the Iowa and New Hampshire primaries to test his viability as a presidential candidate. If he did well, he would give up the Senate and stake all his bets on the presidency. If he floundered, he would withdraw from the presidential sweepstakes and announce his belated candidacy for reelection to a third Senate term.

To those who served as his aides at the time, it seemed that Dole oscillated between being "Mr. Caution" and "Mr. Reckless." From day to day, his mood would swing like a pendulum.

On a warm May morning in 1979 in his hometown of Russell, Dole announced his candidacy for president. "Everything I have ever become I owe to Russell," he told the audience and then went off to celebrate what the town had declared Bob Dole Day. It was a sentimental moment, recalling his appearance three years earlier, with his running mate President Ford in tow, to launch his vice presidential campaign, and it underscored the personal nature of Dole's candidacy. Most of his rivals opened their campaigns in Washington, where they hoped to wind up governing the country; Dole acted out his own personal drama in the small town of Russell, offering America his leadership as a "small-town man, a mid-American man."

Yet Dole did not *look* like a small-town middle American. Tall and dark, lean and mean, he projected a somewhat sinister aura. Dole's words seemed hollow, devoid of fire and conviction. Here he was, a man who had spent the past twenty years in Washington, campaigning as an outsider. A group of farmers was in attendance protesting—with signs such as WHERE WERE YOU WHEN WE NEEDED YOU?—because they felt that Dole had done little to help them.

In his maiden campaign speech, Dole spoke awkwardly of his dream "to let America be America again," chided the federal bureaucracy for vitiating the "small-town values of America," and promised a return to those very values. He didn't say what those values were, and he offered no specific prescriptions for lifting the country out of the slough of stagflation and apathy into which President Carter had led it. Voters, though generally disenchanted with Carter's uninspiring performance as president, saw little promise in what Dole had to offer. In stark contrast to the charismatic candidacy of Reagan, Dole spoke vaguely of free enterprise and seemed unable to articulate a credible, inspiring rationale for his own candidacy. He spoke of being the most qualified candidate, in the sense of managerial competence, but Americans were looking for a lot more than that.

Appearing nationwide on the "MacNeil/Lehrer NewsHour" a few days after opening his campaign with campaign manager Tom Bell in tow, Dole presented a fuzzy image as a man uncertain of his beliefs and unwilling or unable to justify his candidacy. He scoffed at the polls and insisted he would win the nomination against all odds. He could not, however, explain how he expected to raise the millions of dollars necessary to mount a viable campaign.

Realizing that Dole lacked money, Bell set him up with a package strategy that included aggressive use of his Senate office to gain publicity on key legislation and a schedule of key appearances in primary states. Bell assigned an experienced political operative to work as Dole's administrative assistant in his Senate office, to get free publicity through sponsorship of controversial, conservative legislation. The problem was that Dole was not a true conservative but a maverick. "I'm my own manager," he boasted, and he distrusted and resented anyone managing his campaign.

Less than three months later, Dole parted company with Bell, blaming him for spending money without his authorization and failing to raise his standing in the polls. With his fierce independent streak and his inveterate distrust of "experts," Dole was an unmanageable candidate who insisted on doing things his own way and rarely listened to advice.

"He's impossible to plan for, we never could articulate a clear position, and could not decide on a strategy," said Gerry Mursner, Dole's Midwest campaign coordinator. "We had five different strategies that could have beaten George Bush in Iowa, but Dole didn't stick with any one," Mursner added. Dole rejected his managers' advice not only because he resisted all authority and advice, but also because he found it difficult to stick his neck out and take a stand on controversial issues.

In his brief, quixotic presidential campaign, Dole went through five campaign managers, discarding each one after a few weeks.

Back in Washington, he was the only senator who carried on his Senate duties with no administrative assistant at all; office management duties were divided among several aides.

From the opening of his campaign in May 1979 to the first presidential caucus in Iowa in January 1980, Dole virtually vanished from public sight and became the invisible candidate. He made few campaign trips outside of Washington and Kansas, choosing to stay sequestered in Washington and attend to his Senate duties rather than compete for votes in Iowa and New Hampshire. His name rarely appeared in print or on the television screen. With astonishing naïveté for a seasoned politician, he told his disbelieving Senate staff that they were his "only real staff" and that he would win the presidential nomination by impressing voters with his record of accomplishment and high attendance in the Senate. As one veteran GOP stretegist said to me, this was a "mighty peculiar campaign."

In my opinion, Dole was a victim of Potomac myopia, a peculiar malady affecting many senators who believe the country shares their exalted view of themselves and that voters will choose a man who spends most of his time on the Senate floor over an unemployed showman who spends his time kissing babies and shaking hands on the hustings. Wherever he went campaigning, Dole called himself "the working candidate," and contrasted himself with Bush and Reagan, who were not employed. "I'm the one with the full-time job; I'm the guy who has to work for a living," he would tell audiences. Potomac myopia had affected many senators with presidential ambitions, including Lyndon B. Johnson in 1960 and Henry "Scoop" Jackson in 1976. Each of these men saw his candidacy collapse in the face of more active rivals.

That Dole was playing political solitaire is evident from the fact that many of his Senate aides secretly supported one of his opponents for the Republican presidential nomination. "I hope he withdraws soon, so we can wear our Reagan buttons to work," they joked.

In light of his chronic inability to rise in the polls and to raise money, everyone expected this Don Quixote to face reality and withdraw. His presidential campaign staff was reduced to a handful of people in a tiny office across the Potomac. When a reporter showed up and asked them if Dole was really running, one of them replied, "He says he is. But we're not sure."

Meanwhile, many Kansans criticized Dole for failing to declare whether or not he would be a candidate for reelection to the Senate. Widely condemning his cat-and-mouse tactics, movers and shakers questioned his political judgment and attacked him for putting his personal ambition above the interests of Kansans. He was viewed by many as attempting to use his Senate seat as a springboard to higher national office.

Dole remained oblivious to these voices and blind to reality, marching instead to the beat of a different drummer: his wife. Elizabeth was completely devoted to Bob's campaign. She influenced his strategy, coordinated his few appearances, and, when in town, charged into the Senate office (where she was quite popular with Bob's staffers) like a range boss, cheerfully directing everyone's activities. She often flew to New Hampshire and Iowa to appear as a surrogate candidate, reveling in pressing flesh and making speeches. Though well-intentioned, her appearances on Bob's behalf probably did more harm than good, for voters wanted to see the candidate himself. Clearly, the "working candidate" strategy was not working, but the Doles clung to it nevertheless.

Why a man of Bob's independent bent listened so long to a woman with no campaign experience is an intriguing question. Perhaps he realized that he stood no realistic chance of winning the primaries and chose to remain an "invisible" candidate so that when the inevitable defeat came he would have the readily available excuse that "I had to stay in Washington, so I *didn't really try* to win the presidential primaries." At the same time, by keeping his hat in the ring, he was able to mollify Queen Elizabeth, as he sometimes referred to her, and to retain his own pride. Yet he still seemed to be waiting for a miracle.

While the press ignored Dole, it was obsessed with the undeclared presidential candidacy of Democratic senator Edward M. Kennedy, whom it all but forced into challenging President Carter for the Democratic presidential nomination.

To Dole, this lionization of Kennedy was particularly irksome. "They [reporters] are attracted to Teddy like flies," Dole com-

Bob Dole (center) with his brother, Kenny, and sister, Gloria, standing in front of their father's 1927 Whippet, circa 1931. Though the Great Depression was at its height, the Dole family was never down-and-out poor. (Courtesy of Russell Townsley and Kenny Dole)

Back home in Russell, Kansas, Dole exercises his wounded right arm, atrophied by neglect while he lay in Army hospitals. (Courtesy of Russell Townsley and Kenny Dole)

Bob Dole as an Army gunner at Fort Breckenridge in 1944, just before he embarked for Italy. (Courtesy of Russell Townsley and Kenny Dole)

The Russell County Courthouse, where Bob Dole worked as county attorney from 1953 to 1960. (Courtesy of Russell Townsley)

Dole in his office as Russell county attorney. (Courtesy of Russell Townsley)

Dole's parents, Bina and Doran, on their forty-ninth wedding anniversary in Russell, February 28, 1970. (Courtesy of Russell Townsley)

Congressman Wint Smith (left), Bob Dole (center), and U.S. Senator Frank Carlson (right), when the GOP political caravan visited Russell in October 1956. Dole was destined to replace both men in the U.S. House of Representatives and the Senate.

Dole campaigning in his first congressional race in Russell, on July 23, 1960, with his traveling team of females, later dubbed Dolls for Dole. The Bobolinks are the four girls wearing Bob Dole hats. Bob's niece and his daughter, Robin, are to his immediate left. Notice the uniformity of the girls' campaign outfits. Dole's first wife, Phyllis, and his mother, Bina, helped make the girls' campaign dresses. (Photos courtesy of Russell Townsley)

*The Dolls for Dole honor Bob's daughter, Robin, during Dole's tough 1974 Senate reelection campaign. Attractive young women had been a Dole campaign hallmark since the 1960s, when they were called the Bobolinks. (Courtesy of Russell Townsley)*

*A recent photograph of the Dole family home at 1035 North Maple Street, Russell, Kansas, where Bob grew up. (Courtesy of Russell Townsley)*

*Bob and Elizabeth Dole in 1976, a few months after their marriage. (Courtesy of Russell Townsley)*

Dawson's Drug Store (now called Rogers') as it looks today on Main Street in Russell, Kansas, where Bob Dole worked as a soda jerk every night during high school. (Gene DeForrest)

Returning to Russell on August 20, 1976, with his running mate, President Ford, Dole is overcome with emotion as he recalls the generosity of townspeople who contributed $1,800 for an operation on his arm after the army refused him further treatment. (UPI/Bettmann Newsphotos)

Dole and President Gerald Ford in the Oval Office of the White House during the 1976 campaign, when Dole was Ford's running mate. "The vice presidency is indoor work, with no heavy lifting," Dole joked. (Courtesy of Russell Townsley)

The huge billboard greeting visitors to Bob's hometown is a vivid testimony to the fact that "Bob Dole is Russell, and Russell is Bob Dole." (Courtesy of Russell Townsley)

Dole campaigning for the vice presidency outside his house in Russell on November 2, 1976. (Courtesy of Russell Townsley)

Dole with wife Elizabeth (at his left) and mother Bina (at his right) in front of Russell County Courthouse on January 6, 1978, for the dedication of a plaque commemorating the 1976 Ford-Dole campaign. (Courtesy of Russell Townsley)

*Bob Dole at election rally outside his home in Russell on November 2, 1976 ("Bob Dole Day"), when he ran for vice president. (Courtesy of Russell Townsley)*

*(left to right): Elizabeth Dole, Nancy Landon Kassebaum (Alf Landon's daughter, elected junior U.S. senator from Kansas) and Bob Dole, Labor Day, 1978. (Courtesy of Russell Townsley)*

*Dole with Dole pineapple juice cans, May 1985. He used the pineapple juice to gain name recognition and to differentiate himself from rival Phillip Doyle in 1960. (Courtesy of Russell Townsley)*

Bob and Kenny Dole in 1987 at the Dole family house in Russell. Bob is pulling the arm exerciser his father made for him forty years earlier. (Courtesy of Russell Townsley)

At a sentimental homecoming in Russell on November 9, 1987, Dole announces his candidacy for the Republican presidential nomination and accepts from Bub Dawson (left) the very same cigar box used to collect money for his surgery in 1947. (Courtesy of Russell Townsley)

December 17, 1987. Sharing the spotlight with President Reagan, Dole announces his support for the INF medium-range missile treaty and vows to lead the fight for Senate ratification while Vice President George Bush "doesn't even get to vote." (AP/Wide World Photos)

plained to me, often giving vent to feelings of envy and loathing of Kennedy, whom he branded "a phony, a limousine liberal, a big spender raised on a silver spoon." In August 1979, he startled and amused the media by announcing, in a National Press Club speech, that he would run his campaign "against Kennedy" even before the latter had officially announced his candidacy. "Senator Kennedy is unique in American politics," Dole told the audience, explaining that he was "running against Kennedy because the press and the Democratic Party had already anointed him the Democrat nominee and dismissing President Carter as a sure loser.

On the Senate floor and in Judiciary Committee hearings, Dole harassed Kennedy with snide remarks. Taking potshots at the seemingly invincible Goliath of American politics made him feel like David, the underdog gallantly trying to score an upset. Kennedy ignored him, turning up his nose at the Kansas bumpkin and treating his candidacy as a joke.

After Kennedy declared his candidacy in early November, Dole worried that reporters would wander down the hall and catch his Senate staff in some activity, such as campaign work, that "might look bad." Dole complained, "The media will let him [Kennedy] get away with anything, but if I did it, they'd cordon off my office and shut me down the next morning." Instead, the media turned on Kennedy and resurrected the ten-year-old scandal of Chappaquiddick. As Kennedy fumbled and sputtered, Dole privately ridiculed him as "needing a bridge over troubled waters" and "making a big splash," elated to see Goliath felled by the media mudslingers.

Kennedy's decline did nothing to revive Dole's own invisible candidacy, however. Ever hesitant, Bob remained silent and broke. When a mob of Iranians seized the U.S. Embassy in Tehran and took fifty-two Americans hostage, Dole toyed with several controversial anti-Iran legislative proposals that might have won him some publicity but held back for fear that the press would say, "Dole's going to get us into a war." Typically, he ordered his staff to draft tough bills imposing sanctions and embargoes on Iran, but he never saw them through.

As Dole stood idly by, other candidates stole his ideas and got the credit. On November 8, 1979, on the Senate floor, Dole accused Carter of failing to stockpile oil because of Saudi Arabian threats, thereby leaving the country dangerously vulnerable to another Arab oil embargo. Dole told the clerk of the Senate that he wanted to introduce an amendment to an energy bill that would force the president to stockpile oil in the nation's "strategic petroleum reserve." Then Dole retreated to the GOP Senate cloakroom, just off the floor, unable to decide whether to actually introduce the amendment.

When the clerk of the Senate called out his name on the loudspeaker and told him it was time to fish or cut bait, Idaho Senator Jim McClure went up to him and said, "Come on, Bob, make up your mind. What if you were president and the Russians were attacking? What would you do?" Thus goaded into action, he finally did walk onto the floor and introduce the legislation.

The controversial amendment passed, but not before meeting stiff opposition in a House-Senate conference. Dole had no stomach for such a fight and dropped out of the picture, leaving other senators to take credit for his amendment. Democratic Senator Bill Bradley of New Jersey led the fight. Dole was afraid that the Saudis would impose an oil embargo on America and that he would be blamed. Finally, the bill was signed into law by Carter, and the Saudis' bluff was called, but Dole was nowhere to be found.

In a rare interview with the *New York Times* in November 1979, Dole said that he still thought it possible that he would receive the presidential nomination and explained his hope that the party would run to him in 1980, as it had in 1976, as a compromise dark-horse candidate. But it was hard for most people to see why the party would turn to a candidate who did very little active campaigning.

On national television in late 1979, Johnny Carson ridiculed Dole in a famous line that summarizes what the country thought of the Kansan: "Bob Dole is not the most exciting, charismatic personality around. He recently willed his body to science, and they contested the will." In the "parking lot of life," Carson quipped, "Bob Dole is a Chrysler."

Dole's invisible campaign rode into the sunset on January 5,

1980, when six of the seven GOP hopefuls gathered in Des Moines, Iowa, for a nationally televised debate two weeks before the "baptismal font" of the Iowa precinct caucuses. Dole showed up to give a maudlin, inappropriately sentimental pitch for votes. His *de facto* campaign manager, Elizabeth, and some other aides had prepared him for the debate by advising him to appear compassionate and to appeal for a sympathy vote by parading his handicap on the stage. "She wanted me to take off my shirt, show 'em by arm, and say, 'Here, this is what I did for my country. Now, vote for me,' " Dole later commented acidly, in the only time I ever heard him express disillusionment with advice from his alter ego.

At the Iowa debate, Dole summarized his qualifications for the presidency by giving vent to his frustration at being ignored:

> I've been wondering for some time as I stood on the Senate floor day after day after day, if the voters in Iowa really appreciate my nineteen years' experience in the House and Senate. I've wondered from time to time whether Iowa voters were aware of my role in World War II, and the strength I've gained through adversity. I've wondered sometimes if the Iowa voters know about my chairmanship of the Republican Party, my work in the party, and my campaign with Jerry Ford in 1976.

Thus, in the most personal terms imaginable, the physically handicapped candidate made his pitch for votes. This self-pity evoked media scorn. *Time* magazine columnist Hugh Sidey criticized Dole's "focus on self, on the I, I, I," remarking that "audiences are too sophisticated for that in this age."

Two weeks later, Dole finished in last place in Iowa, with less than 3 percent of the total vote. His dismal showing was particularly humiliating since Iowa was a farm state contiguous to Kansas. Pundits wrote him off as finished.

Virtually all of his political advisers—except his wife—counseled him to withdraw from the presidential race after the Iowa debacle, but Dole arrogantly dismissed them with a wave of his hand and rushed headlong into the next primary state, New Hampshire. What propelled him into New Hampshire was the surprise victory of the despised George Bush in Iowa. With a strong grass-roots organization in Iowa, Bush had upset the front-runner, Reagan, and had gained in the "five M's" that Dole felt were necessary to win—money, momentum, manpower, media, and management. Overnight, Bush had become the front-runner for the GOP nomination. If he could win in New Hampshire, where he now led in the polls, he would probably sew up the nomination.

"We have to stop Bush," Dole told his staff the day after the Iowa vote, adding a number of expletives in his description of the new front-runner. Stopping Bush now became an obsession that profoundly altered Dole's campaign persona and tactics. The hitherto invisible candidate now became a self-proclaimed Nemesis, out to wreak destruction on his hated rival.

Determined to demolish Bush at all costs, Dole spent $50,000 on a ten-day, last-minute campaign blitz in New Hampshire. Gagging at the thought of Bush as president, Dole aimed personal barbs at him in private. He resented Bush's wealth and string of "appointed figurehead positions"[4] and still bristled at Bush's replacing him as RNC chairman in 1972.

With monomaniacal ferocity, Dole suddenly abandoned his Senate duties and practically moved into New Hampshire, with staffers in tow. Casting off the mask of "silent compassion" he had worn since the outset of his campaign, he now mounted an anti-Bush campaign with a vengeance. Becoming active and effective only after targeting a specific enemy, he seemed like Captain Ahab chasing Moby Dick, hurling harpoons at his old nemesis, seeking to dismember his dismemberer.

In his search for an issue on which to hang Bush, Dole resorted to appealing to the dark underside of American politics: a fascination with conspiracy and an appetite for witch-hunting. Learning that Bush had once been a member of the Trilateral Commission, an elitist "Eastern Establishment" organization founded by David Rockefeller in 1973 as a forum for promoting economic and political cooperation among the United States, Europe, and Japan, Dole

[4]Bush had been an elected congressman from Texas from 1967 to 1971, but had then been defeated for the Senate twice before being appointed GOP national chairman, United Nations ambassador, and CIA director. He was born in Massachusetts, reared in Connecticut, and educated at Yale before moving to Houston and starting his oil business. His father was a U.S. senator and a Connecticut patrician.

identified Bush as a card-carrying member of the Trilateral Commission, which he labeled a supra-national group. Slipping into the role of witch-hunter, Dole implied that the Trilateral Commission was a conspiracy to undermine American economic and political interests by grooming what he considered candidate clones like George Bush and Jimmy Carter. Noting that Carter and virtually every one of his cabinet secretaries had been Trilateralists (both Bush and Carter had resigned from the commission in order to campaign for president), Dole equated Bush with Carter, denouncing them both as the bankers' puppets and "the Rockefeller candidates" who wanted to put foreign interests before American interests and who would subvert the First Amendment. Giving vent to his populism, Dole mounted a crusade against "the bankers and their marionette." The Trilateral Commission was a favorite target of many distressed farmers in western Kansas, who blamed it for conspiring to keep down crop prices.

Because Reagan wanted to maintain a congenial and affable image in New Hampshire, he declined to savage Bush personally and let Dole do his dirty work. Dole's anti-Bush attacks found a receptive audience in William Loeb, Reagan supporter and right-wing publisher of the influential *Manchester* [New Hampshire] *Union Leader*, who shared Dole's views. Though he had completely ignored Dole for the past nine months, Loeb suddenly gave the Kansan an arena in which to air his anti-Bush views. Increasingly, news stories and op-ed pieces appeared in the *Union Leader*. Loeb followed through with savage editorials lambasting Bush and echoing Dole's allegations of conspiracy. Such attacks damaged Bush's credibility with conservative voters in the Granite State.[5]

On February 23, 1980, three days before the crucial New Hampshire primary election, the *Nashua Telegraph* sponsored a televised debate between Bush and Reagan. Because the *Telegraph* editors considered these two the only "serious" Republican candidates, they excluded Dole, Anderson, Baker, Connally, and Crane. Dole was furious and believed he saw the handwriting of Bush all over the debate rules. He filed a complaint with the Federal Elections Commission and helped orchestrate a scenario that would ultimately take the wind out of Bush's sails.

[5]Loeb died in November 1986.

The ground rules of the Nashua debate had been agreed to by the Reagan and Bush campaign managers weeks before, but now Reagan was trailing Bush in some polls and sorely needed a boost. Dole, who had been acting as Reagan's *de facto* gunslinger by assailing Bush on all sides, was more than glad to supply it. He and the other candidates came up with a plan to sandbag Bush by secretly flying up to Nashua just before the debate started and suddenly demanding to participate in the debate *en masse*. Believing that Bush would panic in a crisis, Dole assured his fellow candidates that they would make Bush look like a wet poodle.

Dole's assessment proved accurate. At the debate, following a carefully written script, veteran actor Reagan feigned righteous indignation when "the Nashua Four" suddenly appeared out of nowhere and were denied the right to participate by Bush and the *Telegraph* sponsors. Reagan, his face red as a beet, seized the microphone and declared, "I'm paying for this microphone, Mr. Green" (paraphrasing a line from *State of the Union*, an old Spencer Tracy movie about a presidential campaign) and insisted he wanted the other candidates to participate. When a pro-Reagan technician turned off the power in the microphone to make the situation appear more oppressive, Reagan started yelling. The power was then turned on. Television cameras recorded everything.

Bush, caught off guard, pointed out that the debate rules had been agreed upon before and therefore opposed allowing the other candidates to participate. He was practically booed off the stage by the angry crowd. "Bad, bad!" Dole shouted while someone in the audience called Bush "a Hitler."

As it turned out, the ground rules stood, and the Nashua Four had to stand on the sidelines and watch Reagan debate Bush alone. But the actual words uttered in the debate were drowned out by the drama of the excluded candidates. Bush never recovered from the fall he took that night. A Washington columnist in the audience commented, "Reagan is winning the election right here tonight." The *Boston Globe* editors later said, "At a high school in Nashua, the Gipper grabbed the class ring."

Dole's ploy succeeded beyond his wildest expectations. The ornery New Hampshire voters turned on Bush overnight. His poll standings plummeted, and he was soundly defeated by Reagan in the primary election three days later. Reagan won 51 percent of the vote to Bush's 22 percent.

Ironically, while these gunslinger tactics helped demolish Bush, they destroyed Dole's own campaign. Out of a total of over 100,000 votes cast in the New Hampshire Republican primary, Dole received a puny 608, less than 1 percent.

Dole reacted to the New Hampshire disaster—the worst single election defeat of his entire political career—with a mixture of pride and anger. With his campaign totally bankrupt, with no support whatsoever in the country, he strutted about the Senate like a conquering Caesar, telling colleagues how he had turned the tide against Bush in New Hampshire. He steadfastly refused to withdraw from the race and insisted that he could still win the GOP presidential nomination. Once again, the cripple had become the crippler, and demolishing a hated foe made him feel powerful. He continued to attack Bush, even while jeopardizing his own chances for reelection to the Senate from Kansas. "He's committing political suicide," said his Senate press secretary, Bob Waite. "If he keeps this up, he won't have any credibility left in Kansas." Everyone else on his staff echoed this view, but no one dared broach the subject of withdrawal with Dole, for fear of incurring his ire.

Dole's vast reservoir of antipathy was directed not only against Bush but also against the press. Two days after the New Hampshire debacle, a reporter who had written critical articles asked Dole if he had a statement. His face dark with anger, Dole thundered: "Not for you—not now, not tomorrow, not ever."

Dole was being attacked by Kansas Democratic congressman Dan Glickman for "pursuing the impossible dream" in seeking the presidency. "At some point," Glickman warned, "the Kansas voter is going to believe that Bob Dole is acting foolishly. He is going to start asking questions about his credibility."

As the full magnitude of the New Hampshire disaster became apparent, Dole became increasingly dejected and caustic. He lashed out indiscriminately at his staff, blaming them for his defeats. Bill Fritts, Dole's executive assistant, was reduced to a punching bag and endured endless tirades. Withdrawing into his inner sanctum, Dole lapsed into a bunker mentality, feeling surrounded by enemies and incompetents and convinced that his political career was doomed.

Longtime adviser Dave Owen openly urged him to get out of the race, but Dole still demurred. Seeing his presidential candidacy as a personal test of his worth, he vowed never to be the first candidate to withdraw. He was determined to hang on until one of his opponents preceded him to the gallows. His lifelong self-image as a finisher, not a quitter, was on the line. Alone among Dole's advisers, Elizabeth urged him to continue his hopeless presidential bid. Forever expecting a miracle, the Doles seemed oblivious to reality.

With the Kansas primary filing dates just ahead, Dole flirted with political disaster by considering *not* putting his name on the ballot for reelection to the Senate and toying with the idea of running only as a presidential candidate.[6]

Nonetheless, even though he stayed in the race, Dole was the only GOP candidate who failed to put his name on the ballot for the Kansas presidential primary on April 1. Fearing embarrassment at losing even his home state, where he was a favorite son candidate, he preferred the fantasy of staying in the race without being on the ballot. Still hoping that Reagan would stumble and that Bush would be discredited, he held on.

As if misfortune at the polls were not enough, fate treated Dole to embarrassment on two further counts: his health and his creditors.

His health had been good since his last hospital stay during the late 1940s and obviously he was strong enough to consistently work long and hard. But because he had only one kidney and a virtually useless right arm, and experienced occasional numbness in the fingers of his left hand, Dole sometimes worried that the status of his health might become a campaign issue if he ran for president. In the past, his opponents had graciously avoided mentioning his physical handicaps. But now he was running for the presidency, and the rules were different. With his finger on the

---

[6]Dole had until February 12, 1980, to file for the April 1 Kansas presidential primary—which he did not do. A second primary, for the Senate office, held in August, required that he file by June 20.

nuclear button, a president had to be in tip-top physical shape, and voters would be zeroing in on his health.

On February 18, 1980, the *Medical World News* published a report on the health status of each major presidential candidate. The magazine did not claim that Dole's useless arm would inhibit him in carrying out his presidential responsibilities, and it included the conclusion of Dole's personal physician, Dr. Freeman Cary, that Dole was "in excellent health" and said there was no medical reason why he should not seek the presidency. However, it did refer to a vectorcardiograph (VCG) as indicative of an "old inferior myocardial infarction," and stated "one candidate seems to have had a silent heart attack three years ago." Dole hit the ceiling at this charge when it was reported in Kansas newspapers as a reference to him.

The medical issue became moot, because he was never taken seriously as a candidate, but Dole's problems with his creditors did not. In late 1979, Computer Business Supplies Inc. filed a lawsuit against Dole and his campaign committee for unpaid bills of $166,000, and his former campaign manager Tom Bell's organization, Response Marketing, sued Dole for total lawsuit damages of $237,000 for unpaid bills.

Dole had refused to pay these bills because he claimed his creditors had violated an agreement with him not to engage in deficit spending and to incur no expenses without his authorization. Dole vigorously opposed the suits and in February 1980 filed his own lawsuit against Bell and Response Marketing for $1 million in damages, alleging fraud, breach of contract, and negligence.

Bell was infuriated at the suit and threatened Dole with a defamation action. "This is typical Bob Dole," Bell was quoted in the press as saying. "His attorney said all along they were going to file some kind of suit to try to scare us out of our money. . . . I'll be damned if I'll let him slander me . . . and get away with it."

The suits became very ugly, and embarrassing to Dole. A settlement was reached eventually.

Finally, Dole was bailed out of his dilemma by Howard Baker, who on March 5, became the first GOP candidate to quit the presidential race. Sarcastically joking that Baker, the shortest candidate, "can always open up a tall men's clothing store—in Japan,"

Dole took a breath of fresh air. Now, he suddenly decided, he could bring about peace with honor by bowing out gracefully. On March 15, at a news conference in Lawrence, Kansas, he announced his withdrawal from the presidential race and his candidacy for reelection to the Senate. He thanked his supporters and complained, "The basic irony is a bit painful. My greatest asset, my experience and performance as a senator, turned into my greatest liability" in the presidential campaign. Deploring that "campaign skills are valued more highly than leadership skills," he went on to hint that he might reenter the presidential sweepstakes at some future date. As their candidate finally terminated his forlorn presidential bid, his longtime supporters breathed a collective sigh of relief. People on his staff were relieved. In another week, it would have been too late.

Even after his withdrawal from the presidential race, the atmosphere in Dole's Senate office reflected his campaign fortunes. There was a sense of being on a sinking ship. Dole seriously considered resigning from the Senate before the term expired, perhaps giving up his seat to his wife or to one of his protégés. He told me in April, "I haven't decided if I'm going to run again." When someone mentioned a potential rival who wanted to run for his seat, Bob remarked, "I can't understand why anyone would want to come in here. Better to be going out." Newspapers reported rumors that he would not run again, and in late April 1980, a Kansas newspaper printed a story stating that Dole had categorically decided to resign and join an East Coast law firm.

Finally, on May 22, just a few weeks before the June 20 deadline for filing his candidacy for reelection, he announced that he would seek a third Senate term after all.

Dole easily won reelection to his third Senate term, campaigning vigorously with Elizabeth at his side. "Elizabeth is my American Express card," he joked. "Don't leave home without her."

The November 1980 election belonged to Ronald Reagan and the GOP. Reagan and his running mate, George Bush,[7] won by a landslide over the hapless Jimmy Carter and Walter Mondale, with

[7]Less than thrilled with the prospect of Bush as vice president, at the Republican convention Dole had unsuccessfully tried to bring about a Reagan-Ford ticket.

a margin of eight million popular votes and 489 to 49 electoral votes, winning forty-five states and sweeping in a Republican majority in the Senate.

For the first time in a quarter of a century, the GOP had seized control of the Senate, by a margin of fifty-three to forty-seven seats. This meant that Dole would now have a committee chairmanship and real power. For the first time in his career, he would be among the majority. The man who had nearly given up his career in disgust just six months earlier, the man whose campaign had seemed a sinking ship, had now been transformed—literally overnight—into one of the most powerful figures in Washington.

The question was: How would he handle power?

# 12
# THE TAX MAN
# COMETH

I visited Bob Dole in Washington shortly after the November 1980 election. He seemed like a man transfigured, a political Lazarus who had risen from the dead and transformed himself into a mighty beast of prey as he prepared to assume his new role as Senate Finance Committee chairman.

Lean, tanned, basking in his newfound power and celebrity, he bore no resemblance to the hapless creature struggling against impossible odds just eight months earlier, the critically wounded gladiator who had come within an inch of throwing away his political career. And the national press corps, which had previously avoided his press conferences like the plague, were now queuing up outside his office waiting for interviews.

The impression Dole gave me as he was about to embark on a new phase of his career was that of a man hungry to get even with all those who had excluded him from power and "real" success for so long. He joked about "going after those Guccis," and he talked of new initiatives in taxation. Within two years, the whole country would know what he meant by that.

"Taxation is my new weapon," Dole boasted to me, as he went about planning his strategy to become king of the hill.

True to form, he played Mr. Independent as reporters mobbed him and asked if he would act as President-Elect Reagan's errand boy in shepherding new tax-cut legislation through the committee. He remained coy about this issue, claiming he had to think about it.

"How do you plan to use your new power as a bargaining chip to get what you want on other bills?" a reporter asked him in his first news conference following the election. "I don't know," he shot back. "I never had any power to bargain with."

Now he had power galore. As chairman of the Senate Finance Committee, he would be the gatekeeper for virtually every major piece of legislation affecting the massive federal budget. His committee would pass judgment on every bill on tax, welfare, Social Security, foreign trade, Medicare, and a host of other issues affecting fiscal policy. Next to President Reagan, he would be the most powerful man in Washington.

Meanwhile, Elizabeth Dole was busy securing her own position in the White House as special assistant to the president for public liaison. She took with her some of Dole's key Senate staff, including Ernie Garcia, the man who had worked on Dole's controversial cult hearings two years earlier. Now part of Reagan's "truth squad," she had to stick much closer to the Reagan line in public than her husband did. She loyally modified her hitherto staunch support for the Equal Rights Amendment, settling for a Reagan bill that removed sex-biased language from federal statutes but did nothing about state sex discrimination. As always, she proved flexible in order to advance her career.

Quipping that his wife had "made it to the White House first," Dole predicted that he "might have to run against her in a couple of years," a comment that thinly veiled his longstanding and invigorating rivalry with Elizabeth. Jealous that she was more popular than he, even among his own staff, Dole engaged in some heavy kidding with her, in public and off camera.

But for the most part, he carefully planned a strategy that would give him great prominence while minimizing Reagan's role. While he had managed to stay on good terms with Reagan, Dole had always had a great deal of contempt for the man as an intellectual midget in the Oval Office and a "programmed line reader" as an actor. It was a strategy that Dole hoped would lead the "septuagenarian" and "befuddled" Reagan into quitting the White House in 1984, after one term, so that he could run on the Republican ticket instead.

Unlike most GOP senators, who blithely fell into line as "Reagan's rubber stamps" when the Ninety-Seventh Congress convened in January 1981, Dole stood out as an ornery and temperamental committee chairman who was firmly in control.

He found a map of the country, circled the Midwest with a red crayon, and sent it to Senator Paul Laxalt, a member of Reagan's inner circle. He demanded an agriculture secretary who was from the Midwest. Reagan complied and approved Dole's personal choice, John Block, for the post. It was the first of many concessions that the "befuddled Methuselah" would grant to the much cleverer Dole.

As a man with an insatiable appetite for publicity, Dole was in paradise when he was handed the gavel to the Finance Committee. He had always wanted to be a committee chairman. He relished the publicity, the power, and the chance to really make a contribution. But he also found his new position a bit unnerving. As an outsider in Washington for twenty years, he had developed a pattern of attacking the Democrats with his ever-sharp tongue. But now he and his party were in power, and negativism would not do.

Dole told me shortly after the election that he thought the GOP had a real opportunity to become the majority party in the country "if we can show that we're responsible." He had often criticized his own party in the past for being too negative, too antipeople, and too enamored of the wealthy. But few Republicans had listened to him, least of all Ronald Reagan. Reagan was a man for whom wealth meant worth and to whom big business was sacrosanct. Now that Reagan was president, Dole feared that his administration's policies would not be compassionate toward the poor but would instead favor the rich and that Reagan would squander the opportunity his party had.

As Finance Committee chairman, Dole was "the ball carrier," as he called himself, whom Reagan would have to rely on to get his policies enacted by the Senate. Reagan feared that Dole might prove recalcitrant on the Hill, and his appointment of Elizabeth to a big position on his White House staff may have been, at least in part, an effort to secure Dole's loyalty.

The White House also knew that there was a strong element of ruthlessness in Dole, a proclivity to ride roughshod over anyone who stood in his way. Authority figures, whether committee chairmen, Senate elders, or presidents, were seen by Dole as targets for his barbs and his maneuverings. He seemed to relish poking holes in their armor.

Keeping Dole in tow might thus prove a major problem for the new president, especially since the senator had never had any great respect for him. Dole would not fall into line easily just because Reagan wore Republican colors. He might strike alliances with liberal Democrats on some issues, just to defy Reagan and to stand out as an independent star. With an eye toward 1984, he might not be content to play the role of ball carrier for the White House. When Dole became ill with kidney stones in early March 1981, Reagan personally visited him at Walter Reed Army Hospital. When Dole barked, Reagan shuddered.

Almost immediately following his inauguration on January 20, 1981, Reagan instituted his new program, dubbed "the Reagan Revolution" by his supporters. He began by putting an immediate freeze on all federal hiring and by promising to send up a package of legislative proposals to Congress that would cut back the bloated federal bureaucracy by targeting "waste, fraud, and inefficiency" and by systematically cutting back on a wide array of social programs. Almost immediately, critics on the left accused Reagan and Republican congressmen and senators of attempting to repeal the New Deal and to eliminate the social safety net.

Ultimately, both critics and admirers of Reagan's policies settled on the word *Reaganomics* to describe them. This new word embraced the president's simultaneous attempts to balance the federal budget, increase defense spending dramatically, and slash income taxes by 30 percent over three years.

Reagan promised miracles, and he couched his promises in glowing terms. As the media politician *par excellence*, with a trained actor's voice and gestures, Reagan went on national television to sell his promises to the millions of viewers. "We don't have to choose between inflation and unemployment—they go hand in hand," he said, two weeks after being inaugurated. "It's time to try something different." The media wizard promised simultaneous fast growth, low unemployment, huge military budgets, and balanced budgets.

Reagan sought cuts of $35 billion in programs and got them, thanks to a coalition of Republicans and conservative "boll weevil" Democrats in both the House and Senate. The Reagan steamroller seemed destined to flatten Congress as easily as it had bulldozed the electorate.

In this atmosphere, Dole thought it politically inexpedient to oppose Reagan for going too far in cutting back social programs. Instead, he criticized the president *for not going far enough.* Characteristically, Dole introduced his own proposal for budget cuts, exceeding Reagan's by $1 billion, and called a press conference to publicize his more drastic proposal.

Dole's initial budget proposal angered many people in both the White House and the Senate. Some White House aides complained that Dole was trying to outdo Reagan at Reaganomics. His committee was responsible for tax bills, not budget proposals (although the two are related, of course), and he was seen as an opportunist seeking to take credit for the implementation of Reaganomics.

The man who had campaigned just a year before on the need for government to act responsibly toward the underprivileged, the man who had championed federal spending programs to aid the poor and the handicapped, was now doing an about-face and calling for massive cutbacks in these very programs. If Congress was in a budget-axing mood, Dole was eager to pick up the hatchet and thereby increase his own political stature.

As he proceeded to shape a tax bill for the year, Dole tried hard to put his own mark on it. He searched for a way in which to differentiate himself from Reagan, even while promoting Reaganomics. In the meantime, his characteristic indecisiveness was taking its toll, and he was criticized heavily for stalling on the bill and sending out ambiguous and conflicting signals. One disgruntled presidential aide called him a "prima donna," while the *Wall Street*

*Journal* criticized him in an editorial titled "Where's the Dole Bill?"

Dole apparently remained unflappable in the face of such censure, however, perhaps because he was basking in the glow of media attention. The publicity Dole craved throughout his career was finally his. Television and newspaper cameras photographed him in committee, on the White House driveway after important meetings with Reagan, and in the many press conferences he called. His every word suddenly became newsworthy. If he dropped a hint to the press that he didn't think a Reagan proposal would pass on Capitol Hill, the media flocked to him like hungry birds. If he said he had a "problem" with a presidential proposal, the press went to work analyzing his position.

The abortive assassination attempt on Reagan by John Hinckley on March 30 boosted the president's popularity enormously on Capitol Hill and throughout the country, extending his honeymoon with the press and Congress. It contributed greatly to his securing congressional passage of his proposals. When he appeared on national television while addressing a joint session of Congress four weeks after the assassination attempt, Reagan was at the peak of his popularity.

Despite that popularity, it was after the assassination attempt that Dole made an about-face: he began to criticize Reagan for going too far in cutting back on food stamps and other social programs, just a few weeks after criticizing the president for not going far enough. Apparently realizing that it was not practical to outdo Reagan at Reaganomics, he tried his luck in attacking the president from the left. If he appeared contradictory, so be it. He had never been a genuine idealist willing to go down fighting for a cause. He was more attuned to pragmatic politics, in which compromise and reversal of positions were the name of the game.

Dole measured the political winds with a sensitized barometer, and he moved in what he thought to be the prevailing wind direction. In the spring of 1981 he sensed, earlier than most of his GOP colleagues, that, while the president was personally popular, the public perceived Reaganomics to be unfair—that poor people were being hurt, while the rich had never had it so good.

Reaganomics, the most radical tampering with the national economy since the New Deal, sought to effectuate three fundamental shifts in the allocation of the nation's scarce resources: from the public sector to the private sector, from the civilian sector to the military sector, and from the poor to the wealthy. The justification of the new program rested upon the so-called trickle-down economic theory. According to this hypothesis, also known as supply-side economics, the transfer of wealth to the wealthy individuals and corporations (primarily through massive tax cuts and breaks) would lead these entities to invest more money in capital equipment and research, thus ultimately stimulating the economy and producing jobs for all. According to the theory, greater revenue would ultimately accrue to the government through tax cuts because a vibrant economy would produce more overall taxable income. Thus, less welfare spending would be needed, since everyone would have a job. Ultimately, the tax cuts (and consequent cuts in social programs) could be justified as "incentives" given to the rich for the benefit of all.

Reaganomics espoused a definite normative value system, namely, that government subsidies to the poor were inherently wrong and demoralizing, while such subsidies to the rich were deserved and productive. Reaganites and supply-siders believed that poor people were poor because they were lazy, not because of some fundamental unfairness in the economy and the society. The government's program of doling out welfare checks and food stamps served only to further weaken the character of such people; hence, it had to be ended.

Ronald Reagan, a showman at heart, managed to symbolize the great value that he bestowed upon the rich by leading a personally opulent lifestyle at the White House. He and Nancy became symbols of the New Luxury. They appeared elegant, exuding good taste, and were invariably clothed beautifully. Millionaires and their families were frequently invited to the White House to shine before the television cameras. Nancy Reagan, espousing what *Washington Post* columnist Mary McGrory called "a concern for things—not people," raised $822,641 to redo the White House living quarters and another $209,508 from private donations to pay for a setting of gilt-edged china. At a time when Reagan was drastically cutting social programs for poor *people*, this lavish expenditure on *things* struck many as callous and inhumane.

The growing popular perception of Reagan as a president of the rich, by the rich, and for the rich was not lost on Dole, who was often invited to the lavish White House parties. With an eye on Reagan's job, Dole perceptively concluded that Reagan's wealthy image might prove his ultimate undoing.

Reagan had campaigned in 1980 by appealing not only to the rich but also to the average man. He had won largely because he had been able to convince the average voters that he was one of them. His average-guy demeanor, his "aw shucks" expression, and his promise to create "jobs, jobs, jobs" had played a significant role in his winning a large portion of the blue-collar vote. But once in the White House, Reagan began looking and acting very much like the rich man's president, and a lot of the people who had voted for him were becoming increasingly frustrated.

Almost immediately after taking office, Reagan faced a wave of unemployment largely of his own making. Despite the promises of Reaganomics, people were losing their jobs at an astounding rate throughout 1981. Unemployment, which had been slightly over 7 percent on Inauguration Day, rose steadily upward toward 8 and 9 percent. Factories were shutting down at an alarming pace and capacity utilization was heading below 70 percent. The financial markets reflected great pessimism during the early months of the Reagan presidency. It seemed that Wall Street had little confidence in supply-side economics. The only positive factor was the declining interest rates. Reagan had inherited a prime rate of 21 percent when he took office, and it soon fell—largely because of the recession.

Dole had never believed whole-heartedly in the reasoning underlying supply-side economics. As a skeptic when it came to "experts" of all kinds, he viewed all economic theories with suspicion. Supply-side Reaganomics had always seemed a classroom theory to him, and he harbored great doubts about its efficacy. Privately, he thought that Reagan had been "sold a bill of goods" by supply-side "charlatans."

The former actor, Dole thought, simply lacked the intellectual capacity to understand the theories he was espousing. "His mind is simple, primitive . . . he thinks in terms of slogans," Dole had said to his staff about the man who was now occupying the White House. Dole called supply-side economics "the napkin theory," a reference to the fact that one of its founders, Professor Arthur Laffer, had allegedly conceived his theory one day at a restaurant, when he drew a curve on a napkin. When candidate George Bush had ridiculed Reaganomic theory as "voodoo economics" during the 1980 presidential campaign, Dole had remarked acidly, "Bush has his head on right, for once."

But now Bush was vice president, Reagan was president, and Dole found himself as point man in affirming this questionable economic theory by weaving it into law.

Dole's genuine doubts about the validity of the supply-side economic theory exacerbated his natural indecisiveness and his tendency to wait and see which way the political wind is blowing. Indeed, he seemed virtually immobilized on the tax bill. In the May 15th *Wall Street Journal* editorial that pointedly asked where *Dole's* bill was, he was skewered for being unconstructively dubious about Reagan's bill.

"Perhaps it is time to remind him [Dole] that he is no longer in the opposition . . . and that man in the White House, Ronald Reagan, is a fellow Republican," the *Journal* editors wrote. "He [Dole] wallows in doubts . . . hems and haws. . . . Chairman Dole's performance would be a bit more understandable if he had a tax plan of his own."

In fact, Dole did have a tax plan of his own, but he was reluctant to bring it forth. While a senator in the minority, he had become notorious for waiting until the last minute to make up his mind on bill after bill, and sometimes changing his mind during a vote. Now that he was in the majority, he still found it difficult to make timely decisions.

Criticisms from the *Journal* and other influential sources may finally have helped galvanize Dole into action. Fearing that his indecision might make him appear weak and soft, he unveiled his own tax plan two weeks later. His plan, he said, was a compromise measure that reduced the total amount of the tax cut from 30 percent to 25 (over three years), proposed a number of tax incentives to stimulate savings and investment, and was "leaner" than Reagan's.

He tried to induce the Reagan Administration to accept his tax proposal *after* he announced it to the press so that he would be able to take credit for it. He claimed that his committee "just doesn't have the votes" to pass Reagan's initial proposal, although this was probably not accurate. In fact, on a vote along strict party lines, Reagan's proposal would have passed by a narrow margin. But Dole preferred to impose his own version of the tax bill, and he had the power to do so.[1]

He enjoyed toying with Reagan's aides, cajoling and pressuring them to embrace his bill. "He was harder on us than on his committee members," one aide complained. Reagan went along, and the bill sailed through the committee by a bipartisan 19–1 vote. Dole was able to accurately call it a compromise bill. He relished playing the role of Great Compromiser, able to bring liberals and conservatives and Democrats and Republicans together. Because he had no real coherent political philosophy of his own, he could see all sides of an issue and give opposing groups some of what they wanted while denying them "the whole pie." More than once he had demonstrated a natural skill as a swing man, able to process a compromise amendment or bill that appealed to everyone.

In this regard, he was quite different from the true ideologues, those who valued principle over compromise. Dole's voting record was once, in his early days in the House and Senate, consistently conservative like theirs, but he had changed a lot over the past ten years. He now thought he could carve out a niche for himself in the political marketplace, "right straight down the middle," by appearing as a uniquely gifted deal maker. "Our form of government needs a compromiser," he often said in my presence.

Shortly after the resulting tax bill—called ERTA (the Economic Recovery Tax Act)—passed the Senate in June 1981, Democratic senator Lloyd Bentsen of Texas praised Dole as "a very compassionate man with a great sense of fairness. Dole's press image as a tough, caustic hardliner does him a great disservice," Bentsen said.

[1]Dole also successfully inserted in the tax bill a provision requiring income tax rates to be indexed to the rate of inflation.

Yet the benevolent Great Compromiser was only one side of Dole's complicated personality. He was still an intensely driven, ambitious man. His role as a compromiser was undoubtedly motivated, in part, by his desire to outmaneuver Reagan, to gnaw away at the vitals of Reaganomics. This was just his opening shot in what was to become a long, drawn-out, subtle war to make Reagan appear as an emperor without clothes. The 1981 tax bill gave Reagan most of what he had asked for, but Dole had shown his independence. More importantly, the contest over the tax bill did much to convince Dole that Reagan would not challenge him when defied on an important bill. This was to have important consequences in the future.

For Reagan, 1981 was a year of victory. The former actor was being hailed by the media as a master of Congress because most of his economic and defense proposals had been enacted. In addition to income tax cuts, Reaganomics brought about huge tax breaks for oil production, capital gains, stock options, estates, interest income, IRAs, savings certificates, and other items. The tax bill even allowed companies to sell their tax breaks to other companies if they couldn't use them in a particular year. While social spending was cut by about $30 billion, military spending was increased by a corresponding $28 billion—the largest single increase in U.S. peacetime history. Critics pointed out that Reagan was just transferring money from the social sector to the military—that that was all there was to Reaganomics. To pay for the new weaponry, child nutrition programs and workers' unemployment insurance were reduced drastically, as were welfare payments, Medicare, and Medicaid aid to the states. CETA public service jobs were eliminated entirely, as were college education benefits previously provided under Social Security.

Even the food stamp program, which Dole had stood up for, was reduced by $1.7 billion, thereby eliminating more than a million recipients. Were it not for Dole's influence leading to compromise, the cuts here would have been far greater, perhaps as high as $5 billion, which Reagan wanted.

With virtually all cuts in social spending going to the military, nothing would be done about remedying the federal budget deficit—then projected at about $49 billion for the year. (The 1981 budget deficit turned out to be even worse: $57.93 billion.) Indeed, with taxes cut by a whopping 25 percent, it seemed obvious that the budget deficits would dramatically *increase*, thereby violating one of Reagan's main campaign promises: to balance the budget by fiscal 1984. People were being forced to sacrifice not so that the budget would be balanced, but in order to give more money to the Pentagon and the super-rich.

The only way out of this dilemma was for the supply-side economics theory to work. That is, the massive tax cut would have to lead to a dramatic increase in business investment and productivity so that the government could take in more revenue at lower tax rates and thereby reduce the deficit.

But with unemployment rising and the worst recession in fifty years being proclaimed by virtually every economic analyst (except the ever-optimistic supply-siders), it did not appear likely that this would occur. Why would a businessperson invest more money in equipment when his factory was 30 percent idle?

Dole wanted to give Reaganomics a chance to prove itself, and he must share responsibility for having implemented it. Whether such an "experiment" could justify the economic hardship of millions of people was a question he preferred not to think about. But his Kansas constituents forced him to think about it, as they mailed him an avalanche of letters protesting Reaganomics. Unemployed construction workers mailed him heavy wooden blocks to dramatize the plight of the housing industry.

By November 1981, it was clear beyond doubt that the economy was deteriorating and that the country was in a recession. Unemployment had increased by 13.6 percent in the last ten months; housing starts had declined by 44 percent; new car sales were down by 30 percent; total industrial output had declined by 0.5 percent. The bond and stock markets were taking a nosedive. On November 10, Reagan admitted publicly that he expected some "hard times" ahead. The phrase *hard times* was repeated in banner headlines around the country and, for ten million unemployed people, became synonymous with Reaganomics.

In December, *The Atlantic Monthly* magazine published a sensational article by William Greider entitled "The Education of David Stockman." This article, based on a series of taped interviews with Reagan's budget director, Stockman, revealed the fundamentally phony theoretical basis of Reaganomics. Stockman, who had appeared as Reagan's whiz kid in masterminding the massive social budget cuts enacted by Congress, turned out to have had strong doubts about the very program he had sold so effectively to Congress. In effect, he admitted to having pulled figures out of the air and fed them into the computer of the Office of Management and Budget so that he could represent to the Congress that Reagan's policies would lead to a balanced budget by 1984.

Stockman also admitted that the great Reagan tax cut was really "a Trojan horse to bring down the top [tax] rate" for the rich. He denigrated supply-side economics as nothing more than a dressed-up version of the old trickle-down theory, which had been around for decades.

Stockman's revelations seriously undermined the credibility of Reaganomics. The embarrassment induced David Stockman to offer his resignation, but it was declined, allegedly out of fear of what else Stockman might say if he parted company with his boss. Thus, Reagan was stuck with having his budget prepared by a man who did not even believe in Reaganomics!

When Stockman went before Congress again, to present the budget for fiscal year 1983, he was met by angry and sarcastic congressmen, whose attitude was summed up in a statement made by one of them: "I have no questions for you, sir, because I frankly don't believe anything you say."[2]

At about this time, Dole met with other congressional leaders and planned a strategy for attacking the looming budget deficits. While Reagan pleaded for patience and asked the country to "stay the course" and give his program a chance to work, Dole was already planning the moves that would undermine that program. Against the advice of his more conservative colleagues, he decided to challenge Reaganomics directly.

---

[2]After leaving the government, Stockman revealed his story in a book, *The Triumph of Politics: The Inside Story of the Reagan Revolution* (New York: Harper and Row, 1986), in which he said, "Never before was the game of fiscal governance played so seriously and brilliantly as it was in [Dole's] office.

In January 1982, the administration announced that it expected the federal budget deficit to reach a record of $91 billion; this was assuming the most optimistic of circumstances. Other sources estimated it would exceed $109 billion.

This announcement, made by an administration that had promised to balance the budget, created a major credibility gap in the minds of the public and even in the business community. The previous record for budget deficits, $66 billion, had been set by the Ford Administration in 1976. Now Reagan was rewriting the book of deficit spending. After spending his whole career preaching about the evils of big government, Reagan was actually increasing the size of the bureaucracy while floating it on a sea of red ink. At that rate, he would build up more deficits during his four years in office than all previous American presidents *combined* had built up in two hundred years.

Dole was disturbed by the fact that Reagan was apparently oblivious to these problems of his own creation. Reagan was still acting as if "life is just one grand sweet song, so start the music." His optimism stunned even some of his closest advisers, who told him privately that his program was not working.

In the forefront of nonbelievers was Bob Dole. He began complaining that Reagan's policies were "unfair" and proposed the enactment of a minimum tax on the wealthy.[3]

Reagan, who initially opposed the idea of a minimum tax on the grounds that it would stifle productivity and weaken incentive, eventually went along with Dole and agreed to some kind of a minimum tax. This encouraged the senator to go after more.

On February 19, 1982, in his home state of Kansas, Dole announced that he intended to repeal the "safe harbor leasing" rule that had been sanctioned by his Finance Committee the summer before. This rule enabled less profitable companies to sell their tax breaks to more profitable ones, which used the breaks to lower their own tax liability further. The rule was strongly favored by the business community, which began a massive lobbying effort to preserve it. Dole, relishing a battle, declared that "leasing is indefensi-

[3]Dole said he was bothered by the fact that many corporations and wealthy individuals paid no tax at all, thanks to loopholes in the tax laws and generous tax breaks.

ble in a year in which the federal deficit will reach nearly $100 billion" and called it "corporate welfare." With combative flair, he declared that his repeal would be applied retroactively to all leases entered into "as of the date of this speech" and warned that henceforth anyone who chose to engage in such a swap of tax breaks would "do so at their own risk."

Characteristically, Dole acted alone in proposing this dramatic measure. He had not consulted President Reagan before making the speech. Valuing the elements of surprise and secrecy, he struck like lightning, catching the White House completely off guard.

Dole, who had always resented "those sharp New York tax lawyers," watched with glee as his words set off a scramble in executive suites and law firms to enter into proposed lease transactions by midnight. Business lobbyists, who had long regarded Dole as a friend on Capitol Hill, wondered where he had gotten this "radical idea." They would have more to wonder about as the year progressed.

Immediately after Dole's speech, Reagan's aides went on the air to denounce his proposal. Treasury secretary Donald Regan said it would be "extremely unwise" to repeal the rule, while White House chief of staff James Baker told CBS-TV's "Face the Nation" that Reagan supported continuation of the rule.

Ten days later, Dole said on "Face the Nation" that Reagan would have to accept changes in the ERTA tax-cut bill that had been enacted just the year before. He suggested a repeal of the 10 percent tax cut scheduled to go into effect in July, as well as imposition of a minimum tax on the wealthy and the closing of tax loopholes. He fingered rich doctors and other professionals who routinely used such loopholes.

At about this time, the Congressional Budget Office released a report proving that the 1981 tax cut was producing very little benefit to low- and moderate-income taxpayers, while gently benefiting the wealthy. Dole seized on this to hammer away again at the unfairness of Reaganomics.

When Reagan claimed his programs did not hurt "the truly needy," Dole responded that Reaganomics was just helping "the truly *greedy*." Increasingly, he delivered his speeches with populist gusto that struck many observers as "radical" and "liberal." On one national television program, a well-known panelist said in reference to the finance chairman, "If I didn't know any better, I'd think that person sitting next to me was Teddy Kennedy."

There was a certain sting to Dole's words, a certain fire in his delivery, that reminded many people of his old days as a partisan gunslinger. The only difference was that now he was attacking big business and the wealthy (and, indirectly, Reagan), while in the past he had attacked Democrats as left-leaning marshmallows.

Many who did not know Dole thought that he had seen a blinding light and become converted to liberalism. The reality was that he had always had strong populist leanings, but until now the political climate had not been right for their expression. Now, however, with Reagan tainted by the stigma of unfairness and with the economy in a definite tailspin, Dole's political antennae told him that Reaganomics was ripe for the plucking. Dole took off his gloves and began to do what came naturally to him: *fight*. And, as usual, he acted on his own, as his political timing and his conscience suggested. In making his proposals, he defied not only the White House and the conservative wing of his own party but conventional political wisdom. He kept his true thoughts to himself, often surprising staffers with his seemingly sudden decisions.

Dole at this time generally defied the New Right gurus who sought to place extremist "apparatchik" conservative staffers into every senator's office. Gloating over their successful role in achieving a Republican Senate and a Republican White House by means of massive financing of the 1980 campaigns, New Right fund-raisers and organizers wanted to control Dole, a notion the Kansas maverick found totally intolerable. He ridiculed and took on some of the more extreme right-wingers and made it clear he was going to be his own man.

He moved in contradictory directions, keeping everyone guessing his next move. He was considered unpredictable to ideologues of both the right and the left.

In March 1982, Dole went into the camp of big business, the Chamber of Commerce, and told the businessmen to their faces, "There is a perception out there that this administration lacks sensitivity, lacks compassion, and spends most of its time dreaming up programs to help the rich . . . you see it on a daily basis: morning, noon, and night."

Dole attacked the rich and said he was trying to broaden the base of the Republican Party by bringing in people of all classes and races. Judging issues on the basis of political practicality, he thought that his party had a golden opportunity to capture the mainstream of American public support by following a moderate course that stressed fairness. Kemp and the "purer" conservatives, on the other hand, sought to make the GOP the party of the conservative idealists. They regarded compromise as anathema and thought that the American voters had given them a mandate to implement stark conservatism.

As Dole sized up the opposition in his own party, he observed that Reagan was far more pliable than Kemp and the other more ideologically "pure" conservatives. Reagan liked to say that his feet were "fixed in concrete" over economic policy issues, but Dole believed that the concrete was not solid. As governor of California 1967–75, and as a presidential candidate in 1976 and 1980, Reagan had modified his positions so many times that he simply lacked credibility with Dole.

With midterm elections coming up in eight months, Dole realized that he had an important factor going for him in trying to influence his colleagues in Congress to support his proposals. One-third of the Senate and the entire House would be up for reelection in November. With many voters seething over the unfairness and ineffectiveness of Reaganomics, many Republicans stood to be defeated. They would not be willing to go down in defeat for Reagan. If Dole offered them a chance to jump ship, by voting for his moderate measures, they would do so. Then, once he had the votes for his proposals, Dole would present Reagan with a *fait accompli*. The president could either support the proposals or veto them—and thereby anger the majority of his GOP colleagues and the voters.

Dole used this strategy throughout the year to undercut Reagan's position. In April, Reagan proposed a massive cut of $2.3 billion in the food stamp program. Dole countered with a proposal to cut back only one-third as much and rounded up enough support among his Senate colleagues to force Reagan to back down.

In May, Dole again defied Reagan by proposing a crucial amendment to the Voting Rights Act, which preserved the teeth in the act's provisions against discriminatory voting booth practices. Acting independently, Dole mustered enough support among Judiciary Committee senators to pass his "compromise amendment" and again presented Reagan with a *fait accompli*. The president, who had initially tried to gut the key provisions of the bill, again backed down. As a result, Reagan was made to appear as an opponent of civil rights progress, while Dole earned the accolade of "the Dirksen of the eighties" from civil rights lobbyist Joseph Rauh, who then considered him an ally in the war against what was felt to be an insensitive Reagan Administration.

Dole's crowning achievement of 1982 was his single-handed success in proposing and spearheading through Congress his tax reform measure, dubbed the Tax Equity and Fiscal Responsibility Act of 1982 (TEFRA). More than any other piece of legislation, this tax bill elevated him to the status of a political star and greatly enhanced his prospects for winning a future presidential nomination, as far as the media were concerned. It also cast him in the role of being pro-tax and therefore alienated Reaganites, however.

In June, Congress was stalemated over a budget impasse caused in large part by Reagan's unwillingness to offer a practical and acceptable budget proposal. In contrast to Congress's eager rubber-stamping of Reagan's budget a year before, this time the legislators showed no tolerance for the massive social budget cuts the president proposed. His budget proposal was overwhelmingly rejected, and he declined to offer a substitute. Meanwhile, hundreds of different budget proposals were introduced in both the House and Senate, but none stood any chance of passage.

In an election year, the politicians did not want to vote for unpopular budget cuts or tax increases. There was a clear vacuum of leadership and a paralysis of congressional will. Dole decided to step into this leadership vacuum by proposing a major tax compromise package that he judged likely to appeal across the board to Democrats and Republicans, liberals and conservatives. The keystone of his proposal was the repeal of many of the tax benefits that had been given to business and rich individuals in the previous year's tax bill. He set a clear goal of raising $98 billion in taxes through such a repeal. This was a startling and original idea, which appeared utterly impractical in an election year.

But Dole was not a conventional man. He dreamed up novel ways to sell his proposal to his colleagues and, ultimately, to Reagan. He presented his idea to conservatives as a means for reducing the monstrous budget deficits, while he sold it to liberals as a reform measure intended to come down hard on big business and the rich.

On June 28, Dole told reporters that he would "step on a lot of toes" with TEFRA. "There's a perception that we've been too hard on poor people," he said. "Now we have to make sure that corporations pay taxes." Social programs should be left alone to "stabilize for a couple of years," he said, and he vowed to direct his fire at "some of the other programs that have escaped" spending cutbacks.

Dole outlined a number of proposals designed to raise revenues and thereby decrease the deficit. In addition to repealing the safe harbor leasing rule and closing corporate and rich people's loopholes, as he had suggested earlier in the year, he proposed increasing numerous taxes that would chiefly affect the middle class: taxes on airline tickets, cigarettes, and telephone calls would all be hiked. Medical payment deductions would be reduced significantly. The three-martini lunch—that is, the standard business entertainment deduction—was also targeted for repeal. In addition, Dole proposed more stringent reporting requirements for taxing waiters' and waitresses' tips, an immediate 10 percent withholding tax on savings account interest and stock dividends, and enhanced enforcement powers for the Internal Revenue Service.

TEFRA was the largest single tax-raising measure in history—$98 billion over three years—and these proposals shocked and angered the business community and conservative Republicans. If TEFRA were passed by a Republican-dominated Senate and supported by a Republican president, it would seem quite strange. After all, this was the party that had promised to cut back taxes, give big business a stimulus, and get the government off the backs of the people.

The tax bill, by its very nature, seemed a repudiation of Reaganomics. Conservatives like Kemp realized this and said so vociferously. Dole, however, declined to characterize his bill as a step backward and insisted that he was not reversing Reaganomics.

In a lengthy op-ed piece he wrote that appeared in the *Washington Post* on August 8, 1982, Dole said he was "not trying to make a U-turn. We are merely adjusting the route to keep from going off the road." He insisted that he was *still* a "conservative" and claimed, "I am not a liberal . . . neither am I a lemming." He wrote, "I never defined conservatism as the religion of the propertied few or of those whose voices carry in direct proportion to their wealth." He went on to praise "working people" and insisted that "the current debate is not one of conflicting philosophies, but over how to put conservative theory into practice in a way that won't invite popular rejection."

Somewhat ingeniously, Dole attempted to define the term *conservative* to fit his own political philosophy. He wanted to avoid being branded a *liberal*, which he saw as a term of opprobrium in the political climate of the time. He also declined to use the word *moderate* to describe himself. While he had acted independently and contrary to the Republican president's inclinations, he wanted to be accepted as a leader by his own party, and he feared being written off as a renegade. He was not about to become a lemming, in *any* sense.

The flavor of the tax debate was caught brilliantly in a political cartoon by Clyde Wells accompanying Dole's piece in the August 8 *Washington Post*. The message of the cartoon was clear: Dole was trying to steer economic policy in one direction, while Reagan did not know where he was going.

Dole met with Reagan in the Oval Office in an effort to convince him to come aboard. Kemp and other conservatives urged the president to denounce the tax bill. Reagan was caught in the middle, hardly an impressive position for the presumed leader of the nation. Elizabeth Dole, ever alert to the inner dynamics of the Oval Office, reported to her husband the utter disarray among Reagan's top aides. Many urged the president to embrace the Dole tax bill in order to modify his image of a rich man's president. Some aides thought that if the tax bill failed and the huge deficits persisted, the Republican candidates would be massacred in the

November elections. Dogged by a stigma of unfairness, they would melt under the Democratic candidates' heat.

In the end, Dole managed to convince Reagan to actively support his tax bill. Reagan went on national television to ask the American people to call and write to their representatives in Congress and urge them to pass this "necessary" measure. Characteristically, Reagan insisted that the bill did not amount to a tax hike and that it was just a "reform" measure needed to close the budget deficits.

The tax bill barely passed the Senate, by a 52–47 vote. Several liberal Democrats who viewed the bill as an attack on the rich provided the margin of victory. In the House, though bitterly opposed by Kemp and a contingent of die-hard conservatives, the bill was finally passed in August and became law on September 3, 1982.

Dole has often been criticized for the fact that, after twenty-eight years in Congress, his name is not attached to a single piece of major legislation, but TEFRA is one bill that deserves to be called the Dole Bill, for it originated largely through his own initiative and he steamrolled it through Congress. The magnitude of his accomplishment can be seen in the fact that tax bills normally originate in the House Ways and Means Committee rather than the Senate Finance Committee. To his credit, Dole stepped in where no one in the House dared to tread and crafted TEFRA on his own terms and on his own turf.

With TEFRA, Dole had managed to cut a rift between Reagan and his conservative supporters in the Republican Party. Pried loose from his bastion of support, the president was in danger of finding himself in a political no-man's land, branded as a weak-willed chameleon. But as his star faded, Dole's shone brighter.

Several national newspapers and broadcast networks focused on Dole, showering kudos on him for his extraordinary role as the Great Compromiser in the enactment of the new tax bill. They spoke of "the new Dole," a man to be reckoned with as "a potential president," a courageous leader who was willing to stand up to big business for the good of the country, while the rest of his colleagues cowered in fear.

The stock market, which had hit a two-year low below the 800 level in June, suddenly began to rise in mid-August, marking the beginning of a five-year bull market.[4] Though the ultimate causes of the market's dramatic rise were complex, Dole felt that passage of his tax bill was a key factor. "By passing the bill," he said, "we [Congress] showed that we're responsible, that we're going to do something about lowering the budget deficits."

Dole may have been right. Shortly after his bill was passed, interest rates began to drop dramatically—a fact that helped the stock market rise. The tumbling of interest rates may have resulted from an expectation among the financial community that the government would not need to compete with the private sector as much as in the past for funds to finance the budget deficit.

In late August, Dole paid a visit to the floor of the New York Stock Exchange, where he received a hero's welcome from brok-

[4]The bull market raged on through the summer of 1987, reaching a peak of more than 2,700 on the Dow on August 25, 1987. It then began to decline, falling a record 508 points on October 19, 1987, a drop attributed to huge budget deficits, according to many economic analysts.

ers. Eyewitnesses said they had never seen any politician so lionized by Wall Street. The bull market that Dole allegedly ignited was eventually to drive the Dow Jones Industrial Average to an all-time high.

While in New York, Dole addressed a convention of the Sheet Metal Workers Union.[5] He was the only Republican invited, an extraordinary recognition of his reputation for standing up in the Senate for the working man. Dole followed several prominent Democratic liberal senators to the podium in what was billed as a "parade of presidential hopefuls." Symbolically, through his opposition to Reagan, he had made his connection to the left, demonstrating his affinity with the interests of the working class. In his address, he spoke of the need to recognize and satisfy those interests in Washington.

While Dole was addressing the workers, he was being pilloried by the bosses. Businessmen and their lobbyists expressed perplexity and dismay at his unshoeing of big business. During the tax bill hearings before his committee, Dole had kept them at arm's length. When a whole line of such lobbyists stood outside his hearing room to plead their clients' causes, Dole remarked, "There they are, lined up Gucci to Gucci. They'll all be barefoot by morning." He attacked business lobbyists for their "high-handed tactics" and "campaigns of distortion" against his bill. When they threatened to lobby against a provision, he countered by threatening to impose an even tougher measure against them. "Nobody wants to give up a good thing he's got going," Dole said of big business. "What you don't want to do is to let some amendment slip in that helps some big corporation."

Horace Busby, a major business lobbyist and former aide to Lyndon Johnson, castigated Dole for having "undergone a transformation this year" and described Dole's tax bill as being "very much in the mode of a Democratic liberal bill, lightly taxing individuals, coming down heavily on investors and businesses."

Dole told *Fortune* magazine, "We shouldn't favor big business

[5]Dole said this was the first union he had addressed since his early days in Kansas. He had acquired an anti-union reputation during the 1960s and 1970s. He once blasted Walter Mondale for "never making a speech more than two blocks from a union hiring hall."

over small business. We shouldn't favor any business over any
individual enterprise or partnership." He continually criticized
corporations for their abuses and wealthy individuals for their
greed and their exploitation of tax loopholes. "I think it's unfair,"
he said, "that we have to take money away from a disabled man
who's trying to get along on food stamps, so that doctors and den-
tists can put $40,000 away in a tax-free shelter."

In August, Dole seized another opportunity to expose business
abuses. The Johns-Manville Corporation, a very profitable company whose assets exceeded its liabilities by $1 billion, and which
had sales of $2 billion per year, filed for bankruptcy under Chapter
Eleven of the federal bankruptcy code. Its purpose was to shield
itself from liability for thousands of claims and lawsuits filed by
victims of asbestosis and other lung disease allegedly caused by
Manville's products over many years. This was an unprecedented
use of the bankruptcy laws by a financially sound company. Dole
attacked the maneuver as "dubious at best" and held hearings in
his Senate Judiciary Subcommittee to draft legislation preventing
companies from exploiting the bankruptcy laws in this way. He
featured witnesses who suffered from exposure to asbestos and
who testified about the cynical legal maneuvers used against them
by Manville.

Dole intensified his criticism of the "enormous" influence that
big business was wielding over Congress through its financing of
campaigns via political action committees (PACs). He told the *Wall
Street Journal* in 1982, "When the PACs give money, they expect
something in return other than good government. It is making it
much more difficult to legislate. We may reach a point where if
everybody is buying something with PAC money, we can't get anything done."[6]

Such talk was remarkable, coming from a Republican leader.
PACs were largely responsible for financing the great Reagan–GOP
landslide in the 1980 elections. They were usually criticized by
liberal Democrats, whom they had targeted for defeat. With 3,100
PACs in existence, contributing an estimated $80 million to con-

[6]In 1987, however, he vehemently opposed a Senate bill that would have placed a cap on
campaign spending.

gressional campaigns in 1982, it was generally thought that conservative Republicans had the most to gain from them.

Yet here was Dole, Mr. Independent, going against the grain of his own party. Perhaps Dole was expressing his populist leanings. Or perhaps he was remembering that when he ran for president in 1980, PAC money had gone to his rivals, chiefly Bush and Reagan, while his own campaign had gone bankrupt.

Whatever his motives, Dole knew that by coming up with the unexpected he would attract publicity. The media were always on the lookout for the unusual—a Republican attacking the president and the supporters of his own party, a hatchet man who turns into a compassionate defender of the poor and oppressed—and he attracted the cameras.

He drew more publicity by calling for a special lame-duck session of Congress between the November 1982 election and Christmas to deal with the Social Security issue. When the election came in November, and the GOP lost twenty-six seats in the House, most Republicans tried to pooh-pooh these losses, but Dole went against the flow and called attention to them, making news by declaring on television that "Reagan has taken a bath in the House."

Two weeks after the election, he staged another sensational media event by leading a delegation of congressmen and American businessmen to Moscow, where he addressed the Soviet Trade Council and called for more trade between the United States and Soviet Union. At a time when Reagan was denouncing Russia as an "evil empire," Dole calmly walked up to the gates of the Kremlin and shook the Soviet leaders' hands. The media loved it.[7]

Speaking on American television via satellite from Moscow on November 21, Dole said, "I understand the profit motive that some of the [American] companies had. . . . They are very sophisticated businessmen. . . . If we can improve our trading relationships with the Soviet Union, it might lead to other areas of improvement." He urged Reagan to start a dialogue with Moscow on reducing nuclear weapons, noting that "we could literally bankrupt both countries if

---

[7]Dole was generally critical of the magnitude of Reagan's defense budget increases, which he saw as wasteful and deficit-producing.

we continue the arms race." He stopped short of embracing a nuclear freeze, however, and engendered some criticism from his Soviet hosts when he advocated placing some conditions on trade relations with them. As for selling grain to the Soviet Union, however, he was all for it, apparently without conditions. He called for "consistency" in American grain export policy and noted with dismay that America's share of the Soviet grain market had dropped from 70 percent to 17 percent because of Carter's grain embargo. Dole had played a leading role in convincing Reagan to lift that embargo in 1981.

By advocating a web of interdependence with the Soviet Union, Dole angered many conservatives in this country. Columnist George Will accused him of appeasement and of "sinking into the fudge."

Dole's criticism of the Pentagon spendthrift mentality, like his criticism of big business, further alienated him from the conservative mainstream of the GOP. But at the same time it increased his appeal to the general population. In 1982, for the second year in a row, Dole was the most sought-after senator in the country. His honoraria from articles, lectures, and speaking engagements in 1982 came to $135,000, far exceeding those collected by any of his colleagues (the second most sought-after senator, Scoop Jackson, earned only $52,000). Dole was in demand on college campuses, before public interest groups, business meetings, conventions, citizens' groups, and—of course—the news media. He was a familiar face on the nightly news broadcasts, the weekly talk shows, and the news specials. Newspapers from around the country invited him to submit articles for their op-ed pages. His name appeared in editorials everywhere.

Dole now projected an image of respectability and statesmanship. He was looked upon as a sage, a solon. His brand of populism mixed with liberalism made him stand out as the conscience of the GOP. By moving further away from his party, he had managed to carve out a unique niche for himself in the national political market. In many ways, 1982 was his banner year and might well have propelled him directly into the presidency in 1984 if Reagan had chosen not to seek reelection.

Dole's frequent criticism of the Reagan Administration's policies put him in an awkward situation on many occasions when he followed his wife to the podium and addressed a group. When Elizabeth worked for Reagan in the White House, she was obligated to defend her boss's policies regardless of what she may have really thought about their efficacy and fairness. This was a role she had become accustomed to long before Reagan, when she had served under Presidents Johnson and Nixon. Her husband, by contrast, felt no obligation to defend the president's policies. When he followed his wife in public speeches, he often began by saying, "Elizabeth has told you so and so; now, let me tell you the real story. . . ." Privately, he joked that he had a "direct line" to the White House.

Many believed, however, that a conflict of interest existed. The Doles shrugged off this touchy problem by telling the press that they "compartmentalized" their lives and jobs.

The alleged conflict of interest was particularly visible because Dole made no secret of his ambition to replace Reagan. Probably partly as an effort to blunt the Kansan's attacks on him and as a diplomatic way of resolving the conflict of interest, Reagan offered Elizabeth a graceful way out of his inner circle by nominating her as secretary of transportation in January 1983. She eagerly accepted and set off a chorus of oohs and aahs when she appeared at her confirmation hearings before the Senate Commerce Committee with Bob in tow. Speaking "in support of" his wife, Dole quipped, "I regret that I have but one wife to give to my country's infrastructure" and added that he saw "no conflict but plenty of interest."

Elizabeth was confirmed with no opposition and went on to preside over the massive Transportation Department bureaucracy for the next four and a half years. She became a field marshal in the Reagan revolution, managing an army of bureaucrats during a controversial period that involved airline deregulation, automobile safety, and a host of other problems during the controversial reign.

With the appointment of his wife to a cabinet position in January 1983, Dole acquired a mystique somewhat similar to that which had once emanated from the Kennedy brothers—the mystique associated with a politically powerful family—in this case, Dole and his wife. Elizabeth's cabinet officer status raised speculation that she, herself, might be tagged as a presidential or vice presidential candidate in 1984 or 1988, a prospect that most likely did not exactly thrill her husband, who began to feel somewhat eclipsed by her prominence.

As 1983 progressed, a more serious problem of eclipse faced Dole from other quarters. The economy began to improve dramatically, with unemployment falling, production and GNP increasing, and inflation nose-diving below 5 percent. The recession bottomed out in late 1983. As a result, Reagan's standing in the polls skyrocketed, and Dole saw his dreams for a 1984 presidential candidacy fade away.

In the Senate Dole was not nearly as successful in 1983 as he had been in 1982. He proposed a huge tax-and-spending package to reduce the federal deficit, but his proposal was bitterly opposed by Reagan and never even got off the ground. The banking lobby mounted a successful campaign to repeal Dole's controversial tax provision requiring a withholding tax on interest from saving accounts and dividends from stocks. The bankers encouraged millions of people across the nation to mail Congress an avalanche of postcards demanding repeal and arguing that "the little guy" would be hurt if his interest and dividends were withheld. Dole was denounced by many as a "tax collector" who wanted to beef up the IRS's tax collecting and enforcing power. Conservative Republican Congressman Newt Gingrich of Georgia denounced him as "the chief tax collector for the liberal welfare state," while other critics accused him of advocating a mindless "austerity" not unlike that of Herbert Hoover (who, at the height of the Great Depression, supported a major tax increase and opposed public relief, which only worsened the Depression).

In his obsessive condemnation of the deficit, which he called "public enemy number one," Dole became something of a Cassandra figure, isolated within his own party, whose Reaganites had come to power on an anti-tax platform and who now maintained that the deficit would "grow away" in a strong recovery, despite Congressional Budget Office forecasts that the shortfall would exceed $200 billion.

With a presidential election coming up in 1984, no politician was willing to listen to Dole's calls for more taxes and spending cuts, and Bob was unable to articulate a clear plan with specific proposals that were palatable to a majority.

Dole's penchant for striking legislative compromises failed not only on economic policy but also on civil rights. Just a year before, he had been hailed by civil rights lobbyist Joseph Rauh as the hero of the Voting Rights Act, but now he found himself bitterly criticized by the same man for his role in a controversial compromise that he engineered on the membership and independence of the U.S. Civil Rights Commission.[8] According to Rauh, Dole had promised to support "our choice of pro-civil rights members" on the commission after its reorganization. Instead, he changed his mind and supported the Reagan Administration's choices, thereby leading Rauh to conclude that the new commission had lost its independence and become essentially worthless. Dole's action on the Civil Rights Commission convinced Rauh that he had been trying to cozy up to the Reagan Administration, which was widely seen as being indifferent at best to civil rights. Civil rights leaders were angry, disappointed, and puzzled. Rauh later called Dole "almost a Jekyll-Hyde" figure because of such contradictory behavior on civil rights.

In fairness to Dole, it should be pointed out that political realities placed him in a familiar dilemma of walking a tightrope between right and left. He realized that in order to be effective he had to appease the right-wingers on some issues, especially within his own party, so he ended up disappointing the civil rights people. Flip-flopping like this put him in danger of trying to appear as all things to all people. As Democratic senator Bill Bradley said, Dole was "a pragmatist, an admirable pragmatist."

[8]The Civil Rights Commission, created in 1957, was charged nationwide with enforcing the laws guaranteeing civil rights, such as voting rights, affirmative action, racial quotas, etc. It had originally been a six-member commission and had been harshly critical of the Reagan administration in 1981–83. In November 1983, the commission was "reconstituted," its membership was expanded from six to eight, and Reagan managed to appoint a majority that supported his policies and which, according to Rauh's personal statement to the author, was basically indifferent or even hostile toward civil rights. The White House and Dole denied that any agreement had been reached with the civil rights lobby as to membership in the newly constituted commission. Rauh claimed the commission lost its independence and was now a "zero," and he seemed bitter at Dole for whatever role the latter may have played. See *Congressional Quarterly Almanac 1983*, 292–95.

Dole's pragmatism tended to alienate the more doctrinaire members of both conservative and liberal camps. Reagan announced he would seek a second term and an economy rebounding from the recession made him a shoo-in for reelection. During the Republican national convention in Dallas in August 1984, Dole received a notably lukewarm reception from the delegates as he mounted the podium to speak. His wife, who also spoke, was greeted much more enthusiastically. She was seen as a Reagan team player and, hence, as more of a party-liner than her husband—besides being personally more likeable than Bob.

Dole was deeply affected by this mild reception from the party he hoped would make him its standard-bearer four years later. He was particularly irked at hearing himself compared to the pallid figure of Walter Mondale, who had committed the *faux pas* of the decade by calling for a tax hike in his speech accepting the Democratic presidential nomination a month earlier. Mondale, like Dole, harped endlessly about the deficit, but the country was not listening. In November, Mondale was trounced at the polls, losing to Reagan in a landslide that gave the incumbent the most popular votes of any president in American history.[9]

Fearful of being branded a Republican Mondale, Dole curbed his tongue concerning tax hikes and shifted gears carefully as he planned for another major career move.

[9]Mondale received only 13 of the 538 electoral votes and lost every state except his native Minnesota and the District of Columbia.

# 13

# THE MAJORITY LEADER
# MAKES
# A U-TURN

The November 1984 Republican landslide gave Ronald Reagan a second term in the White House, with the Republicans still in control of the Senate. Dole, who had crisscrossed the country speaking on behalf of GOP candidates during the election, had busily collected political IOUs as he prepared for his next move.

During his four years as Finance Committee chairman, Dole had built a reputation as a skilled power broker and negotiator, with a knack for crafting legislative compromises palatable to a majority, mainly on tax bills. But now he sensed that taxation was a very hot political potato and that, in light of Mondale's disaster, his colleagues would not be willing to vote for increased taxes.

Furthermore, a vacancy had been created by the retirement of Senator Howard Baker, who had quit the Senate in order to run for president full-time. Baker, the Tennessee veteran, had been Senate majority leader since 1981 and was known as a congenial Reagan rubber stamp who had never really placed his own mark on the office. Now it was time to elect a new majority leader, and nervous GOP senators looked worriedly toward the 1986 elections, when twenty-two of them would be up for reelection (compared with only twelve Democrats), with control of the Senate very possibly hanging in the balance.

With Reagan doomed to be a lame duck for the next four years and his economic policies in a precarious position despite his landslide election victory (the U.S. balance of trade deficit, the federal budget deficits, and the national debt had all reached record highs), the Republican senators were looking for someone of an independent bent to act as majority leader.

Dole considered himself that man. He had been interested in running for Senate GOP leader since his first term in 1970, when he nearly challenged Hugh Scott. When I worked for him, he often spoke of challenging Howard Baker for the post but inevitably backed down because of his fear of being embarrassed in a showdown with the popular Baker.

Dole's interest in the majority leader position stemmed from his natural desire to be in control of everything, as well as from his feeling that the position would give him tremendous national visibility and prominence and would thereby serve as a springboard for his presidential try in 1988.

With his willingness to work to exhaustion and his need to perform at least two or three jobs at the same time, Dole felt more than up to the challenge of serving as majority leader *and* running for president. Baker, on the other hand, felt that running for president was a full-time job incompatible with serving as Senate leader. In thinking he could perform both jobs superbly, Dole also bucked the conventional political wisdom, which held that prominent House and Senate leaders rarely became successful presidential candidates. Since 1920, the only successful candidate to come straight out of the Senate was John F. Kennedy, who had had an erratic Senate attendance record and had never been majority leader.

Bucking conventional wisdom was nothing new to Dole, and he plunged into the wide-open race for majority leader with gusto. Dole lobbied for the position by approaching his colleagues one by one, promising to support their interests if they voted for him and reminding them of his independence and effectiveness as a parliamentarian. Because of his proven indifference to ideology, he was able to secure the support of senators all across the political spectrum, from arch-conservative to moderate-progressive.

One of the key senators Dole allegedly approached (and whose vote Dole reportedly received) was Jesse Helms, the arch-conservative Senate veteran known as Mr. Tobacco on Capitol Hill because of his staunch support for the tobacco lobby, a key interest group in his home state of North Carolina. Helms commanded the right-wing Republican senators who held the key swing votes in the election for majority leader. Dole, a nonsmoker who had spoken about the disabling effect of smoking and had engineered a boost in cigarette taxes in his 1982 TEFRA bill, had never previously been particularly supportive of or interested in bills favoring the tobacco lobby. Indeed, with his overwhelming concern for the handicapped and for budget deficits, Dole had every reason to oppose the tobacco interests. But now this power broker needed Helms's support in his struggle for majority leadership. Subsequently, Dole became a major supporter of bills favoring the tobacco industry. He supported increased federal subsidies to tobacco farmers, helped kill a proposal to raise taxes on cigarettes, and (unsuccessfully) urged Hong Kong not to restrict its tobacco imports from the United States.

Dole was opposed for majority leader in a tight race by Senators Jim McClure of Idaho, Ted Stevens of Alaska, Richard Lugar of Indiana, and Pete Domenici of New Mexico. In general, Dole's opponents had more consistently conservative voting records than he and were thus more palatable to the right-wing majority of the Republican senators. But these men split the vote among themselves, thereby giving Dole a golden opportunity to emerge as the lone "centrist" candidate.

Voting took place in four so-called last-man-out ballots. McClure, Domenici, and Lugar were eliminated in the first three ballots, in that order. In the third ballot, Dole was tied with Stevens, each man winning twenty votes. On the fourth ballot, Dole nosed out Stevens by three votes, winning by a margin of 28–25. He thereby became the first Kansan to hold the Senate majority leader position since Charles Curtis in 1924. Curtis went on to serve as Herbert Hoover's vice president in 1929–33.[1]

[1]Upon Dole's election as majority leader, Elizabeth and his daughter, Robin, presented him with a new schnauzer puppy wearing a big red bow and a sign bearing its name, Leader.

When the new Senate convened in January 1985, the Republicans held a slim 53–47 majority. Dole immediately set about distancing himself from Reagan, stating that communication and negotiation between Senate and White House "has to be a two-way street." Having already pushed through three tax increases (including a rise in gasoline taxes) that Reagan had not wanted but had signed into law, Dole wasted no time in calling for a massive new effort to reduce the budget deficit. Stating that he would look out for "Senate interests" and that he had "enough independence that I won't be a lap dog," Dole set out to take charge.

At Reagan's second inauguration, on January 21, 1985—which, because of inclement weather, was held indoors at the Capitol for the first time since 1837—Dole sported a bright red tie and beamed into the cameras. He stood next to the seventy-three-year-old Reagan and pranced about as if this were his own inauguration. "Senator Dole," asked ABC News reporter Sam Donaldson, "do you expect to be here in this spot, four years from now, taking the oath as the next president?" Characteristically, he responded in a mealy-mouthed fashion, which when one read between the lines clearly meant yes.

In addition to attaining his new Senate post in 1984, Bob created the Dole Foundation, a nonprofit organization headquartered in Washington whose purpose was to raise money for programs to help handicapped and disabled people find jobs. The foundation also served to boost Dole's public image as a champion of the handicapped. He served as its chairman, personally signed letters soliciting foundation contributions, closely supervised and controlled its operation, and appeared at gala fund-raisers. Because the foundation was a nonpolitical entity, it could raise an unlimited amount of money from corporations or individuals. In time, it would raise millions of dollars, much of it in large contributions from corporations. One of the biggest ironies related to the Dole Foundation is that some of its largest contributors have been tobacco companies, whose products disable, injure, and kill thousands of people each year through heart and lung disease and cancer. According to a reporter who was present, Dole was mobbed by dozens of tobacco company officials at one of the foundation's galas. "They all came up to him, patted him on the back, and congratulated him," he told me.

Dole now had become a virtual Washington institution as a fund-raiser, had his name attached to a major nonprofit organization, and because of his status as majority leader, was earning constant attention and space from an attentive national press corps—all of which did not exactly hurt his chances for his upcoming presidential campaign in 1988.

In addition to his Dole Foundation, Dole controlled his own political action committee (PAC), Campaign America, which he used to raise money for Republican candidates across the nation. Campaign America, a legitimate PAC regulated by the Federal Election Commission, was created by Dole in the late 1970s and was entirely separate from the Dole Foundation. Unlike the latter, it could not accept donations of more than $5,000. Nevertheless, its coffers filled up and Dole used the money (including money from tobacco companies) liberally to support his favorite candidates in the elections of 1980, 1982, 1984, and 1986. By doing so, he hoped to reap support from the grateful beneficiaries in his upcoming presidential campaign. In this, he was acting no differently from any of his rivals, who also maintained their own PACs.

With his two fund-raising responsibilities and his Senate leadership position, Dole was a human whirlwind of activity. As majority leader, he received a salary boost and a chauffeured limousine and moved about town like a man in a great hurry.

Wielding the levers of power came naturally to Dole, with his instinct and desire for control. As he had done with everything else throughout his life, he tried to run the Senate as a one-man band, tightening the rules and imposing far greater control on the Senate agenda than Baker had and thus limiting Democrats' ability to oppose his will.

Years before, when he was still in the minority, he used to complain to me that "the Senate is a zoo, it's chaotic, it needs a strongman at the helm." Now he was able to act as that strongman, tightening the rules, inhibiting the proliferation of myriad committees and subcommittees, forcing his colleagues into frequent all-night and weekend sessions, making them follow his schedule and

bend to his will as far as parliamentary rules permitted. By install-
ing his longtime aide Jo-Anne Coe as secretary of the Senate and
his former aide Ernie Garcia as Senate sergeant-at-arms, Bob assured himself of control over the day-to-day administration of the
world's greatest debating club.

Dole knew that support from the right wing was probably necessary if he were to win the 1988 GOP presidential nomination. Since
1964, when Barry Goldwater's acolytes had booed Nelson Rockefeller off the podium in the party's national convention, the right
wing had essentially taken over the financial and organizational
infrastructure of the Republican Party. For twenty years, the GOP
had had a strong leader and symbol (Goldwater and then Reagan),
but now, as Republicans looked to 1988, there was no one in sight.
The New Right had always viewed Vice President Bush with skepticism and mistrust, at best, and still saw him as a remnant of the
old Eastern Establishment, "Rockefeller" wing of the party. Dole's
standing among conservatives wasn't much stronger.

"I'm perceived as a moderate Republican for all the work I've
done on tax reform, voting rights, food stamps, all the stuff for
veterans and the handicapped," Dole admitted in early 1985.
Then, characteristically referring to himself in the plural, he declared: "We're going to make a play for the conservatives. I think I
deserve a shot at them."

The Kingston Coalition, one of the most vociferous and powerful conservative groups in the country, had greeted Dole with stony
silence shortly before he became majority leader. "He was given a
very unpleasant reception," according to Paul Weyrich, a New
Right leader. "There was a great deal of hostility toward him from
the right wing."

"Dole was not number one on any conservative's hit parade
during the 1982–83 period, when he was involved in the tax increases," according to New Right guru Richard Viguerie, who
considered Dole's election as majority leader a disaster for the
right wing.

So, in 1985, Dole saw a vacuum and decided to compete seriously for the right wing's allegiance. He set about to make a U-
turn in his public image and began a process of transformation that
led one major political analyst to call him "the Zelig of American

politics." Just as in the past he had attempted to transform himself into a compassionate candidate by undergoing personality surgery at Speech Dynamics, he now sought to undergo ideological surgery and present himself as the candidate of the New Right.

Dole continued to harp on the swelling budget deficit, but with Mondale's 1984 pro-tax disaster and the right's opposition to all taxes in mind, he carefully avoided any specific proposals for tax hikes. Instead, he coined the euphemistic term *revenue enhancement*, a vague shibboleth that might mean almost anything but that bolstered his image as a sage and solon with the press and the public.

In his first months as majority leader, Dole engaged in "the kind of political high-wire act that Washington loves but rarely sees: a brazen wave to the crowd, then a series of nerve-jangling wobbles, and finally a safe landing for the star performer" as he tried to weave a huge package of spending cuts intended to reduce the deficit by 50 percent within three years without raising taxes. He saw this as a spearhead tactic and launched his gambit from the steps of Blair House, a block away from the White House, before Reagan had even finished writing his own budget proposal.

He became furious when Senate committee chairmen initially rebuffed his efforts to reach a consensus and failed to announce a budget deficit reduction plan by February 1, 1985. He then turned to the Senate Budget Committee to draft a plan, but senators supporting Reagan refused to agree either to cutting the defense budget or to freezing Social Security cost of living adjustments (COLAs), as Dole proposed in a controversial move.

During the bargaining sessions, which numbered six or eight each day and sometimes overlapped, Dole buttonholed his colleagues in countless cloakroom sessions and used all his cagey powers to coax, wheedle, and harangue them into supporting the package. In a fashion unseen in the Senate since Lyndon Johnson's wheeler-dealer days as majority leader in the 1950s, Dole cut deals in which money was restored to senators' favored pet programs in exchange for their votes on the package. Senators who voted for the deficit-cutting plan got money for everything from Amtrak to Urban Development Action Grants to farm programs. In many cases, Dole agreed to introduce amendments he had previously

adamantly opposed in exchange for votes. Demonstrating to the
hilt his tenacity and willingness to change course in order to cut a
deal, Dole simply outlasted the Democrats who had opposed him.
His legendary indefatigability proved too much for the opposition,
as he organized meeting after meeting, rounded up absentee senators for roll calls, and plowed his way through to victory. More
than one senator agreed to go along with Dole's proposal just for
the sake of avoiding further meetings.

Dole finally managed to scrape together a bare one-vote majority by wheeling in Senator Pete Wilson from a hospital bed with an
intravenous tube attached to his arm to cast the forty-ninth vote,
for a 49–49 tie. Reagan supported the measure, albeit unenthusias-
tically, and Vice President Bush cast the deciding vote for the
compromise package. Although this budget resolution barely
passed the Senate on May 10, 1985, it was opposed by Reagan as
well as the House Democrats and was never enacted.

Although Dole's budget deficit reduction plan never became
law, during the 1988 presidential campaign Dole called the resolution one of his biggest achievements in Congress and asserted that
it set the climate for the subsequent Gramm-Rudman-Hollings def-
icit-reduction bill. Also during the campaign, rival Jack Kemp
attacked Dole for the heartlessness of the plan's proposed freeze on
Social Security COLAs.

In ramming his proposal through the Senate, Dole took on some
of Washington's most formidable sacred cows, including the Pentagon, and displayed that jolly irreverence for authority that was
his trademark. He attacked Defense Secretary Caspar Weinberger
for trying to "sit out" his deficit reduction efforts, accusing the
Pentagon chief of using inflated economic figures to exaggerate the
degree of Pentagon belt-tightening. "The Pentagon has been able
to survive without much difficulty," Dole fumed. "I think the rest
of the country needs to survive, too."

Dole was irked by the Reagan Administration's sanctification of
the military, which ran counter to his own longstanding skepticism
about military competence and credibility. I heard him refer to the
Pentagon as "that sandbox across the river" following the failed
rescue of the U.S. hostages in Iran in April 1980. In his twenty-five
years in the House and the Senate, he had never held a seat on any

foreign relations or armed services committee. As a result, he was less experienced than many of his colleagues on matters relating to defense but was also less awed by the Pentagon brass.

Because Reagan refused to budge an inch from his swollen defense budget, Dole found it impossible to craft the type of deficit-trimming deal he wanted. With annual deficits now hovering around $200 billion, a meaningful response to them was not politically palatable.

Dole's anti-Pentagon comments and attempted budget cuts did not endear him to the right-wingers he now courted, but he was as inconsistent as ever, steering his own course and resenting any attempt by special-interest groups, including the right wing, to hem him in. However, for the first time in years, he now refused to back a tax hike as a means of reducing the deficit, and he took several steps to make his "new" ideology known to the zealots of the right. Through his powers as majority leader, he brought to the Senate floor several issues popular with conservatives, including a gun control bill that actually loosened federal gun control and a bill to grant the president line-item veto power. In addition, he made himself far more accessible personally to conservatives, hired them as staffers, and appointed a favorite conservative figure, Don Devine, as head of Campaign America.

Stretching out his arms to the right-wingers, Dole convinced many that he was truly one of them. Howard Phillips, leader of the Conservative Caucus, said in the fall of 1985, "In general, Dole has been able to shed the baggage of appearing to be someone who wants to raise taxes." However, Phillips attacked Dole on another issue, this time for being "wrong on South Africa sanctions, which is the number one issue of the conservative movement in the decade of the 1980s." (Dole supported limited sanctions to protest apartheid.)

Phillips continued to criticize Dole for some of his stands in favor of civil rights and other issues, while other dyed-in-the-wool conservatives, such as Richard Viguerie, remained skeptical about Dole's overall commitment to their cause.

Dole's transformation into a conservative front man ran directly against his institutional role of leading his GOP Senate colleagues, some of whom did not share the right-wing philosophy. "That's the dilemma he has to resolve," warned Phillips. "He has to decide whether he wants to be a national leader of conservatives who would be in a position to become the Republican nominee in 1988 or thereafter, or if he wants to be the leader of the Republicans in the Senate. He's got to decide whether he's going to be a hero in Washington or a hero to the country."

Dole's courting of the right wing struck many as incredible. Ted Kennedy, for one, chided him acidly. "You've done too much good for the poor, on food stamps and civil rights," Kennedy said, "to be acceptable to those right-wingers."

Dole, who appeared on a daily Mutual Radio Network talk show with Kennedy, dismissed such criticism and continued to walk the political tightrope. He was, after all, a man who had begun his congressional career "somewhere to the right of Genghis Khan" and who had since transformed himself so many times that everyone had lost track. His eclectic pragmatism had taken on a life of its own. He called himself a "realistic conservative," whatever that meant.

Because he was majority leader and because he had a natural performer's talent for delivering punchy one-liners to the media, Dole's national celebrity status grew as he appeared on the nightly news and in the nation's newspapers almost daily. Moreover, despite his contradictory and unpredictable positions, he appeared to be the man at the helm, a man in charge.

In the fall of 1985, Dole shepherded through the Senate the controversial Gramm-Rudman-Hollings bill, which provided automatic budget cutbacks (called *sequestration*) if Congress and the president could not agree to meet certain targets by certain dates each year. The aim of Gramm-Rudman-Hollings, named after its principal authors, was to balance the federal budget by 1991. It was the domestic analogy of the so-called nuclear doomsday machine in that it gave a computer automatic power to shut off billions of dollars of funding on programs across the board if Congress failed to reach specific budget-cutting targets. It was a new approach to the deficit problem, perilous in many ways, and its passage was a bleak testimony to the inability of Congress to solve its own problems. It was, ultimately, a testimonial to the failure of human leadership and decision making. In any event, the magnitude of the budget cuts provided for in Gramm-Rudman-Hollings's bill—$11.7 billion in 1986, its first year in effect—would make only a dent, at best, in the $202.8 billion federal deficit. And whether the results would justify the human suffering such cuts imposed was a question left unanswered.

Nevertheless, Dole was proud of his role in enacting this bill, later referring to it as his greatest legislative accomplishment as majority leader, for it was the first time a serious effort to trim the deficits had been made. And by the end of his first year as majority leader, Dole was able to point to a host of other enacted bills as his accomplishments as well. According to figures prepared by his own staff, as of December 1985, 163 bills were enacted into law and 474 measures were approved during the first eleven months of Dole's reign, as compared to only 84 enacted bills and 413 approved measures during the first eleven months of Howard Baker's reign in 1981.

Apart from his record of bill passage, Dole won mixed reviews in the Senate for his performance as majority leader. Kansas's junior senator, Nancy Kassebaum, characterized Dole as by nature "more aggressively partisan than Howard Baker. Dole is very much the eye of the hurricane. He's right there with an enormous amount of energy sort of battling through each issue as it comes up and trying hard to engineer a compromise."

With his horror of delegating authority, Dole sought to control legislation in floor debate in a manner unseen in any of his predecessors since Lyndon Johnson. For example, when Senator Helms, chairman of the Agriculture Committee, brought his 1985 agriculture bill to the floor, Dole personally took control of it and steered it in debate.[2] Most majority leaders permit the committee chairmen to control floor debate. "My view," Dole said on this matter, "is that I have the responsibility to make it happen. I make decisions on the theory that I'm elected the leader and if I make the wrong decisions, they can get a new leader. I don't wait for the consensus. I try to help build it."

[2]Although Dole continues to call reducing the budget deficit his top priority, the 1985 agriculture bill of which he was the chief architect accounted for 12 percent of the total deficit for the fiscal year 1987. (Martin Tolchin and Jeff Gerth, "The Contradictions of Bob Dole," *New York Times Magazine*, November 8, 1987.) The bill, P.L. 99-198, gave farmers a record $52 billion in federal price and income supports over three years. (*Congressional Quarterly*, 1985, 517.)

This consensus building generally took place in Dole's impressive office just off the Senate floor. With a window offering a magnificent, picture-postcard view of Washington, this office was converted into a meeting room when Dole installed a hugh conference table. Dole, with his seemingly inexhaustible reservoir of energy, called forty-five meetings in two weeks and routinely kept the Senate in session long into the night as he tried to exert his personal control over virtually every aspect of its operations.

There were complaints that his heavy-handed *modus operandi* often led to the Senate as a whole degenerating into chaos. A top staff director for a Democratic senator, who asked for anonymity, told the *Kansas City Times*, "Other leaders had a more orderly process where they didn't fray tempers, waste time, and keep the Senate in late the way it is now. There was more of a sense of comity and consensus under Baker. Dole has allowed more of a . . . meanness to be rampant."

Complaints were not limited to Democrats. "There is practically no respect left for the institution," Senator Jake Garn complained in 1985, "no respect for individual senators, no respect for party loyalties whatsoever. The Senate has been a disgrace for months. We have no procedure. We have no order."

Garn's feelings were by no means unique. In December 1985, Dole called an unprecedented meeting of all one hundred senators to discuss the Senate's internal troubles. Some criticized the Senate's rules and the trend toward negativity in politics, with the upcoming 1986 elections sparking a more partisan atmosphere. But Dole's leadership was also considered, and not altogether favorably.

Some Democratic senators complained about what they considered Dole's strong-arm style of leadership. The farm bill, for example, was scheduled by Dole for floor action without any hearings, thereby preventing senators from rounding up witnesses to testify for or against its many provisions. Others grumbled that Dole was trying to use the Senate to make himself look good and to promote his own presidential ambitions by appearing to be a strong leader of an active Senate—a charge that was repeated the following year, when he was criticized for keeping the Senate in session through October, thereby depriving his colleagues of precious time needed for campaigning for reelection.

But not all Democrats criticized Dole's leadership. Senate veteran Democrat Thomas Eagleton said at the time, "Dole has done extraordinarily well. I have been pleasantly surprised. I had thought that his temper might run short and he might blow up on an occasion or two. He has held his temper, held his good humor; he has held his patience. I think he's managed himself on a personal basis very, very well indeed."

GOP senator John Danforth echoed Eagleton's praise of Dole, noting that the latter had "done a wonderful job . . . he's an amazingly good senator and leader. . . . The Senate is a very hard place to lead," he said, citing filibuster rules that permit the minority to "stop things from happening."

Despite praise from men as diverse as Eagleton and Danforth, Dole continued to antagonize his colleagues on occasion, when his combativeness and need for control surfaced.

On March 10, 1986, Democratic freshman senator Tom Harkin of Iowa triggered Dole's infamous ire. Harkin had antagonized Dole during the previous year, butting heads with him over emergency farm credit legislation. Also in 1985, the Iowa freshman had dared to call on his own for an adjournment of the Senate, thereby challenging Dole's traditional majority leader authority. Referring to that presumptuous move, Dole said acidly, "He doesn't run this place yet."

In March 1986, Dole mounted a personal attack against Harkin on the Senate floor. "It has come to the point now where it is flat-out politics," Dole snarled, "and I think it is fairly clear where that effort is coming from." Asked if his feud with Harkin was getting personal, he replied, "Almost personal, yeah. I don't mind having disagreements, but not a single soul wants to stop this [change of wording in a resolution] except Tom Harkin. He loves all the attention. Then he runs around and does what he normally does, anyway. So," he added menacingly, "we'll keep an eye on something he wants someday."

Five months later, in August 1986, Dole was in the midst of another feud on the Senate floor, this time against Minority Leader Robert Byrd, whom Dole had campaigned against when Byrd was seeking reelection to the Senate from West Virginia in 1982. On the Senate floor, Dole expressed "surprise and disappointment" at Democratic senators who had just offered a surprise amendment on the bill to override President Reagan's veto of a bill to impose sanctions on South Africa. Furious at having his control of the Senate challenged, Dole barked, "I think it is time we ask ourselves, in all honesty, what kind of game we are playing here."

When Byrd rose to his feet and demanded an apology from Dole for implying that he had sneaked his amendment in behind Dole's back, Dole refused and Byrd shouted, "I have had enough of this business of having the majority leader stand here and act as a traffic cop on this floor." Dole shot back: "I don't intend to be intimidated by anyone in the Senate!" The feud between Dole and Byrd had been simmering ever since Dole had taken over as majority leader in 1985. Dole resented Byrd's attempts to act as copilot. As far as he was concerned, one man had to call the shots, and that man was he and he alone. "I didn't become majority leader to lose," he thundered.

The *New York Times* said that GOP senator Pete Domenici "said he had heard words on the Senate floor that evening that he had not heard before in fourteen years of service. A Republican aide muttered that the Senate was experiencing 'ugly times' and added, 'I don't think I've ever seen anything quite like that.' "

Dole's "I'm in charge here" attitude and determination to control the floor and the flow of legislation with an iron hand irked Senate Democrats. He was a master at using his power to file amendments in such a way that Democrats were blocked from offering their own amendments on key legislation. Some Democrats tried for days to offer amendments but were prohibited by Dole's parliamentary maneuvers. Dole also managed to antagonize House Speaker Tip O'Neill, who complained, "His presidential ambitions put him in a position not to come to me to compromise."

Charges of unfair tactics had also flown during the controversial nomination of Daniel Manion to the U.S. Court of Appeals for the Seventh Circuit in June of 1986. Manion was opposed by some civil rights activists and others who felt he lacked the qualifications to be a federal appeals judge. Manion, whose father had been a founder of the John Birch Society, was considered a conservative and was strongly supported by the conservative groups Dole courted. In a complex series of parliamentary maneuvers orchestrated by Majority Leader Dole, three anti-Manion votes were "paired" with three absentee Senators' votes. Two of the absentees, Republicans Barry Goldwater and Robert Packwood, later said they were undecided, *not* pro-Manion. Then, during a vote on June 26, Republican senator Slade Gorton changed his vote at the last minute from "nay" to "aye," so Manion was confirmed by a two-vote margin, 48–46. Packwood complained he had been "misled," and Democratic senator David Boren charged the GOP leadership with a breach of trust, saying, "The Senate has to be a place that operates on a handshake." Old anti-Dole charges of ruthlessness were revived, and it was whispered that the Manion incident proved that Dole would do anything to win. Dole gave Manion foes a second chance to vote, however, and on July 23 the Senate voted 50–49 against "reconsidering" its earlier vote of June 26. (Vice President Bush cast the fiftieth vote, breaking the tie.)

Thus, Dole had won the battle for his right-wing constituents, but had alienated some of his colleagues with his tactics. Moderate senators said he was confusing his duties as majority leader and presidential candidate and that because of Dole's efforts to accommodate conservatives he was forcing the Senate to grapple with controversial legislation that might have otherwise languished on the calendar.

Despite his efforts to secure conservative backing, Dole came up short on many lists. In the summer issue of *Policy Review*, a publication of the conservative Heritage Foundation, Phyllis Schlafly, president of the Eagle Forum, wrote, "I don't see Bob Dole as somebody who has his heart in any of the issues that conservatives care about. He is trying to do an effective job as majority leader. But he does not seem to be an issues-oriented person." On the other hand, conservative leader Paul Weyrich, in his *Policy Review* assessment, wrote that Dole was "decisive and very tough" and praised him for opening the door to the conservative movement, a door that he said had been closed during Howard Baker's reign. "Dole isn't always in our corner, he doesn't always do what we want, but he is open to us, he listens," Weyrich wrote.

The U-turn in Bob's voting pattern is clear when one looks at his ranking by conservative and liberal interest groups during these years. The American Conservative Union gave him only a 64 percent approval rating in 1983, when he was still advocating tax increases and other ideas condemned by the right wing. However, in 1985 and 1986, Dole's approval rating shot up to 91 percent, a clear indication that he had indeed made a dramatic shift. The Chamber of Commerce of the United States, a key mouthpiece of big business, had given Dole a mere 62 percent approval rating in 1982 and an even lower 56 percent in 1983. By contrast, it gave him a 90 percent rating in 1985 and an 89 percent rating in 1986. On May 7, 1986, the *National Journal*, based on an examination of senators' voting records in 1985, said Dole was more conservative than 86 percent of his colleagues in economic matters and 83 percent in social matters. He was found to be more liberal than none of his colleagues and had a conservative ranking identical to Jesse Helms and Phil Gramm.

On the opposite end of the political spectrum, the liberal Americans for Democratic Action had given Dole a 15 percent rating in 1982 and a 0 rating in both 1985 and 1986. The AFL-CIO, which had given him a 20 percent rating in 1983, also dropped him to a 0 rating in 1986.

In an effort to appeal to the right wing, Dole voted against a proposal to block chemical weapons production, for the MX missile, for aid to the contra rebels of Nicaragua, and against overriding Reagan's veto of economic sanctions on South Africa in 1986, although he had originally voted for sanctions a short time before the veto.[3]

Despite these votes, Dole seemed less than enthusiastic about supporting the very causes he had voted for. When asked by political analyst William Schneider in 1986 whether he supported the overthrow of the Nicaraguan government by the contras, he said, "I wouldn't say yes or no. Generally, no, I don't think so." And yet, he voted for aid to the contras, whose obvious purpose was clearly to bring about that overthrow.

Dole had frequently been a supporter of civil rights issues, but he sided with extreme right-wingers on other African issues to which American blacks were sensitive. He joined Senator Jesse

[3]On October 2, 1986, the Senate voted 78–21 to override Reagan's veto, thereby rejecting Dole's position.

Helms in holding up the nomination of Melissa Wells, the new U.S. ambassador to Mozambique, as a way of pressuring Reagan into dealing with RENAMO, the South African–supported guerrillas in Mozambique.[4] And he wrote a letter to a Kansas constituent denouncing the African National Congress of South Africa, an outlawed antiapartheid organization, accusing it of espousing "necklacing," the gruesome practice of killing suspected government spies in the black townships of South Africa by clamping burning tires around their necks. According to syndicated columnist Anthony Lewis and others, there is no evidence that the African National Congress espouses or condones necklacing, American right-wing propaganda notwithstanding.

Dole's bending over backward to please the right wing after 1985 disappointed many of his Senate colleagues, who had voted him majority leader thinking he would prove independent of Reagan and the right.[5] As the midterm elections of 1986 approached, they grew understandably nervous, realizing that many of their constituents outside Washington did not share their leader's new-found enthusiasm for the right. Their fears proved justified. On November 4, Republicans were trounced at the polls, losing their majority in the Senate to the Democrats, who now took over with a 55–45 majority.

While Dole cannot be blamed entirely for his party's loss of the Senate, the fact remains that the loss did occur on his watch even though he had campaigned actively for Republican candidates in the fall of 1986, reminding voters that it was essential to maintain GOP Senate control.[6]

But now the Republicans' six-year control of the Senate had been lost—by a considerable margin. Dole automatically lost his

---

[4]Dole has supported the rebels battling Mozambique's leftist government, urging the Reagan administration to deal with RENAMO, a far-right cause in which he joins Jesse Helms. Dole has also backed the UNITA rebels fighting Angola's leftist government.

[5]Dole supported Reagan's positions on Senate votes 92 percent of the time in 1985 and 1986—in contrast to 78 percent in 1983. *Congressional Quarterly Almanac*, 1985 and 1986, Appendix C.

[6]In 1986, Dole campaigned in 43 states and 126 cities, on behalf of about 200 candidates, according to the *Kansas City Times*, November 5, 1986. His PAC, Campaign America, gave $240,000 to House and Senate candidates and $64,000 to state and other candidates, according to the *Wichita Eagle-Beacon*, November 3, 1986.

position as majority leader. Nonetheless, he was elected minority leader by his colleagues on November 20, 1986. In his new role, effective January 1987, he continued his confrontational posture in the new 100th Congress. He openly expressed contempt for the Democrats' claims that his goals for deficit reduction could not be met, and he backed Reagan's unsuccessful veto of an $88 billion highway bill. But he now lacked the power to control the Senate's agenda, and being of the minority party, he was no longer even a committee chairman.

In spite of the poor showing of his party, Dole was an easy winner in his campaign for a fourth term. Against token opposition, he defeated his little-known opponent, self-employed investor Guy MacDonald, with 70 percent of the vote. The election itself was something of a charade, in that Dole spent more time campaigning outside of Kansas than inside and raised the vast majority of his campaign funds outside his home state. Dole outspent MacDonald astronomically, raising $2.7 million as compared to a mere $4,400 raised by MacDonald. In what appeared a gesture of arrogance, for the first time in his thirty-five-year congressional career Dole didn't bother to show up in Kansas but remained in Washington on election night.

Dole was now a national institution, and his ambitions clearly ran far beyond the wheat fields of the Sunflower State. Yet he was by far the most dominant political figure in Kansas and was setting a record as the man with the longest Senate tenure in Kansas history.

Nonetheless, there was something about Dole that seemed to bother Kansans, something about the brazen nature of his ambition that made people wonder whether he was somehow too "uppity." In a statewide poll taken shortly before the November 1986 election, the question asked was "Do you think Bob Dole should run for president in 1988?" Of those polled, 45.2 percent said no, while only 32.8 percent said yes, and 22 percent were undecided. Even more startling was the Kansas voters' response to the question "If Dole is a presidential candidate in 1988, would you vote for him?" Only 34.9 percent said yes, 32.1 percent said no, and 33 percent were undecided—an amazingly poor showing for a native son of such prominence. Kansans' resentment of Dole had simmered just beneath the surface of his popularity for some time, and it had become quite evident in 1974 and in 1980, when his career had hung precariously in the balance.

Kansans' ambivalence toward Dole has surfaced in numerous, subtle ways, as in an editorial published in the *Hays [Kansas] Daily News* in August 1986, which chided Dole over a report that his dog had been seen being chauffeured around Washington in a limousine, alone, thereby wasting taxpayer money. The paper obtained its story from the *Wall Street Journal*, which had reported, "Witnesses have occasionally spotted Leader [the Dole dog] being chauffeured alone." Dole responded to the Hays newspaper editorial by sending in a letter with his dog's paw print stating, "I don't mind if you criticize my owner . . . but when you pick on me . . . that really gets under my flea collar."[7]

Although some Kansans had doubts about Dole, there were those who gleefully tooted his horn. The *Wichita Eagle-Beacon*, on November 16, 1986, printed a spectacular editorial endorsing Dole for president in 1988, even before he had announced his candidacy. The *Eagle-Beacon*'s editors said they were "convinced, after watching him grow and develop over the years, that Bob Dole not only is the most qualified person either party has to offer as president: He is superbly qualified to be one of the nation's genuinely great presidents. . . . These are extraordinary times, and they require an extraordinary leader." The editorial went on to predict that Dole would be not only "a pragmatic, courageous, informed, sensitive president;" but also "one of [the nation's] most popular presidents. There hasn't been a platform performer like him since John F. Kennedy."

Such an editorial surely warmed Dole's heart. As he surveyed

---

[7]A steal from Franklin D. Roosevelt's famous quip in 1944 in response to criticism of his alleged decision to send a navy ship to bring his dog from the Aleutian Islands to Washington: "These Republican leaders have not been content with attacks on me or my wife or my sons. No, not content with that, they now include my little dog, Fala. Well, of course, I don't resent attacks, and my family doesn't resent attacks, but . . . Fala does resent them. . . . His Scotch soul was furious, he has not been the same dog since." (James MacGregor Burns, *Roosevelt: Soldier of Freedom 1940-1945*; New York: Harcourt Brace Jovanovich, 1970; 523-24.)

the wreckage of the 1986 elections, he toyed with the idea of resigning from the Senate—ostensibly in order to be free to campaign full-time for the presidency, but in reality because he could not stomach the thought of yielding up his power as majority leader to the Democrats. Dole's flirtation with "retirement" in the face of impending failure (a trait he shared with Lyndon Johnson) paralleled his behavior at the end of his disastrous presidential campaign in the spring of 1980 when, rather than accept defeat, he considered ending his career in politics.

In November 1986, he began dropping hints about a "last Senate term" but was encouraged to stay in Washington by a series of unforeseen events that enabled him to emerge from the shambles of disaster with another phoenixlike regeneration.

Far from being blamed by his party and the press for the Senate election debacle (in sharp contrast to receiving blame for his role in the GOP's loss of the presidency in 1976), Dole saw his standing in the polls actually increase after the 1986 election. In September 1986, before the election, Dole had ranked a distant second to Bush in virtually every poll of Republican voters. By January 1987, Dole was widely considered to be the GOP's hottest property, the most sought-after speaker, and the rising star in the presidential sweepstakes. What had brought on this latest transformation?

In one of those great coincidences that have favored Dole throughout his life, an obscure weekly magazine in Beirut, Lebanon, had published a story on the day before the 1986 election—a story that eventually took on great significance and turned out to have miraculous consequences for Dole.

# 14
# THE 1988 RACE
# FOR PRESIDENT

T he Lebanese magazine *Al Shiraa* reported on November 3, 1986, that in 1985 and 1986 President Reagan had been secretly selling spare parts and ammunition to the fanatical Iranian regime of the Ayatollah Khomeini. Subsequent reports revealed that the sales were worth about $30 million, included weapons and missiles, and were an effort to "improve" relations with Iran and to secure its help in pressuring Lebanese Islamic terrorists to release several Americans held hostage in Beirut.

The revelation that the U.S. government had been secretly paying ransom for the release of hostages created a storm of controversy and a blizzard of daily news reports throughout November and December 1986, as the media pilloried Reagan, who until then had seemed immune to criticism.

The Iranscam, as the press called it, began to resemble the Watergate scandal, as scores of would-be Woodwards and Bernsteins revealed ever more damaging proof of a cover-up.

On November 24, Attorney General Ed Meese told the nation he had just discovered that millions of dollars of the profits from the Iranian arms sales had been secretly channeled to the Nicaraguan contra rebels in 1985 and 1986—after Congress had passed the Boland Amendment banning all U.S. government aid to the contras. Meese, in a statement many found difficult to believe, claimed that Reagan had been completely unaware of the diversion of funds to the contras. Instead, Meese pointed to an obscure Marine lieutenant colonel, Oliver North, who Meese claimed had been acting as a self-appointed loose cannon out of the White House basement while serving as an aide to national security adviser Admiral John Poindexter. On November 25, Reagan fired North and accepted Poindexter's resignation on the spot, vowing to "get to the bottom of this."

Dole, who had always privately considered Reagan a geriatric basket case, recognized a great opportunity to gain favorable publicity for himself and jumped directly into the fray, appearing on nationally televised news programs and criticizing Reagan—and, implicitly, Bush—for allowing the Iran-contra scandal to occur. He called the contra diversion "a bizarre twist." In lambasting Reagan, Dole was doing what he did best—attacking a vulnerable opponent on an issue when the prevailing political winds were already blowing strongly in that direction.

Still majority leader until January 1987, Dole made national headlines by calling for a special session of Congress to convene immediately. Dole's call for a special congressional session won him national publicity but was politically naive. When Reagan opposed the idea, and few of Dole's colleagues shared his interest in holding marathon emergency sessions during the holidays, Dole lost his last chance to hold the reins of Senate power for a few more weeks.

However, the scandal helped Dole in other ways—mainly by damaging Reagan's copilot, Vice President George Bush, whose standings in the polls plummeted, particularly in the heartland of America. As Bush plummeted in the polls, Dole skyrocketed. In September 1986, Dole was the choice of about 10 percent of Republican voters, far below Bush's 40 to 50 percent ranking. By January 1987, two months *after* the Iran-contra disaster, he had increased his poll standing to 30 percent of the national Republican vote. He still trailed Bush by a narrow margin; but in Iowa, scene of the first presidential caucuses in 1988, Dole had actually moved ahead of Bush.

While the freewheeling Dole took potshots at Reagan for his handling of the Iran-contra scandal, Bush was reduced to the unenviable position of mouthing support for the president and claiming that he, himself, had also been kept in the dark by Colonel North. He appeared somewhat foolish by offering as part of his defense that he had been attending an Army-Navy football game during a crucial White House meeting in which the Iran-contra affair germinated. Aided by the national press corps's tendency to portray Bush as a wimp, Dole now began to attack his hated rival in campaign speeches throughout the country. "George Bush is a fine vice president," Dole sarcastically told a Chicago audience in early 1987. "And he should stay there."

Presented with an excellent opportunity to take the lead on Iran-contra criticism, however, Dole again revealed his cautious side and did an about-face.

That spring the House and Senate agreed to set up a joint select committee to investigate the Iran-contra affair. As minority leader, Dole had the power to appoint whomever he wanted—including himself—to this committee. Although the position would have raised his national profile, Dole did not appoint himself, fearing that he might alienate too many conservatives who still backed Reagan. Instead, he appointed Senators Rudman, Cohen, and Trible to the panel, which began televised hearings in May. Meanwhile the President's Special Review Board, called the Tower Commission, appointed by the president, published its own report exonerating Reagan and Bush of any complicity in the affair. Bush was hardly mentioned at all, a fact that led Dole to grumble privately in his Senate office, "He never leaves any footprints, wherever he goes."

Avoiding the political hot water of Iran-contra, Dole backed off in his criticism of Reagan and began spending more time campaigning for president in Iowa, New Hampshire, and other key primary states. Dole claimed to be running on "a record" while Bush was running on "a résumé." He accused Bush of being an "observer" as vice president for the past seven years.

Dole's hope for a Bush collapse was not fulfilled, however, as public ennui over the Iran-contra affair set in, and even the commercial television networks bypassed the hearings (until the photogenic secretary Fawn Hall and her charismatic former boss, North, took the stand in midsummer).

As it became clear that Bush would survive the scandal and continue to collect endorsements and contributions as the GOP frontrunner, the minority leader began looking for new ways to attack Bush. His dilemma, however, was that any frontal assault on Bush might well resurrect his old hatchet man label. In March 1987, he formed a presidential exploratory campaign committee with his old Kansas friend Bob Ellsworth[1] at the helm. And, in contrast to his ill-fated 1980 presidential bid, he declined to declare his candidacy early. When he declared on November 9, 1987, he was the last major candidate in either party to do so.[2] At the age of sixty-four, one year older than Bush, he was also the oldest candidate.

In May, a remarkable political event took place that gave all the presidential candidates much food for thought. Former senator Gary Hart, by far the frontrunner for the 1988 Democratic presidential nomination, was caught by reporters of the *Miami Herald* entertaining a stunning model-actress named Donna Rice at his Washington home over the May 2–3 weekend. Hart, who had been dogged for years by rumors of womanizing, found his picture alongside Rice's on the front page of every newspaper in the country on May 4. It was the beginning of an avalanche of devastating news stories and editorials attacking his alleged adultery, but especially his character and judgment. Four days later, despite his overwhelming lead in the polls, Hart withdrew from the presidential race.[3]

[1]A former congressman from Kansas and Defense Department official under President Nixon.

[2]All eight Democrats and five Republican presidential candidates had declared their candidacies for the 1988 nomination long before Dole. Democrats included Bruce Babbitt, Richard Gephardt, Michael Dukakis, Jesse Jackson, Paul Simon, Albert Gore, Gary Hart, and Joseph Biden. Republican candidates included George Bush (declared on October 12, 1987), Alexander Haig, Jack Kemp, Pierre du Pont, and Pat Robertson.

[3]On December 15, Hart made a surprise reentry into the race for the Democratic nomination, but soon dropped behind in the polls following overwhelming ridicule from the press.

Within a few weeks, rumors and news stories began to appear hinting that Vice President Bush also was an adulterer with a longtime extramarital affair. Bush was convinced these rumors were being spread deliberately by Dole's campaign staff. George Wittgraf, Bush's Iowa campaign director, directly accused the Dole campaign of spreading rumors. "The only Republican presidential campaign from which any such news came to us in Iowa was the Dole campaign," he said. "I think it is unfortunate," he added, "that any other presidential campaign, and particularly the Dole campaign, is resorting to something that is unsubstantiated by fact. . . . It is unfair to Senator Dole, who has been trying to move beyond the mean and nasty image he has had in the past."

Wittgraf's public accusation infuriated Dole, who denied that anyone on his staff had spread rumors against Bush. He lashed out at Wittgraf, taking the latter's charge as a personal affront. "It seems to me it might be an effort by Mr. Wittgraf to sort of turn the thrust of the story in our direction," Dole growled. "He's pretty good at that."

In June, while attending a Republican picnic near Des Moines, Dole spotted Wittgraf and accosted him in what he thought was a location far from reporters' cameras. "Listen," Dole said, "I'm tired of being stabbed by you every time I come out here. . . . If you wanna play that game, I'll be glad to play it with you."

Unknown to Dole, a CNN-TV camera crew had been standing by and recorded his confrontation with Wittgraf. The incident, which showed Dole as a snarling bully who personalized his political feuds, was reported in newspapers across the country.

A few months later, Ted Koppel announced on ABC's "Night-line" that someone had been planting rumors with news organizations throughout Washington about Bush's alleged extramarital affair. Koppel and ABC had refused to run the story, Koppel said, because they suspected that "one of Bush's rivals" had been the source. Dole was not named, however, and no one had ever been able to prove that he was in any way responsible for planting rumors. Bush denied that he had ever had an extramarital affair, and the whole issue faded away.

Such incidents are not uncommon in politics. The Democrats had an internecine feud of their own three months later, when the campaign staff of Massachusetts governor Michael Dukakis surreptitiously leaked a videotape to the press that showed how rival candidate Senator Joe Biden had plagiarized speeches from British Labor Party leader Neil Kinnock and the late Robert Kennedy. Acutely embarrassed over the disclosures, Biden dropped out of the race within a week. Dukakis denied playing a role in leaking the video and blamed his campaign manager, who resigned. Dukakis, who had been emerging as the Democratic front-runner among the so-called Seven Dwarfs then in contention, was hurt by his new reputation as a campaign hardballer. (When Dole was asked what he thought about Dukakis, he sarcastically retorted, "Dukakis? Never had it.")

Dole has always used humor as a club against rivals. As the campaign ground on in 1987, and he continued to trail Bush in the polls (though only slightly), he let loose a barrage of savage jokes at his opponents, though presented in a manner designed to be socially acceptable. New York congressman Jack Kemp, a former professional football quarterback who worshiped at the altar of supply-side economics, became a favorite target.

Dole saw Kemp as his main rival for the right-wing vote he now courted, and he had always envied and resented him, possibly for becoming the athletic star Bob had always dreamed of being. Believing himself vastly superior in intelligence to that "jock," he developed an exhaustive repertoire of jokes to tell about this rival. After Kemp had espoused his economic theories in a nationally televised debate, Dole dismissed him with the barb "You've been playing quarterback too long." Another time, he referred to Kemp's supply-side "busload" of supporters as follows: "The supply-side bus went over the edge of the cliff. The bad news is that everybody on board got killed; the good news is that all of the seats were empty." And on numerous occasions he told jokes about "a certain football player who forgot his helmet and then started talking supply-side theory."

Dole uses his Russell-bred razor-sharp humor like a stiletto to pierce and wound an opponent. Stabbing swiftly and unexpectedly into a target's hide, he then withdraws immediately and goes on to other matters, escaping before his victim has a chance to retaliate or make any response at all. Dole is a master at this type of guerrilla political warfare. His caustic jokes, usually delivered with a deadpan facial expression, sink into the minds of his audience and germinate there like seeds.

*Washingtonian* magazine, in July of 1987, ranked Dole as "the most humorous senator." But it has often been said that a funny man is an angry man, and in Dole's case this maxim is probably not far from the truth. Anger is a force for much, but not all, of his humor. Being an intensely private man who is reluctant to reveal his emotions, Dole is a person whose true feelings can often be discerned only between the lines of his jokes.

Besides lending support to his hatchet man image, Dole's humor has gotten him into trouble in other ways. In the fall of 1987, he told a crowd in Milwaukee that "Central America wouldn't mind a three-day invasion of Nicaragua." When called to task for this remark on national television, he retreated and said he had just been quoting someone else. But at the time he made this remark, Dole was desperately seeking the conservative vote in order to win the GOP presidential nomination. He was well aware that many right-wingers would love nothing better than a three-day invasion of Nicaragua and has always felt that wars should be prosecuted "as quickly and as painlessly as possible." His "three-day invasion" comment was a joke, but it was loaded with meaning.

Typically, Dole speaks of enemy countries in terms of their leaders. He has attacked Nicaraguan president Daniel Ortega, whom he referred to as "Mr. Ortega" instead of by his title, calling him "the biggest stumbling block (to peace) in Central America." He has spoken in similarly personal and biting terms of Iran's Ayatollah Khomeini, Saudi Arabian oil minister Sheik Yamani, and former Soviet leader Leonid Brezhnev.

Dole's aggressive style against domestic opponents is legendary. On November 14, 1987, for example, just five days after Dole announced his own candidacy in Russell, George Bush won a stunning victory in the Florida GOP straw poll, with 57 percent of the vote and 1,322 votes. Dole, who won only 14 votes and finished in fifth place, immediately blasted the straw poll as "rigged" by Bush's supporters.

Calling his opponents' tactics "unfair" or "rigged" has always been a Dole trademark when he has felt on the verge of losing. In his tough 1974 Senate reelection campaign in Kansas against Dr. William Roy, he complained it was "unfair" for Roy to use Watergate as a campaign issue against him and said he wanted to "retaliate" by using a Democratic scandal (an architectural fee dispute involving a Democratic Kansas governor) against Roy. After his infamous 1976 vice presidential candidate debate against Mondale, he said he had blasted Mondale because he felt it "unfair" for the Democrats to be using Watergate against him and Gerald Ford. I recall a scene in a Senate elevator during the 1980 campaign in which Dole began railing against Bush after seeing a new poll showing the latter ahead in the Granite State. "That SOB is fixing that primary!" he thundered, accusing Bush of "buying" the election with "big oil money" and vowing to "set things right."

Because he regards every campaign as a "must win" situation, Dole has a tendency to lash out against critics, whether they be other politicians, the press, or even voters. Once, when a former supporter and contributor voiced criticism of Dole's vote on an antitrust bill, Dole flew into a rage because he felt he had to write a conciliatory letter. Riding in the Senate subway car from his office to the Capitol, he told me, "The thing I hate most about this job is that you're not supposed to 'offend.' " With a look of disgust on his face, he added: "How are you supposed to accommodate every incompetent [constituent]?"

Dole's tendency to follow the unofficial town motto of Russell and to "tell it like it is," regardless of whose toes he steps on, has often troubled his dealings with constituents. Once, when a whole parade of Kansans, complete with babies and cameras, walked into his office, he winced visibly and froze like a statue. Loathing the thought of kissing the babies, a difficult chore for him because he can only use one arm, he went through the motions and then retreated on some pretext that he had to "go vote." After the visitors left, he clenched his fist in the air and snarled, "This place is like a barber shop. I ought to hire a look-alike to go through the motions with these idiots. You can't waste your time massaging every clown who comes in here."

Dole's contempt for "little people" is based largely on his belief that he is smarter than everyone else. It is not unusual for him to refer to people in pejorative terms such as *idiot* and *incompetent*. He considers himself a great intuitive intellect, one who has such a gut feel for issues that he need not read books or listen to would-be mentors. Other than congressional reports and bill-related material, I never saw a book in his office or heard of his reading one or discussing a single book or idea in the abstract. His rival, Jack Kemp, jokes, "There was a fire in Dole's home, and both books burned down." Dole is primarily a *doer*, a man of action who scorns intellectuals and "bookworms" and insists he doesn't have the time to read books because he is always so busy.

Just as he ridicules and demeans small-fry constituents, he also looks down on intellectuals and would-be intellectuals. He has repeatedly ridiculed Kemp for "trying" to write a book on supply-side economics—Kemp has written such a book, in fact—and has no patience with economists who create theoretical models for how the economy is supposed to work. A former Harvard classmate of mine[4] once presented him with an autographed copy of his new book on Harvard. Dole took it, threw it in a corner, and gave it away without so much as looking at it. When another constituent presented him with an intellectual treatise, he threw it in the garbage can.

[4]John LeBoutillier, author of *Harvard Hates America* (South Bend, IN: Gateway Editions, 1978).

Dole's contempt for books, intellectuals, and experts probably has its origins in his identification with the values of his hometown in central Kansas. As one of his old-time friends from Russell explained it to me, "We here in the heartland think we know better than people from either coast. We spend our time waiting for the coasters to make a decision when we already knew the right answer before."

When Dole radios his brother from his Lear jet and makes a stop in Russell, Kansas, in order to touch the ground while flying between coasts for major campaign stops and, as he says, "change his shirt," he is symbolically and literally touching his heartland roots and getting his bearings straight.

On November 9, 1987, he came home again, this time to declare his candidacy for the 1988 Republican presidential nomination. In typical Dole style, there was little organization, and his candidacy debut was chaotic up to the last minute. While TV reporters from around the world prepared to film the event, Dole's advance men were scurrying around trying to get the props and the seating arrangements settled just right. "What should we do? What should we do?" they asked one another, distractedly. Then the candidate himself appeared. Furious at the chaos, he put his foot down and thundered, "You know damn well what you'd better do! Now, just go out and do it!"

An hour later, the candidate, clad in a heavy overcoat for the chilly thirty-degree weather, took the stand. He was surrounded by thousands of blue and gold balloons around a huge sign that read, somewhat presumptuously:

## DOLE
President

The man of Russell stepped to the microphone and barked in a voice as flat as the Kansas plains: "I offer a willingness to work hard, to hang tough, to go the distance. . . . I offer the strength and determination, molded in America's small-town heartland and tempered during a career of public service, to bring common-sense answers to the complex problems facing America in its third century." Comparing himself to "America's great heartland presidents . . . Lincoln . . . Truman . . . Eisenhower . . . Reagan," Dole said that he and they were "plain-speaking men whose clear-eyed vision enabled them to make the tough choices."

Standing on the corner of Eighth and Main streets before a crowd of five thousand, Dole slipped into his Cassandra role, calling the federal budget deficit the "single greatest threat to a prosperous and dynamic America." Taking a slap at supply-side economists and Jack Kemp, Bob said that the country can no longer "rely on stopgap economic fixes." Then, in a phrase reminiscent of his controversial days as Senate majority leader, Dole vowed to "sit down with congressional leaders during my first weeks in office [as president] and we'll stay there as long as it takes, and we will not stop until we come up with a renewed commitment to a multiyear plan—a new compact—that ends with a balanced budget in the near future." Arguing that "someone must make the hard choices," he implicitly promised a program of austerity aimed at trimming the deficit.[5]

In the speech, Dole also criticized America's allies for failing to "assume their rightful role and bear their rightful burden in the defense of our common interests. We must stand in support of genuine freedom fighters," he insisted, by which he presumably meant the contra rebels in Nicaragua.

After his speech, Dole made a sentimental journey down Main Street to Dawson's Drug Store (now called Rogers' Drugs), where he had worked in high school and where townspeople had collected the $1,800 in a cigar box to pay the hospital fees for his surgery forty years earlier. This time he was presented with the identical cigar box, by Bub Dawson, a high school chum whose father had placed the "Bob Dole Donation Fund" cigar box on his counter in 1947. (Dole had kept the box for forty years in his desk in Washington.)

From his nostalgic trip into the past, Dole rushed into the harsh realities of the present. Leaving Russell in the early morning, he flew to Waukee, Iowa, to make an identical speech at a farm rally. There he was greeted by about twenty-five civil rights pickets led

---

[5]The *Washington Post*, in its headlines the next day, November 10, 1987, actually said that "Dole Stresses Austerity as Theme for '88," even though he did not use that word.

by Randall Robinson, the head of an anti-apartheid lobby group called Transafrica. The pickets waved placards charging Dole with being indifferent toward apartheid in South Africa because of his support for Reagan's veto of a bill imposing sanctions on South Africa—a complete about-face after he had voted for the sanctions in the first place. Dole was infuriated. Pointing at the pickets, he shouted, "The signs are wrong. There's not a racist bone in my body."

This ugly incident marring his presidential debut illustrates the fundamental dilemma Dole faces as an ideologically inconsistent politician. While he needs the support of the right wing, which is opposed to sanctions, I can testify that he has genuine feeling for blacks and other minorities and that he identifies with them as an outsider and a member of a minority (the handicapped). But Dole has alienated civil rights supporters by taking inconsistent positions on numerous civil rights bills. He has shown himself at times willing to side with those deemed by civil rights activists to be hostile to civil rights. In fact, members of Transafrica have followed Dole around to picket him at various stops during his campaign.

Indeed, Dole may be in the wrong party on civil rights, because a majority of right-wing Republicans appear to be indifferent or hostile to civil rights, and Dole must secure their support in order to win the GOP presidential nomination. He has said, "I wish our party were as sensitive as the Democratic party" and has bucked the GOP mainstream by demanding rhetorically that it act more compassionately toward minorities.

In his role as deficit Cassandra, too, Dole seems out of step with most Republicans. By and large, the Republican Party of the 1980s has become synonymous with conservatism and is fundamentally opposed to raising taxes. For the most part, conservatives seem to consider the budget deficit to be little more than a minor head cold for the economy, while Dole considers it to be a life-threatening cancer. His implicit call for austerity does not sit well with conservatives (during the 1988 campaign in New Hampshire, Jack Kemp called Dole "the candidate of austerity, pain, and sacrifice"), and his previously well-documented role in raising taxes and in attempting to freeze Social Security COLAs to shrink the deficit has found few receptive ears among right-wingers, whose support is essential to his bid for the nomination.[6]

Indeed, Dole has often bucked the GOP and voted with Democrats as liberal as George McGovern and Ted Kennedy, overriding the advice of his own staff, which has often been far more staunchly conservative than he. Fundamentally, Dole is so eclectic and pragmatic that he is truly a blend of both liberal and conservative, Democrat and Republican. I recall one incident in the Senate when some Democratic Kansans come in to see him, urging him to support a Carter Administration program being opposed by GOP conservatives. "My parents were Democrats," Dole told the group. "And when I first ran for the Kansas legislature, I was being courted by both parties. . . . You might say I'm a 'Republicrat.' "

Dole's self-described status as a Republicrat seemed to spring involuntarily from his mouth during a nationally televised debate of GOP presidential hopefuls on October 28, 1987. William F. Buckley, conservative guru and host of the debate on "Firing Line," asked each of the six candidates which U.S. presidents' pictures they would hang up on the wall of the Oval Office if they became president. Dole mentioned Lincoln, Washington, and Reagan and then added, "And then I would put up a picture of my parents . . . my father in his overalls, and my mother, who meant so much to me." That Dole would place his parents on the same level as presidents tells us much about the enduring influence and inspiration of their values on him. Those values included hard work and self-reliance, to be sure, but they also included Democratic Party affiliation and a fundamental identification with the common man.

The boyhood memories of desperate farmers in the Depression and of Russell as the great extended family in which everyone helps everyone else and lends a hand if you only work hard and meet them halfway shaped Dole into what he is today. But Russell is not the national Republican Party, and Russellism is not national Republican conservatism.

Whether Dole can bridge the considerable gap between Russell-

---

[6]At a New Hampshire debate on January 16, 1988, the Panglossian Kemp proclaimed, "It's morning in America." To which the pessimistic Dole countered, "It's high noon in America."

ism and the Republican Party remains to be seen. Because he is an eclectic Republicrat who pays lip service to the traditional Democratic compassion for the needy, he would be a far more formidable presidential candidate in the *general* November 1988 election than would the more loyal Republican George Bush or the more purely conservative Jack Kemp, and Democrats naturally fear him more than they do any of his GOP rivals. With his genuine concern for the underdogs of society, Dole has the potential of appealing to voters of all ideologies and races.

Although in 1988 Dole is a major threat to Republican frontrunner George Bush and, unlike in 1980, is a serious contender for Republican presidential nomination, some aspects of his latest campaign have been true to past form.

The campaign has been plagued by disorganization from the start. When Bill Brock resigned his position as Reagan's secretary of labor to come on board as Dole's full-time campaign manager in late 1987, he found, according to *The New Republic*, that "the campaign has no record of its expenditures or even a rundown on Dole's Senate voting record." Position papers on issues had not yet been released in early February 1988. And Brock himself took a ten-day Caribbean vacation at the height of the primary campaign.

Dole still talks of being a compassionate candidate, but his main issue of concern seems to be reducing the budget deficit. Characteristically, he presented no proposal for how he would do so until January 1988. At that time, he offered the rather vague notion of a spending freeze, saying that it would save the government $50 billion a year. Without saying how, he also said that low-income people would be exempt from any hardship such a plan may cause. And in an interview with Marvin Kalb on PBS-TV in January 1988, Dole promised that no one would go homeless or hungry if Dole were president. Subsequently, he also proposed a 2 percent limit on Social Security COLAs.

Dole's stump speech, heard all over Iowa and New Hampshire before the February caucuses and primary, was almost a rehash of his record in the Senate and seemed more appropriate for a candidate for Senate leader than for a presidential candidate. The speech referred to his past record and was almost completely devoid of ideas and plans for the future. Despite the viability of his current

campaign, Dole still seems unwilling to stick his neck out.

For example, as of mid-December 1987, Dole was the only presidential candidate of either party who had taken neither a pro nor a con position on the Intermediate Nuclear Forces (INF) Treaty signed by Reagan and Soviet leader Mikhail Gorbachev in December 1987. Though supported by a majority of Americans, the treaty was vehemently opposed by the right wing of the Republican party. Characteristically, he waffled on it, saying he "had to read it first." Finally, after realizing that he was losing support in Iowa because of his waffling, Dole suddenly announced his support on December 17, appearing at the White House with Reagan (much to the chagrin of George Bush) to offer his strong endorsement of the treaty. After hedging his bets, Dole then demanded to be the leadoff witness for the treaty in the Senate committee hearings on its ratification.

Another example of Dole's inconsistency involves his stand on Bill S.2, a campaign finance reform measure that would have limited campaign spending and PAC contributions in Senate election campaigns. When the bill was introduced on January 6, 1987,

Dole supported it and said on the Senate floor, "I do not believe there will be any effort to stall any such legislation." In May, however, he led a filibuster on the Senate floor against the measure, saying that the bill would have made it even more difficult for new legislators to be elected and thereby perpetuated incumbency. After several attempts to break the filibuster failed, majority leader Robert Byrd withdrew it on September 15, 1987. It was resubmitted in 1988.

Dole's controversial role in leading the filibuster against S.2 earned him the enmity of Common Cause, the public interest lobbying group, which took out huge ads in the *Washington Post*, picketed Dole's campaign appearances, and mailed anti-Dole leaflets to voters in Iowa and New Hampshire. Common Cause denounced Dole for blocking campaign finance reform and alleged that he had received more PAC campaign contributions than any other Senator during the past fifteen years.

Dole was pilloried in the nation's media as a creature of the PACs and special interest groups. Stories in *Nation* magazine and the *New York Times* cited his sponsorship of Senate bills favoring the tobacco, ethanol, and insurance industries and listed massive campaign contributions received from executives and PACs of companies in these industries. *Newsday* reported that Dole had regularly solicited and accepted corporate jet rides for campaign appearances from companies whose interests he supported in Senate voting.

Dole's PAC connection is likely to become a major campaign issue if he becomes the 1988 GOP presidential nominee. In January 1988, Dole was embarrassed by a series of revelations appearing first in the Kansas Harris News chain of newspapers, and picked up by the national news media across the country. The articles alleged that Dave Owen, Dole's longtime political protégé and then-presidential campaign finance director, had had a possible conflict of interest in his role as investment adviser to Elizabeth Dole's blind trust. It was established in 1985 after she had become secretary of transportation and it contained $2.3 million in assets as of January 1988.

The allegations against Owen were threefold: (1) that Owen had set up a network of Kansas companies which drew investments from Elizabeth's blind trust, thereby presenting the appearance of impropriety and conflict of interest, as well as poor judgment by Mrs. Dole in allowing Owen to serve as the trust's investment adviser; (2) that Owen may have used a black businessman and former Dole aide, John Palmer, president of EDP Enterprises, as a front in getting the Small Business Administration (with Dole's help) to award EDP Enterprises a $26 million no-bid minority set-aside government contract to provide food to the Army's Fort Leonard Wood (Missouri) complex. Though Owen is white and therefore ineligible for an SBA minority no-bid contract, Owen's company drew a $4,500 monthly consulting fee from EDP. Finally, (3) that several months after the Army awarded Palmer's EDP the $26 million food contract, Palmer's firm signed a $279,000 promissory note as partial payment for EDP's half interest in an office building (College Park-2 in Overland Park, Kansas) owned by the trust. (Owen brokered the purchase of the $1.6 million office building for a commission.)

The office building transactions are complex and fogged in mystery, but several government agencies (the FBI, SEC, SBA, U.S. Department of Justice, and Kansas Attorney General) began investigating the matter in January 1988, and Dole rapidly dismissed Owen and distanced himself from his ex-protégé's affairs completely.

Though Owen announced that he had "temporarily" removed himself as Dole's presidential campaign finance chairman, Dole said he didn't want him back at any time and told the press that the ongoing investigations of Owen's affairs were "his problem, not mine."

The Owen scandal was potentially damaging to Dole because of his close fifteen-year association with Owen and intervention with the SBA on behalf of Palmer's EDP. It raised new questions about Bob Dole and Big Money, cronyism and poor judgment, which George Bush tried to make into a campaign issue. Under pressure to divulge his finances, Dole released his tax returns for the past

---

[7]Dole still likes to emphasize his humble roots, even to exaggerate the degree of his boyhood poverty. While his roots are certainly more humble than those of his arch-rival, financial disclosures during the 1988 campaign revealed that today the Doles are at least as wealthy as the Bushes. In 1986, each family had earnings of more than $600,000 as well as

twenty years, revealing that he has become a multimillionaire—
due mainly to his marrying into Elizabeth's family fortune.[7] No
one has yet proved that he either knew about or condoned Owen's
financial activities with regard to Elizabeth's blind trust or the
College Park-2 building. On the other hand, allowing a crony like
Owen to serve as investment counselor to the blind trust, whose
very purpose was to prevent Elizabeth from knowing where her
money was being invested, must go down as a colossal error in
judgment, if only because of the potential appearance of impropriety that Dole should have foreseen.

As 1988 progressed, Dole was making an effort to maintain his
new, mellower image, Bush went on the attack, eager to belie his
somewhat "wimpy" image. In January 1988, Bush tore up a
schoolgirl's leaflet critical of him, then had to apologize after she
called a news conference and said he had "humiliated" her. During
a speech before the National Rifle Association, Bush pulled a pistol
out of his jacket. And in a live interview, Bush aggressively castigated CBS-TV's Dan Rather for questioning him about the Iran-
contra affair. Afterward Bush was overheard boasting, "The bas-
tard didn't lay a glove on me."

In early February, just a week before the Iowa caucuses, Bush's
campaign released some leaflets blasting Elizabeth, charging that
she and her blind trust were under investigation by three government agencies. The leaflets further accused Bob of "cronyism,"
"mean-spiritedness," and "single-handedly" bringing about the
defeat of the Ford-Dole ticket in 1976. Ever protective of his wife
and furious at Bush's "cheap shot," Dole suddenly cast off his
mask of low-key benevolence and angrily confronted Bush face to
face on the Senate floor. Waving a leaflet in the vice president's
face, a livid Dole denounced Bush for "a new low in campaigning"
and for "groveling in the mud" and demanded an apology—which
Bush refused to give.

Dole beat out his five Republican rivals in the Iowa caucuses on

---

substantial trust funds. The Doles contributed 17.5 percent of their income to charity,
however, while the Bushes gave away only 6 percent of theirs. James O'Shea, "Tax Records
Show Bush, Dole Alike," *Chicago Tribune*, February 2, 1988; "Returns of Rich Rivals,"
*Topeka Capital-Journal*, January 22, 1988.

February 8 with 37 percent of the vote. Pat Robertson made a surprisingly strong showing, winning 25 percent of the vote, and Bush was humiliated by a third-place finish with a feeble 19 percent of the vote.[8]

Bush won the New Hampshire primary eight days later, however, with 38 percent to Dole's 29 percent.[9] Blaming his poor showing on "distortion" of his record and "desperation tactics" by Bush, Dole vowed to set the record straight. On the night of the primary, Dole confronted Bush face to face on NBC-TV and warned him, "Stop lying about my record." After being "a model of political decorum," according to the *Chicago Tribune,* after the primary Dole served notice that "he is no longer going to be Mr. Nice Guy."

[8] Jack Kemp received 11 percent, Pete du Pont 7 percent, Alexander Haig 0 percent, and no preference 1 percent. Haig subsequently dropped out of the race, endorsing Dole as he did so.

[9] Kemp received 13 percent, du Pont 10 percent, and Robertson 9 percent.

# 15
# BOB AND ELIZABETH: RIVALS AND PARTNERS

lizabeth Dole must get some of the credit for her husband's ascent to serious contention for the presidency, for undoubtedly she influenced the transformation of Bob's public image from that of embittered hatchet man into the calmer and self-professed compassionate candidate of 1988. Whether his actual character has changed is something only Bob himself can know.

The political star of Elizabeth, as ambitious and indefatigable as her husband, has risen along with that of Bob in recent years. And, if the nation elects Bob Dole to the White House, it will be electing not just an individual but a team—"Dole & Dole in '88," as the buttons at the 1984 Republican convention read.

These two highly motivated and fiercely independent people have somehow managed to keep their marriage and their careers happily intact. They seem the model dual-career couple of the eighties. When Elizabeth, under fire for being on the campaign trail and away from the job so much, resigned her position of secretary of transportation to campaign full-time for Bob in late 1987, some thought she had sold out by giving up her job for the sake of her husband's career. The *Louisville Courier-Journal and Times* said Elizabeth lost touch with the spirit of the women's movement "by using a stereotype about politicians' wives as an alibi for quitting." Others criticized her for deserting a department beset by problems, particularly air safety. Elizabeth countered the criticism by saying, "This is a personal decision, and that's what we women have fought for, the right to decide what is best in our own lives. I think playing a meaningful role, a substantive role in the democratic process that leads to the selection of the leader of the free world is meaningful work."[1] Also, by helping Bob, Elizabeth will be gaining national exposure and furthering her own cause as well as his.

The spirit of the Doles' campaign partnership and rivalry was captured in political cartoons such as this one shortly after Elizabeth's resignation.

Jim Borgman, *Cincinnati Enquirer.* © 1987 King Features Syndicate, Inc. Reprinted with special permission.

[1] However, Elizabeth was clearly none too pleased when, before she had announced her resignation, Bob publicly commented that of course she would have to quit her job to help him campaign.

Sometimes Elizabeth's prominence has irked Bob, a man who cannot stand being upstaged by anyone. His fear of being eclipsed by his wife is undoubtedly aroused whenever some reporter suggests that she might become the first woman president or the GOP vice presidential nominee in 1988 or 1992. He is particularly annoyed by speculation that Elizabeth might become the running mate of his despised rival George Bush in 1988.

Bob's fear that his wife is more popular than he is probably well grounded. A week after he had announced his 1988 presidential candidacy in his hometown, a local woman walked into the drugstore where Bob had worked in his teens and announced loudly, "I wish he would step down so that I can vote for her." And, in Savannah, Georgia, where Elizabeth was campaigning for Bob in 1987, a woman in the audience was heard to declare, "She's got my vote. I think they're running the wrong Dole."

Elizabeth's popularity has exceeded her husband's even among his own staff in the Senate. When I worked for him, she frequently visited the office, and because of her buoyancy and charm, everyone there preferred her to her husband. Bob's Senate and campaign staffers have been known to jump ship to work for her.

The rivalry between Bob and Elizabeth is by no means bitter, however. Instead, their competition with each other seems to have an invigorating influence. "We like to see who gets home last at night," Bob once told me, pointing out that neither he nor his wife is the domestic type.

"I'm a terrible cook," Elizabeth has boasted, noting that they usually dine out or skip meals altogether. Because of their perpetually busy schedules, they have never found the time to look for a house; they still live in Bob's bachelor apartment in the Watergate complex. Both Doles have frequently pointed out that their home life is minimal. The shared experiences and family intimacy that bring happiness to most couples—a home, children, nightly dinners—are completely lacking in the Doles' marriage. But the absence of traditional family life seems never to have bothered either Bob or Elizabeth, each of whose main interest has always been work. Elizabeth, however, claims that she has changed since her single days and has undergone spiritual growth in recent years. She attends Foundry United Methodist Church in Washington, where she delivered a sermon in 1983 in which she bore witness to the satisfaction brought on by prayer and which her ambition, perfectionism, and success could not provide. Nevertheless, she still exhibits many traits of the ultimate modern career woman, and her public image is that of a working woman who happens to be married rather than a married woman who happens to work.

I am convinced that by far the most influential person in Bob Dole's life has been Elizabeth. The man who has become legendary as a Lone Ranger is not at all alone when it comes to Elizabeth. She is the top adviser to the man who hates to take advice and the surrogate candidate for the man who hates to delegate. It is undoubtedly largely because of her influence that he has supported consumer rights bills and the Equal Rights Amendment. When I worked for him, one time Bob's conservative colleagues on the Senate Judiciary Committee urged him to vote for a bill overturning one of his wife's rulings as federal trade commissioner. Bob cracked, "I gotta go home at night, you know. Can't antagonize the queen," and abstained from voting on the bill.

An aura of supreme competence in managing their personal lives as well as their careers is important to both of the Doles. When Bob divorced Phyllis in 1972, he learned that many voters believed that a man who can't even manage his own marriage couldn't possibly manage the country. Yet, when the Doles met in the office, I was struck by the rather impersonal tone of this relationship—more like a business partnership than a marriage. Sometimes they appeared to be putting on a Punch and Judy show, with heavy kidding and bantering, much like a brother and a tough sister. And, in referring to his relationship with Elizabeth, Bob often speaks in curiously abstract terms. "She's my southern strategy," he will say, or "She's my greatest single resource."

In their domestic relationship, I have heard Bob complain that Elizabeth reads too much, that she drags him off to church, and that she owns everything he has. Their private rivalry is clear from Bob's comment to the press in reference to a hotel suite he shared with her at the 1984 Dallas convention: "It's really her room. I'm just a poor senator. She wasn't even here and I walked in. I saw the room said '1988.' Then I learned it was in her name. I think she's trying to tell me something."

In 1984, Dole suggested that his wife be appointed United Nations ambassador to replace Jeane Kirkpatrick, saying "I think she needs foreign policy experience. She likes to learn anything." Nothing came of this suggestion and Elizabeth refused to comment on it, but it was an interesting statement, for the U.N. ambassadorship requires full-time residence in New York, 250 miles from Washington. That he seriously proposed a commuter marriage requiring him to live alone during the week is revealing. Apparently, he simply does not need a full-time wife.

In her career, Elizabeth has shown the same agile pragmatism so amply demonstrated by Bob. Her ideology has changed from liberal to conservative, her party affiliation from Democrat to independent to Republican as circumstances required. After serving Lyndon Johnson from 1968 to 1969, she served the pro-business and anti-consumer Nixon just as devotedly from 1969 to 1973 before Nixon nominated her for the Federal Trade Commission in 1973. Although, at her confirmation hearing, pro-consumer senators on the Commerce Committee questioned the sincerity of her espousal of consumer interests, she proved to be her own woman. Once confirmed, she surprised everyone, and disappointed Nixon, by making pro-consumer and anti-business decisions. By the time she left the FTC in 1979, she had written more than fourteen decisions, many of them ruling against big business.

She served Reagan loyally in the White House from 1981 to 1983. When he appointed her secretary of transportation in 1983—a position in which her salary was slightly higher than Senator Dole's—she had had no experience in transportation or in managing a federal bureaucracy, yet she presided over 102,000 employees in nine branches, with a total annual budget of $28 billion. Among other accomplishments, she was credited with requiring all new automobiles after 1985 to mount a third red light in their rear windows. This brake light became known, unofficially, as the "Dole Light," and was credited with reducing the frequency of accidents by giving drivers extra warning of an impending stop by the car ahead. She was criticized, however, for failing to make public the results of crash performance tests of auto bumpers and for taking too much of a *laissez-faire* position in general.

During her four-and-a-half-year reign, Elizabeth also came under fire for not adequately managing airline deregulation and safety issues. Under her tenure, the skies became dangerously crowded around airports, and the number of plane crashes increased dramatically, passenger complaints of lost and misplaced baggage reached an all-time high, and airports witnessed record delays and canceled flights. Commercial airplane accidents reached a thirteen-year high in 1987, with a record number of near misses, and the fatal-accident rate jumped almost threefold from 1986 to 1987. When she resigned in September 1987, one insider barked, "Well, at least she can't say she quit while she was ahead." And the *Los Angeles Times* published a political cartoon depicting the sky ridiculously crowded with jets, in between which a small biplane hurled a banner reading "Dole for President." The caption read, "I want to do for my husband what I did for the FAA."

By and large, however, Elizabeth emerged relatively unscathed. Her public relations are very good, and she has been able to smile and charm her way through criticism. She herself has received more attention than her job performance has, probably because a powerful woman is a rarity in Washington and because both the press and the public are so fascinated with Bob and Elizabeth as the Power Couple.

In her capacity as transportation secretary Elizabeth once appeared as a witness before Bob's Senate Finance Committee. The press came out in droves, not to hear debate about an obscure bill involving a trucking tax, but to record the historic occasion: the first time that a husband and wife squared off as senator and witness in a congressional hearing. The official topic was all but forgotten as they bantered back and forth, addressing each other as Mr. Chairman and Madame Secretary. Elizabeth testified, "I hope that we can come to quick agreement on these matters that are before us in all three houses." "It looks like you may get home first tonight," Bob retorted, "so you know what to do."

The Doles say that they keep their political and private lives separate, but problems almost inevitably ensue when a husband and wife lead separate prominent careers that intertwine, and they can lead to political embarrassment.

In April 1984, both Elizabeth and Bob attended a party in Orlando, Florida. The party turned out to be a Dole fund-raiser, and fifty developers there contributed a total of about $60,000 to Bob's campaign committee. The same developers were seeking the construction of a certain new federal highway interchange, a project under Elizabeth's jurisdiction. After the press got hold of the story, Bob offered to return all the money to the developers.

The Doles' three-room suite in the posh Sea View Hotel in Bal Harbour, Florida, has also been the subject of speculation by the press. The hotel, a co-op, is managed by a corporation headed by Dwayne O. Andreas, chairman of Archer-Daniels-Midland Corporation in Decatur, Illinois, which happens to be a major producer of ethanol (gasohol), a cause Dole has championed in the Senate for years.

On March 27, 1982, according to the minutes of the annual meeting of the directors of Sea View Hotel, Inc., at which Andreas presided, the board approved "the room transfers made during the previous year." According to the minutes, "Rooms 1210, 1211 and 1212, formerly owned by Mr. and Mrs. David Susskind, were transfered to Senator and Mrs. Robert Dole."

In late 1987 the *New York Times* reported that the Doles apparently received preferential treatment in obtaining shares in the co-op and alleged that the $150,000 price the Doles paid in 1982 is less than the unit's value, according to an independent estimate. Further, who actually owns the unit has been questioned. The March 27, 1982, directors' meeting minutes said the rooms were transferred to Senator and Mrs. Robert Dole, while the original deed names only Mrs. Dole and a subsequent deed lists Elizabeth and her brother, John Hanford, as the owners.

The suggestion that the Doles got a special deal on their co-op in return for Bob's support of gasohol is unfair to Bob Dole. I worked with Bob on legislation promoting the gasohol industry in the Senate and am convinced that his strong support for such legislation was not in any way related to Andreas's financial interests. Gasohol benefits farmers and Dole sincerely believed that it was an excellent alternative fuel. He never based any of his votes on this issue on expected campaign contributions. Moreover, since the Doles are millionaires, the discount they received from Andreas is but a drop in their bucket of assets. It is difficult to see how such a relatively small amount of money could influence Bob's votes.

As tireless as ever, Elizabeth has contributed much to Bob's

1988 campaign. She's traveled all over the country giving speeches and raising contributions, sometimes in tandem with her husband but usually alone, and attracting praise and admiration for her style and personality. Although usually on the road, she undoubtedly has a say in strategy and personally advises the candidate.

Elizabeth's influence on Bob's 1988 campaign is clear from the way in which he often comes across as a restrained, almost mealy-mouthed candidate, much as he did during the first part of his 1980 campaign. It is ironic that even as Bush tries to shed his "wimpy" image by lashing out at the media and other candidates, Dole, despite flashes of his famous wit, tries to shed his hatchet man image by suppressing the embittered, slashing part of his personality.[2]

In the White House, combining the glamorous looks of Jackie Kennedy with the activist soul of Eleanor Roosevelt, Elizabeth would not be content to slip into the mantle of the traditional first lady occupied with trivial projects. Yet, because of a federal anti-nepotism law, she would not be allowed to serve as cabinet secretary or head of a federal agency (unless Congress grants a special exemption).

Bob, being extremely protective of his wife, would almost certainly carve out a unique, semi-official position for her, perhaps as head of a series of blue-ribbon presidential task forces, which would focus their attention on finding unique solutions to problems dear to her heart. As first lady, however, she would almost certainly be his most influential adviser, having a say in political and strategic decisions as well as policy issues—much in the way that other "steel magnolia," Rosalynn Carter, did. Elizabeth told the *Christian Science Monitor* in January 1988, "I will be an active first lady, let's put it that way."

Whatever Mrs. Dole's White House role would turn out to be,

[2]The Doles coauthored a book, *The Doles: Unlimited Partners*, published just as the 1988 campaign was getting in full swing. In it, Bob and Elizabeth take turns telling the stories of their lives and their life together. The projected image of the energetic, confident power couple is heavily laced with compassion.

we can safely predict that she would serve as Bob's *de facto* "brain trust." For a one-dimensional man whose idea of entertainment is pedaling his Exercycle in front of his TV set, Bob Dole has found the perfect glamour queen in his wife. The public and the media, with their insatiable appetite for soap opera glitter, are likely to bite into the "Dole & Dole" apple with relish.

# 16
# DOLE AS PRESIDENT

**W**hat kind of president would Dole make? The answer lies in Dole's personality traits, character, leadership style, values, and experience, as revealed throughout his long career of public service.

The most obvious factor affecting Dole's career is his handicap. Should he reach the Oval Office in January 1989, Bob Dole will be the first handicapped man since Roosevelt to hold presidential power. Would we see a second Franklin D. Roosevelt?

Roosevelt, a victim of polio, turned out to be one of the truly great presidents in history and repeatedly attributed his compassionate and determined nature to his handicap. Bob Dole, too, attributes his most impressive qualities—his phenomenal drive to succeed and his deep identification with the underdogs of society—to his wartime wound.

But there the similarity ends. Unlike Dole, Roosevelt never earned a reputation as a hatchet man and seldom displayed a vindictive spirit.[1] Moreover, Roosevelt showed no distrust of ex-

---

[1]Even Dole's longtime aide and financial whiz kid, Dave Owen, has said that "he [Dole] can be meaner than a junkyard dog, yet there's no doubt in my mind that he's a compassionate person." Stephen C. Fehr, "The Metamorphosis of Bob Dole," *Kansas City Times*, February 6, 1984.

perts, aides, and advisers. On the contrary, he formed a brain trust of intellectuals whose advice he eagerly sought out and respected. It's hard to imagine Dole forming anything like a brain trust, much less seeking advisers. Finally, Dole the loner is temperamentally the opposite of the gregarious, extroverted FDR.

A more likely comparison to Dole might be Nixon.

A fanatical acolyte and soulmate of Richard M. Nixon during his first Senate term, and bearing a striking resemblance to Nixon's dark, brooding appearance, Dole has struck many observers as a Nixon-in-the-making, a Nixon redux. Indeed, almost everyone I interviewed who disliked Dole compared him to Nixon. "They're two peas in a pod," Jim Parrish told me. "Dole has out-Nixoned Nixon," said Norbert Dreiling.

Given Dole's well-documented record of fanatical support for Nixon and his equally strong dislike of the press and of personal criticism, it is fair to consider the possibility that Dole would indeed become another Nixon.

Comparing a prospective president to past presidents is a useful exercise, provided the task is approached systematically and according to certain well-established criteria. Professor James David Barber of Duke University, in his book *The Presidential Character*, has studied all forty presidents and identified three key factors that are determinative of a man's performance as president: his character, his world view, and his leadership style. Of these three, the most important is character, particularly in a crisis.

"The best way to measure a candidate's character," Barber told me, "is by looking at the signals he gives off in private—how he talks and acts around the people closest to him, in unguarded moments—when the press isn't watching."

Barber has put each president into one of four categories: active positive (e.g., John Kennedy, Franklin D. Roosevelt, Harry Truman), active negative (e.g., Lyndon Johnson, Richard Nixon, Woodrow Wilson, Herbert Hoover), passive positive (e.g., Ronald Reagan, Howard Taft, and Warren Harding), and passive negative (Dwight Eisenhower and Calvin Coolidge). This four-pronged typology is based on an assessment of each president's predominant personality traits deriving from his childhood, adolescence, and early personal background.

According to Barber's theory, active presidents are those who expend a great deal of energy in their work, while passive presidents like Reagan tend to be laid-back or lazy.

"I don't think there's any doubt that Dole would be an active president," Barber told me. "The real question in Dole's case is whether he would be active positive or active negative."

Positive presidents tend to enjoy their work, reveling in the give-and-take of politics, joking about the criticism they receive, and generally giving off very positive cues and nuances in their unguarded moments with staff. Franklin D. Roosevelt, for example, was an active positive leader who reacted to media criticism by "sitting on the White House lawn and joking about it with reporters." By contrast, says Barber, Richard Nixon "constantly gave off negative signals to those around him . . . he was always expressing bitterness or anger or unhappiness with his work and with media criticism . . . he didn't *enjoy* his work or his life."[2]

Into which category should Dole be placed? "I find it very interesting that Dole took a course in Speech Dynamics [from Dorothy Sarnoff, following his 1976 election defeat] and that he married an outgoing, positive woman [Elizabeth] as a sort of compensatory exchange," Barber told me. By engaging in such compensatory activities, Barber feels, Dole is implicitly acknowledging a lack of these qualities in himself.

Certainly, a review of Dole's pre-1977 hatchet man phase would lead one to conclude at least tentatively, according to Barber, that Dole is an active negative character. His strident partisan attacks on political opponents, his hair-trigger temper, belligerency, bitterness, and workaholism are indications of an active negative character. As his 1974 Senate campaign opponent, Bill Roy, said: "[Dole] was a bitter, mean son of a bitch. I wondered what was burning so deeply inside his gut." Since 1977, however, Dole has attempted to moderate and mellow his character, with considerable success as far as the media and political colleagues are concerned. The question, however, is whether this represents a real metamorphosis of his character or is just a surface public relations gimmick.

---

[2]Even when he was a young law student at Duke University Law School in 1934–37, Nixon was known as "Gloomy Gus" because of his joylessness and his brooding disposition.

In a November 1987 piece in the *Atlanta Journal-Constitution*, Barber suggested that "Dole's history of anger is extensive, framed in incident after incident." Stories about Dole pile up, negative after negative, noting his anger, his bitterness, his bleak depression, his explosive temper. As to whether Dole has mellowed, Barber says, "we had better verify that with a solid pile of evidence."

"I'm skeptical whether a person can really change his character after the age of fifty," Barber told me. The character forged on the anvil of life's early experiences is generally too ingrained to be changed significantly, at least for the vast majority of people. Of course, Dole is an uncommon man.

In researching his life and interviewing people for this book, I found that Dole has evoked a striking dichotomy of responses from those who have come in contact with him. Many respect and like him, but there are those who literally "hate his guts." Similarly, many people regard him as highly intelligent, while others consider him a dolt. Many find him ethical and honorable, while some view him as "smilingly amoral."

Whether pro or con, so intense is the reaction Dole inspires that one wonders whether the man truly has a bright side and a dark side. Joseph Rauh, the dean of the Washington civil rights lobbyists, referred to Dole as "almost Jekyll-Hyde," and right-wing guru Paul Weyrich described the change in Dole's voting pattern after 1985 as "overwhelming . . . almost impossible to describe." Though these two men were referring to his behavior in Congress, their comments of necessity shed light on Dole's character. What sort of man would be able to elicit such extreme comments from men at opposite ends of the political spectrum?

Whether Dole is *now* an active positive or active negative personality or some kind of amalgam of the two must ultimately be

---

[3]Barber believes that every president's predominant character traits place him squarely in one of the four classes but that he may lean toward a second class and that when a president confronts a crisis his predominant class traits will most likely emerge and determine his conduct.

On February 4, 1988, for example, just four days before the crucial Iowa caucuses, Dole suddenly cast off his mask of low-key benevolence and angrily confronted archrival George Bush face to face on the Senate floor. Waving an anti-Dole campaign flyer in the vice president's face, a livid Dole demanded that Bush apologize. (Bush refused.)

judged by the reader. My personal opinion is that he is indeed a combination of the two and that he tends to oscillate between them, depending on the circumstances he encounters from day to day.[3] Dole is a man who likes to struggle against long odds so that he can continually prove to himself that he is in fact superior to all the competition. Because of this chronic need to compete and win, he tends to place himself in crisis situations calling for great personal exertion and stamina. It is almost certain that he would be a very active president, fiercely determined to meet his self-imposed goals, to achieve for the sake of personal achievement, eager to leave his mark on the country ánd the institution of the presidency. He has identified the budget deficit as "Public Enemy Number One" and would no doubt set deficit-erasing as a primary personal goal, striving to attain it with all the fiery determination of the star athlete he once aspired to become.

Because Dole has displayed active negative traits throughout his life, however, he may, like his former idol Richard Nixon, fall victim to flaws that have destroyed other active negative presidents. "These guys tend to compulsive rigidification in support of a losing public policy," Barber said in discussing active negatives in general. "They often cling to a doomed policy long after its futility has been revealed." Examples of this type of behavior would include Lyndon Johnson's clinging to his fatally flawed Vietnam war policy, Nixon's stubborn stonewalling on Watergate, Herbert Hoover's adamant policy against relief programs and his fiscal niggardliness during the Great Depression, and Woodrow Wilson's equally stubborn and doomed policy of trying to force the League of Nations on America while ignoring the concerns of the senators who ultimately passed judgment on it.

"The critical question for a presidential candidate," Barber explained, "is whether he has demonstrated such a pattern of behavior in his career." Robert Dole certainly has done so. In 1980, for example, he clung to his hopeless presidential campaign long beyond the time when its futility was clear to everyone around him. He nearly wrecked his Senate career, weakened his power base in Kansas, and came within a deuce of not seeking reelection because, for personal reasons, he could not abandon his presidential quest. There is a compulsive, driven quality in Dole that manifests itself in his stubborn persistence in following everything through to completion, in dotting every *I* and crossing every *T*, in campaigning in every single city and shaking the hand of every single voter to be absolutely sure that he has done everything possible to win. Dole's thoroughness is an admirable quality, unless taken to the point where he might become blinded to the practical realities of the situation.

Though Dole is undeniably a compulsive super-achiever driven by a personal ambition that soars far above that of most men, I believe that he lives by a sound moral code that sometimes may serve to check that ambition. Unlike Johnson and Nixon, who trampled over people in their quest for power, Dole has a streak of compassion for those struggling against an indifferent or harsh Establishment and would probably think carefully before adopting a presidential policy that might inflict pain on people he does not see as rivals or threats.

If there is anything consistent about Dole's public rhetoric over the past ten years, it is his call for opening up the party to the outcasts, the poor and the minorities who have traditionally been Democratic voters. He has criticized the GOP for being "too much a country club set," and his criticism has come straight from the heart. Yet, as his longtime friend Russell Townsley says, "Dole is not a social reformer . . . he's not a bleeding-heart liberal."

Dole's concern for the poor and the powerless is an essential ingredient in his world view, the second major category by which Barber judges presidents. A president's world view, i.e., his way of looking at society in positive or negative terms and his conviction as to whether the world should be changed or left alone, is a very important ingredient in determining his actions as the most powerful man in the world. Bob Dole has demonstrated overwhelmingly that he sees the world as based on an unfair pecking order in which some men, like George Bush and the Kennedys, are born with a golden spoon in their mouths while others less fortunate are left to struggle for survival. He started out in life as a man without the advantage of powerful connections, without much money, and without even the praise and affection a child expects from his father.

Dole's ceaseless activity, his dogged perseverance, and his obsession with becoming president all derive from his perpetual quest for the adoration and praise he rarely received at home and from his struggle to overcome his war injuries which left him with the question "Why me?" His view of the world as an unfair and dangerous place has made him eternally vigilant. Like Sisyphus in Greek legend, Bob is a man who must struggle perpetually to roll uphill the huge stone of achievement, yet is destined never to reach the top in his own eyes. For Dole, each triumph calls forth only greater challenge. Each achievement necessarily pales in comparison to the next challenge. As he once told me, "Life is a downward-moving escalator . . . if you don't keep moving up, you go down." It is this perpetual lack of satisfaction that makes him intolerant of the shortcomings of others.

Phyllis, his first wife, recalls that Bob would often come home and criticize his aides for their failure to work as hard as he did and to meet his impossibly high standards. "I told him, 'Bob, you have to realize that your goals are not their goals; your interests are not their interests; so you can't expect them to work as hard as you,' " Phyllis has said. Her words fell on deaf ears, though. Virtually every staffer who has worked with Dole, including the author, has testified to the man's relentless drive and lack of satisfaction with his own and his staffers' output. He is never satisfied, no matter how well performed the task. Like his father, the highest praise Bob can give is, "Not bad—not good, but not bad."

How would Dole's view of life as unfair affect his performance in the White House? As president, Dole would never be satisfied with results under any circumstances and would rely heavily on himself to achieve success in times of crisis. Because he is pessimistic and cynical by nature, he is not likely to underestimate dangers or to discount the strength of an adversary. In negotiating with the USSR, for instance, he would probably be super-vigilant and suspicious of Soviet intentions and skeptical about the value of treaties, yet he would probably seek "verifiable" arms control treaties in order to boost his public image.

Dole's view of the world has also made him extremely self-reliant. And that self-reliance, impressive as it is, may prove to be a double-edged sword. Like Jimmy Carter, as president he would probably immerse himself in the details of everything he approached—a style that could lead to fatigue or burnout.

For Dole cannot relax. He feels uncomfortable "wasting time." Like his father, who never took time off from work, Bob is a human perpetual-motion machine. Indeed, there is something disturbingly machinelike and emotionally cold about him that has bothered many people. In dealing with staff and associates, he comes across as militarily stiff and straitlaced, a man who hides behind his work to avoid human contact. When I worked with him, he never invited his staff to his apartment and rarely attended parties or other social affairs. Because of his icy temperament, he was even called "the Aya-Dole-Ah" by his staff.

Dole's aloofness manifests itself in his curious and frequent use of the second person or the first-person plural when referring to himself or discussing a subject he considers sensitive or painful. His speech is filled with words like *you, we, our,* and *us,* when he should be saying *I, me,* and *my.* When I used to write speeches for him, I was struck by how often he changed *I* to *we* or *the Senator from Kansas* even on the Senate floor.

The detachment and depersonalization revealed by that eccentricity of speech can be chilling. Dole has always been uncomfortable around people, particularly unfamiliar people. I was always struck by his inability to make direct eye contact, his tendency to wander off and ramble incoherently in conversation, and his unease when forced to deal with people on a one-to-one basis.

His ex-wife has said that Dole always had a difficult time communicating with her. "He doesn't like to argue on a one-to-one basis," Phyllis has said. "He's not a mean person. . . . He often does favors for people and doesn't even let them know it." Yet, in divorcing her, Dole characteristically walked in one day out of the blue and announced he wanted out. End of discussion.

Dole's inability to communicate and display emotion has sobering implications for his presidency. As Theodore Roosevelt once said, the presidency is largely "a bully pulpit," a rostrum from which the president can speak out to the American people and the free world, and successful presidents have invariably been great speakers, able to inspire trust and confidence through the spoken word. Indeed, in the age of television *charisma* is virtually synonymous with public speaking and communicative ability.

Despite the counseling of Dorothy Sarnoff, Bob Dole is still not a very good speaker. Indeed, he is a rather poor public speaker whose delivery is somewhat inelegant and whose voice is as flat as the Kansas plains. Because of his difficulties in expressing emotion, his speeches sound uninspired. He appeals to the head instead of the heart. Moreover, the content of the typical Dole speech is often negative or pessimistic—a critique of the shortcomings of the party or the government or his rivals, winding up with a call for austerity and bitter medicine.

Most successful American presidents—Reagan, Roosevelt, and Kennedy, for example—have been able to communicate a positive message of hope and optimism in their rhetoric, their style. Poor communicators, like Johnson, Nixon, and Carter, on the other hand, have generally been unsuccessful and unpopular presidents.

Rhetoric is an essential ingredient of a president's style, as Barber has pointed out. But rhetoric is more than a matter of style; in the final analysis, it is the window that lets the people glimpse the true soul and character of a president. It is an essential bridge between leader and masses. Dole's public image as crafted by his own rhetoric will inevitably determine whether the American people trust and like him, and his effectiveness as a communicator will ultimately determine the success or failure of his presidency.

Should Dole enter the White house in January 1989, he will have to make some hard public-policy choices that will necessarily offend many people, of either the right or the left or both. The question is: How effective and humane will he be in bringing about the belt-tightening he feels is so sorely needed to rectify the record budget deficit, trade deficit, and national debt, and other economic woes created during Reagan's eight years?

Apart from gargantuan economic problems, the next president can expect to confront a formidable set of foreign policy problems, particularly calls from the right wing to intervene militarily in Nicaragua and El Salvador's civil wars, potential Vietnam-type conflicts posing leftists against rightists and, therefore, in the eyes of the right wing, freedom versus communism.

If he is elected, Dole will face pressure from his right-wing backers to send U.S. troops into combat in Central America and elsewhere. He has already gone on record as favoring military aid for the Nicaraguan contra rebels, whom he has called "the freedom fighters," and has denounced the Sandinista government. On the

Senate floor he has been a staunch supporter of aid to the contra rebels since 1985, though he has stopped short of blatantly calling for the overthrow of Ortega's regime. When he visited Nicaragua in August 1987 and "debated" against Sandinista president Daniel Ortega, he immediately denounced the debate as a propaganda ploy and showed little interest in negotiation or discussion.[4]

Dole's tendency to personalize all conflicts could have momentous implications for foreign relations if he were to become president. Because he cannot stand to lose at anything, and because he would probably see foreign opposition to U.S. policies as a personal competitive attack by foreign leaders, he might well react aggressively, as he has to challenges from other senators and politicians within the United States.

And Dole's tendency to exhibit his nasty wit could be divisive. An indiscreet barb or two could wreak havoc on foreign relations. Inappropriate jokes could end up alienating various segments of the U.S. population as well.

Because Dole is such a pragmatic politician and has shown such an ideological nimbleness in order to attract votes and support from various factions whose causes he does not truly embrace, we have cause to wonder how he would perform as commander in chief.

Like Lyndon Johnson, Dole is the type of politician who, in the words of his old Kansas rival Norbert Dreiling, "always accurately reflects the views of the constituency he happens to represent." If the ideology of that constituency is reactionary, or if Dole perceives it to be reactionary (as he did in the 1960s), he will act and vote in a manner consistent with it, in order to be liked, in the words of John Woelk, the Russell Republican who recruited him to run for his first legislative office in 1950. If Dole "still doesn't know if he's a liberal or a conservative as he didn't know in 1950," as Woelk recently said, and if he always waits to see "which way the political wind is blowing," as Kansas's junior senator Nancy Kassebaum recently remarked, he could find himself pursuing presidential policies that he does not really believe in, just to win support from

---

[4]Dole is a master at trimming his public rhetoric on this subject. When interviewed by anti-contra journalists, he has been restrained, careful to stop short of calling for Ortega's overthrow; when addressing right-wing audiences, he has been more bellicose, more outspokenly against Ortega.

powerful politicians and other entities whose goodwill he needs in order to secure passage of his other programs and to get reelected in 1992.

Since Dole is a legislative creature by nature and training, it is difficult to predict his performance in the executive capacity of president. On the one hand, such a president may be the embodiment of the theory that American democracy is based on electing leaders who accurately reflect the opinions and desires of their constituents, rather than elitist leaders who do as they please because of their supposedly superior abilities to gauge the public good. On the other hand, Dole's protean pattern of zigzagging from position to position could get out of hand unless it is checked by a sound set of values, a sort of bottom-line group of deep-seated beliefs that will give his seemingly rudderless boat a sense of ballast and direction.

Whether and to what extent Dole has genuine deep-seated beliefs, and to what extent he is prepared to risk or sacrifice his personal career interests in order to stand up for them, is an open question. Certainly, his record is not entirely encouraging. In 1986, for example, Dole shocked and infuriated black people everywhere by supporting President Reagan's veto of a bill imposing sanctions on South Africa as a protest against apartheid. His action reminded voters of former civil rights leader Roy Wilkins's denunciation of the Kansan in 1976 as "an enemy of blacks" and made people wonder whether he had any real beliefs on racism at all.[5]

While Dole's eclectic pragmatism has led him to embrace contradictory and sometimes unpopular policies, he has an open mind that, if somewhat superficial and intuitive, is rather like a sponge, capable of soaking up ideas from all sides if he feels those ideas will ultimately help him win an election or achieve a goal. This quality is likely to make him an effective president.

As Senate Finance Committee chairman and majority leader in the 1980s, he became a good dealmaker and legislative craftsman precisely *because* he did not approach issues with a clear agenda of his own. As president, he would be able to use this talent and

---

[5]Dole explained his support of the veto by saying (that as majority leader) he was obligated to support the president and that he was for it because the Senate had defied Reagan on just one point, which had precipitated the veto.

character trait and would probably do well in working with Congress in compromising on bills.

In this regard, Dole would contrast starkly with Reagan, whose presidency has been flawed in its terminal years by his stubborn resistance to compromise with Congress on most issues, ranging from the budget to defense. In general, Dole would be far more willing to compromise.

On the other hand, because of his active negative streak, Dole might well show a stubborn unwillingness to bend if he felt challenged or threatened by his foes and rivals or if he encountered a crisis situation in which he felt personally tested. We cannot predict which side of Dole would prevail in a given situation, but in most run-of-the-mill, day-to-day matters involving relations between Congress and the president, Dole would probably prove a very able negotiator and compromiser—unless his temper is so aroused that he antagonizes congressmen and senators he's dealing with.

Finally, Dole's presidential style will be colored by his independent streak. "Dole's an independent cuss," said Washington lobbyist Tom Korologos. "He will do what he thinks is right, and damn the torpedoes." This assessment of the Kansan is quite accurate, as many a lobbyist has found out. On the other hand, Dole has come under fire for allegedly showing favoritism toward heavy campaign contributors, lobbyists, and cronies and has led a Senate filibuster against the campaign finance reform bill that would have limited campaign spending. He has been accused of cronyism and of sponsoring legislation in order to benefit his friends as well.

Would Dole, despite his independent streak, turn into a mere power broker for special-interest groups? Would a President Dole prove the accuracy of his first congressional opponent's charge that he is the candidate of the special interests?

Probably not. Because he ultimately resents Big Money and its efforts to control his conduct, Dole would probably stand as a bulwark against the corrosive influence of special-interest groups and PACs if he had the powers of the presidency behind him. When I worked for him, I was favorably impressed by his independent attitude of "Take their money and screw 'em" and by his resentment of lobbyists' efforts at arm twisting. He has come to share his wife's identification with consumers and the common man as opposed to big business. And he began his 1988 presidential campaign in Iowa by running on the slogan "Bob Dole—He's One of Us"—that is, one of the common people, in contrast to rival George Bush's patrician sentiments and background.

A President Dole would probably make it a priority to establish himself as independent of the special-interest groups in the name of acting as his own man in the White House. He would probably try to revamp the Republican Party's image along populist lines in order to stamp his own personal, lasting mark on the party and on history. Strong rhetoric and action against special interests, such as he displayed when ramrodding TEFRA through Congress in 1982, might become his trademark.

Dole's attitude toward special interests might well become a major part of his "populist" public image, as revealed in the press. He might seek to establish himself as Mr. Independent early in his administration, quite possibly by taking on the special interests as a way of proving his sincerity in opening up the Republican Party to blacks, poor people, and other outsiders. He might well evince genuine idealism if he pursues his avowed populist goal to its logical limit—*and* if he strikes a positive relationship with the press. Ultimately, the press's attitude toward his presidency will play a major role in determining its success or failure. And no one knows this better than Bob Dole.

According to Barber, a president's relationship with the press is a crucial ingredient in the effectiveness of his style. Active negative presidents, such as Johnson and Nixon, have tended to resent and distrust the press and have adopted secrecy as a national policy. They have tried to manage the news by offering favored reporters a highly biased and incomplete account of their activities, thereby engendering much distrust and bitterness with the Fourth Estate. Ultimately, Johnson and Nixon failed because they came to see the press as an enemy and turned reporters into detectives ferreting out the "negative" information denied them by the White House itself.

No president today can manage the news—as much as he might like to—but the ability to handle sharp questions with skill and a touch of humor is an enormous advantage. Though often highly quotable for his acerbic wit, Dole has never enjoyed an easy relationship with reporters and regards the press with hostility and suspicion. A man with an insatiable appetite for publicity, Dole is also acutely sensitive to criticism. He resents the press for ignoring him and is furious when they write unfavorable stories about him. When I was working on his staff, he definitely had favored and disfavored reporters and bore a lasting grudge against any journalist whom he considered unfriendly.

One member of the press, a Washington bureau reporter who has covered Dole more closely than any other reporter in recent years and has written articles critical of Dole, told me in December 1987 that Dole has often shut him out and denied him access as a way of punishing him. Just as he tends to personalize his conflicts with foreign and domestic foes, Dole tends to personalize his relations toward the press. If you are a reporter, you are either for him or against him. This reporter, by the way, requested anonymity in this book.

Another reporter, who also requested anonymity, wrote a widely read feature story on Dole that was critical in general. That reporter told me that Dole had been "leaning on" some of the people who had spoken to him. "He's a vindictive guy," the reporter added.[6]

And, reportedly, after the appearance of the *New York Times Magazine* article including Senator Nancy Kassebaum's barb about Dole's tendency to sail in the direction of the political winds, Dole called in an aide to Kassebaum for a verbal thrashing over the article. Then Kassebaum herself wrote a letter to the *Times* claiming she had been quoted out of context.

Dole's acute sensitivity to press criticism is evidenced also by the fact that many of his present and former aides declined to be interviewed for this book or would talk only on condition that I not reveal their names in print, because they feared Dole's retaliation. Dole himself did not respond to my numerous requests for an interview, and his spokespersons similarly refused to respond.

Apart from shutting out reporters deemed to be critical of him, Dole spends enormous effort making certain that he gets positive press. Being a perfectionist obsessed with his public image, Dole

---

[6]The fear Dole inspires in his colleagues is one secret to his power in the Senate and would contribute to his effectiveness in the White House as well. People know that he plays hardball.

often insisted when I worked with him that his press releases and articles for print be rewritten over and over again, ten or twelve times on occasion, so that they would sound just right. His constant anxiety about adverse publicity derives not only from his long-standing distrust of reporters but also from his innate fear of failure. Because he cannot stand to lose, and because he always plays to win, Dole seeks to control every story about his office and his campaigns.

This tendency to control the tone and content of press accounts was graphically illustrated by his relationship with the reporters and editors of *Cosmopolitan* magazine. In January 1986, *Cosmopolitan* printed a glowingly positive article about Dole and his wife, Elizabeth. The article had a fairy-tale, "perfect couple" quality about it, slathering praise on the Doles and recommending them to the country as the perfect dual-career couple. The article was not unique by any means in its praise of the power couple. Ever since the resurrection of Bob's image in 1981, "Bob and Liddy" articles have appeared in numerous magazines, featuring the inevitable interviews and photographs of the couple. Invariably, such articles comment uncritically on Bob's remarkable mellowing since his marriage to Elizabeth Hanford and slavishly praise the eternally smiling and genteel Mrs. Dole as the driving force behind her husband's metamorphosis.

The fairy-tale articles seem awfully good until one learns something about their genesis. In the case of the *Cosmopolitan* article, editor Helen Gurley Brown later revealed that the Doles had demanded to see the manuscript of the article before it was published. When she showed it to them, they vociferously objected to the inclusion of statements that "rumors are all over the Hill" that "the marriage is shaky."

"I have never, ever had so much concern on the part of an interviewed person," Brown later complained. "They were just crazed with anxiety," claiming that the article was filled with "inaccuracies." *Cosmopolitan* yielded and permitted the Doles to delete offending passages before the article was printed.

If the *Cosmopolitan* incident is a harbinger of President Dole's press policy, trouble could lie ahead. Reporters are notoriously independent-minded and resent any efforts by a president to control or limit what they say in print or on the air. They are not likely to give Dole a veto over their stories, and they are bound to resent any efforts he may make to shut out their critical colleagues and to control the news.

Like his combative and sometimes manipulative attitude toward the press, Dole's attitude toward life in general may well be summarized by the phrase "I fight; therefore, I am." In the final analysis, Bob Dole is a man who literally lives to fight. His obsession with the tactics of fighting to get a bill passed in the Senate or to win an election is truly phenomenal. He is a man who revels in a good fight, who is always thinking of all the angles necessary to win, and who is a very sore loser. Even Vince Lombardi's motto, "Winning isn't everything; it's the only thing," is far too mild to describe the intensity of Dole's drive. Because he is a man who always plays to win and who always plays for keeps, he has the potential to become one of the truly great presidents. On the other hand, because his character has revealed some active negative traits, he also has the potential to wrap himself stubbornly around a truly flawed policy and to become a very unpopular president. His ultimate fate will depend on the extent to which he permits his brighter side to prevail over his darker side. And that, ultimately, will depend on the nature of the challenges and crises he confronts as president.

While we cannot divine the future, we can safely predict that Bob Dole's presidency would reflect his personality to the hilt. History may yet deny him the greatness he so craves, but it cannot relegate him to the status of a footnote. Because Dole has such an overpowering desire to become truly great, and because the fiery engine burning inside him is constantly working at 110 percent capacity, Dole seems destined to make his mark on history. Whether the final judgment is negative or positive, the one thing we can be sure of is that Dole would not become an asterisk president. He would be a hands-on leader, very much in charge of everything going on around him in the government. Following the detached, hands-off style of Reagan's presidency that has brought about the Iran-contra scandal and the worst deficits in American history, the American people may be looking for a hands-on, take-charge president. If so, Dole, with his fierce drive to achieve greatness, may well be their man.

# CHRONOLOGY

1923:  Born on July 23 in Russell, Kansas. Oil discovered in Russell County on Thanksgiving Day.

1929:  Stock Market crashes on October 29, ushering in the Great Depression. Dole attends public schools in Russell.

1930's:  Dole family rents top floor of its house to oil companies and moves to the basement. Bob enters Russell High School, stars in basketball, football, and track. Dust Bowl and Depression rack Kansas.

1941:  Graduates from Russell High School and enters the University of Kansas at Lawrence, joins fraternity, waits tables, and participates in athletics.

1942:  Enlists in U.S. Army in December.

1943:  Called to active army duty in June.

1944:  Trains with army, enters Officer Candidate School, and is assigned to Rome, Italy, in December as a second lieutenant.

1945:  Assigned to the army's elite Tenth Mountain Division in northern Italy in February, is wounded slightly in March, and sustains severe injury to his right arm, shoulder, and spine while attacking German position on Hill 913 in Po Valley on April 14. Dole is hospitalized in Italy and shipped back to Kansas in a body cast, is admitted to Winter General Army Hospital in Topeka, Kansas, and transferred in November to Percy Jones Army Medical Center in Battle Creek, Michigan. Dole loses a kidney and sustains severe infection at hospital, nearly loses his life twice in the hospitals.

1947:  Receives operation in Chicago on his right arm and shoulder, using $1,800 raised by citizens of Russell for hospital fees.

1948:  Marries Phyllis Holden in June, is discharged from the army, and enters the University of Arizona in the fall.

261

1949:   Transfers to Washburn Municipal University in Topeka, Kansas, seeking both an undergraduate and a law degree.

1950:   Runs for a seat in the Kansas House of Representatives, while still a student, and wins his first public election.

1952:   Graduates from Washburn University and is elected Russell county attorney.

1953–60:   Serves as Russell county attorney, builds up his personal political base, and gains the support of the Alf Landon machine old-boy network of GOP power brokers.

1960:   Elected to Congress in November.

1961–68:   Serves in Congress as a conservative, championing agriculture and opposing most of the Great Society programs.

1968:   Elected to the U.S. Senate in November.

1969–72:   In the Senate, Dole is a fanatical defender of President Nixon, lashing out at Nixon's critics.

1971:   Selected by President Nixon to serve as Republican national chairman, having earned a reputation as Nixon's "Doberman pinscher" on the Senate floor.

1972:   Divorces wife Phyllis in January and is fired by Nixon as GOP national chairman in December.

1974:   Plagued by Watergate fallout and narrowly defeats Bill Roy in his Senate reelection bid in November.

1975:   Marries Elizabeth Hanford in December.

1976:   Nominated as GOP vice presidential candidate in August, earns reputation as "hatchet man" during campaign, and Ford-Dole ticket is defeated in November by Carter-Mondale ticket.

1979–80:   Mounts unsuccessful, quixotic campaign for 1980 GOP presidential campaign, finishes in last place in Iowa caucuses and New Hampshire primary, drops out of race in March 1980 and wins reelection to Senate in November. Republicans win control of Senate and Reagan wins presidency in November.

1981:   Dole becomes Senate Finance Committee chairman, shepherds through Senate Reagan's massive tax-cut legislation (ERTA), while Elizabeth Dole becomes a Reagan White House assistant.

1982:   Pushes through Senate a massive tax-raising bill (TEFRA) that raises nearly $100 billion in revenue.

1983:   Elizabeth Dole is appointed U.S. secretary of transportation by Reagan in January.

1984:   Elected Senate majority leader in November.

1985–86:   Serves as Senate majority leader until GOP loses control of Senate in November, when Dole is elected Senate minority leader.

1987–88:   Mounts campaign for 1988 Republican presidential nomination while simultaneously serving as Senate minority leader. Elizabeth Dole resigns her cabinet post in September 1987 in order to campaign for her husband.

# NOTES

### Chapter 1: BOB DOLE AND THE AMERICAN DREAM

Page 1.   **"Jekyll-Hyde" figure:** Joseph Rauh, quoted in Thomas B. Edsall, "Dole's Transformations," *Washington Post*, March 9, 1987.

Page 1.   **a disaster:** Richard Viguerie, quoted in *Wichita Eagle-Beacon*, November 29, 1985.

Page 1.   **"the Zelig of American politics":** William Schneider, "The Republicans '88," *The Atlantic Monthly*, July 1987.

Page 2.   **climb all the rungs on the ladder of success:** Dole frequently used the image of a ladder of success in my presence and in speeches before groups, including a nationally televised debate with his GOP rivals on October 28, 1987, on "Firing Line," broadcast on PBS.

Page 3.   **"hatchet man":** Nationally televised vice presidential debate, October 15, 1976, in Houston, Texas.

Page 5.   **"contradictory character":** Howard Fineman, "The Contradictory Character of Bob Dole," *Newsweek*, November 16, 1987.

Page 5.   **"contradictions":** Martin Tolchin and Jeff Gerth, "The Contradictions of Bob Dole," *New York Times Magazine*, November 8, 1987.

Page 5.   **"lack of clear vision":** "Dole Buries the Hatchet," *Time*, November 16, 1987.

Page 5.   **"unguided missile":** Lyn Nofziger, quoted in Jules Witcover, *Marathon: The Pursuit of the Presidency 1972–1976* (New York: Viking Press, 1977), 613.

Page 7.   **"To make a difference"** . . . **"greater opportunity":** "The MacNeil/Lehrer NewsHour," broadcast on PBS November 9, 1987.

### Chapter 2: BOB DOLE COUNTRY, U.S.A.

Page 11.   **"gritty prairie values":** Laurent Belsie, "Robert Dole," Part 5 of a series on 1988 presidential candidates, *Christian Science Monitor*, January 15, 1988.

Page 11.   **Dean Banker:** Personal interview.

Page 12.   **Kenny Dole:** Personal interview.

Page 12.   **The population:** According to personal interview with Russell Townsley.

Page 13.   **Gloria recalls:** Personal interview with Gloria Dole.

Page 14.   **Bub Dawson recalls:** Personal interview.

Page 14.   **"He didn't give out praise":** Personal interview with Gloria Dole.

Page 15.   **"my father in his overalls":** Statement by Dole on "Firing Line," broadcast on PBS-TV October 28, 1987.

Page 18. **Russell Townsley:** Personal interview.

Page 18. **"Poverty is a relative thing":** David Frost's interview with Bob Dole on ABC-TV's "The Next President," January 3, 1988.

Page 18. **John Woelk:** Personal interview.

Page 20. **"Wall Street owns the country . . .":** Mary Elizabeth Lease, quoted in Margaret Canovan, *Populism* (New York: Harcourt Brace Jovanovich, 1981), 33.

Page 20. **"hard to get to close to":** According to Bub Dawson, "From the Pages of the Presidential Yearbooks," *USA Today*, December 24, 1987.

Page 21. **Harold Elliott:** "The Dole Decision," *Time*, August 30, 1976. Elliott died in 1985 at the age of seventy-five.

Page 21. **George Baxter:** Personal interview.

Page 22. **"The Dawson brothers, Chet and Bub . . .":** ABC-TV's "The Next President."

Page 23. **Alice Mills:** Quoted in Irene H. Jepsen, "Alice Mills Reports Bob Dole Good Student," *Russell Record*, November 5, 1987.

Page 23. **Mabel Lacey:** Quoted in Irene H. Jepsen, "He Was There to Learn What Was Before Him," *Russell Record*, November 5, 1987. In 1986, Lacey was inducted into the Kansas Teachers Hall of Fame in Dodge City upon the recommendation of Dole.

Page 23. **Faith Dumler:** Quoted in Irene H. Jepsen, "Dole Good Person, Leader in School," *Russell Record*, November 5, 1987.

Page 23. **"When he started using that wit . . .":** Personal interview with Phyllis Holden Dole Macey.

Page 24. **"I must have done something wrong":** Martin Tolchin and Jeff Gerth, "The Contradictions of Bob Dole," *New York Times Magazine*, November 8, 1987.

Page 25. **"I wasn't quite the athlete I thought I was":** ABC-TV's "The Next President."

### Chapter 3: "THAT DAMNED ARMY ALMOST KILLED HIM"

Page 28. **"King Franklin":** FDR was frequently referred to as "King Franklin" by many people in Russell in the 1930s, according to Dean Banker. Personal interview.

Page 28. **"roof over my head and a floor under my feet":** Personal statement by Bob Dole.

Page 29. **"You're not doing very well . . .":** According to David Frost's interview with Dole on ABC-TV's "The Next President," January 3, 1988.

Page 29. **convinced that they would be drafted:** Personal interview with Kenny Dole.

Page 31. **"the real cannon fodder of World War II":** Personal interview with Al Nencioni.

Page 31. **Tenth Mountain Division:** Information in this chapter about Dole's experiences with the Tenth Mountain Division comes from personal interviews with Walt Galson, Devereaux Jennings, and Al Nencioni. All quotes of Galson, Jennings, and Nencioni from personal interviews.

Page 35. **"raw anger" and a "protective instinct":** Frank Carafa quoted in Bob and Elizabeth Dole, with Richard Norton Smith, *The Doles: Unlimited Partners* (New York: Simon and Schuster, 1988), 44.

Page 36. **his dog, his parents, and childhood friends:** Doles and Smith, *The Doles: Unlimited Partners*, 45.

Page 37. **"Jesus was with us that night":** Lew Ferguson, "Veteran Recalls Helping to Save Sen. Dole's Life," *Topeka Capital-Journal*, October 18, 1984.

Page 37. **"like furniture in a crate":** Dole's remark to the author in 1980.

Page 37. **"out of Dachau":** Personal interview with Bub Dawson, in the presence of Kenny Dole.

Page 38. **"That damn army almost killed him":** Personal interview with Bub Dawson, in the presence of Kenny Dole.

Page 39. **"why did I have to get hit?":** ABC-TV's "The Next President."

Page 39. **"completely helpless":** Personal statement by Bob Dole.

Page 39. **still has trouble looking in the mirror:** Doles and Smith, *The Doles: Unlimited Partners*, 47.

Page 39. **"get back the ten years I lost":** According to personal interview with Kenny Dole.

Page 41. **Humor became his antidote:** Doles and Smith, *The Doles: Unlimited Partners*, 50.

Page 41. **"He just can't stop . . .":** Personal interview with Kenny Dole.

Page 44. **telegram:** Myra MacPherson, *The Power Lovers* (New York: Putnam, 1975), 225.
Page 44. **"little red Chevrolet":** Personal interview with Kenny Dole.

## Chapter 4: THE MAN WITH THE WITHERED ARM

Page 45. **"You think nobody could have it worse . . .":** Gail Sheehy, "The Whole Robert Dole," *Vanity Fair*, April 1987.
Page 46. **"You have to make a decision":** This is one of Dole's favorite phrases. He used it when explaining his sudden decision to divorce Phyllis in 1972.
Page 46. **the "Little Man" from Independence:** Personal comment by Robert Dole.
Page 47. **A bare three months after meeting:** Personal interview with Phyllis Holden Dole Macey. Many facts and all quotations in this section are based on a personal interview with Phyllis.
Page 50. **John Woelk:** Quotations and information from personal interview with John C. Woelk and from James M. Perry: "Ferocious Ambition Drives Political Junkie Dole, But Candidate Lacks Carefully Fixed Philosophy," *Wall Street Journal*, September 25, 1987.
Page 51. **"As John Woelk told me . . .":** Dole on ABC-TV's "The Next President," January 3, 1988.
Page 52. **"selling pencils on the street corner":** Sheehy, "The Whole Robert Dole."
Page 52. **2,576 to 1,805 votes:** According to personal interview with Russell Townsley.
Page 52. **"only three months of each year":** Personal interview with Phyllis.
Page 52. **"do-nothing, part-time debating club":** According to personal interview with Russell Townsley.
Page 53. **Eric "Doc" Smith:** Quoted in Gene Murray, "Sen. Bob Dole . . . a Long Way from Russell, Kan.," *Kansas City Star*, September 24, 1972.
Page 53. **John Woelk recalls:** Personal interview.
Page 53. **"The tailor would mumble . . .":** Personal interview with Dean Banker.
Page 54. **"Probably the most important thing I did":** Don McLeod, "The Grass Roots Senator Who Never Left Kansas," *Washington Times Insight* magazine, June 1, 1987.
Page 55. **"maybe a little too independent for my own good":** McLeod, "The Grass Roots Senator."

## Chapter 5: A LIGHT BURNING LATE AT NIGHT

Page 57. **John Woelk:** Personal interview.
Page 58. **Bob Earnest:** Personal interview. Earnest and Dole have remained close and Earnest says he advised Dole to "be a statesman" after his abortive 1976 vice presidential campaign. His advice was heeded, he says, and he takes credit for helping transform Dole's image into a mellower, more positive one since 1976.
Page 58. **"less than the janitor made":** Quoted in Irene H. Jepsen, " 'Cause I Like Him,' former Sheriff says," *Russell Record*, November 5, 1987. According to Russell Townsley, this was probably a slight exaggeration.
Page 59. **Dean Banker:** Personal interview.
Page 59. **Judge C. E. "Ben" Birney:** Personal interview. Judge Birney retired from the bench in 1978 and lives in Hill City, Kansas. As a lawyer, Dole often appeared before him in the 1950s. "He was a brilliant conversationalist and very respectful," Birney says of Dole.
Page 59. **John Woelk:** Personal interview.
Page 60. **Bub Dawson:** Personal interview.
Page 61. **Russell Townsley:** Personal interview.
Page 61. **three thousand oil wells:** These statistics were compiled by Russell Townsley.
Page 62. **an opinion:** Kansas Supreme Court opinion, reported in Vol. 182, *Kansas Supreme Court Reports*, 437–38, January 30, 1958. The unconstitutional statute levied and imposed "an annual privilege tax upon every person engaging or continuing within this state in the business of producing, or severing oil or gas from the soil or water for sale, transport, storage, profit, or for commercial use. The amount of such tax shall be measured by the value of the oil and gas produced, and shall be levied and assessed at

the rate of one percent (1%) thereof at the point of production."

The *quo warranto* action was technically brought "by the state of Kansas on the relation of" Dole and the other county attorneys, but Dole was the driving force behind it.

Page 62.   **John Woelk:** Personal interview.

Page 63.   **Holland's mother:** "Dole, Physical Therapist Meet and Get Married," *Russell Record,* November 5, 1987.

Page 65.   **Dole "just took over":** Personal interview with Norbert Dreiling.

Page 65.   **"Bob channeled his competitive energies":** Personal interview with Bob Earnest.

Page 65.   **Harry Morgenstern:** Jepsen, " 'Cause I Like Him,' Former Sheriff Says."

Page 65.   **abused and neglected children:** Dole described his activities relating to this issue in a nationally televised interview with David Frost on ABC-TV's "The Next President," January 3, 1988.

### Chapter 6: "SOMEWHERE TO THE RIGHT OF GENGHIS KHAN"

Page 67.   **the right man to succeed him:** According to personal interview with Russell Townsley.

Page 68.   **anti-communist as well as anti-Kennedy sentiment:** According to a personal interview with Norbert Dreiling.

Page 68.   **Mary Humes:** Quoted in John Marshall, "The Most Influential Kansan," *Hutchinson News,* June 1, 1986.

Page 68.   **"the candidate of the special interests":** "Davis Says Dole Is Wint Smith's 'Fair-Haired Boy,' " *Wichita Eagle-Beacon,* November 6, 1960.

Page 69.   **Bob's brother Kenny recalls:** Personal interview with Kenny Dole.

Page 69.   **bringing booze into a church:** This story is from a personal interview with Jim Parrish, now Kansas state Democratic Party chairman. The alcohol issue was also mentioned in Martin Tolchin and Jeff Gerth, "The Contradictions of Bob Dole," *New York Times Magazine,* November 8, 1987.

Page 71.   **the many interviews he gives to the media:** See, for example, David Frost's interview with Dole, ABC-TV's "The Next President," January 3, 1988; Gail Sheehy, "The Whole Robert Dole," *Vanity Fair,* April 1987; Kandy Stroud, "Robert and Elizabeth Dole: America's No. 1 Power Couple," *Cosmopolitan* January 1986.

Page 71.   **The Bobolinks began:** Personal interview with Dorothy Voss Beecher and Phyllis Dole Macey.

Page 74.   **Garner Shriver:** Personal interview.

Page 74.   **Larry Winn:** Personal interview.

Page 76.   **sent his wife and daughter home:** According to personal interview with Phyllis Dole Macey.

Page 76.   **"It is hard to justify fighting communism":** *Congressional Record,* November 6, 1963, 21189–21190.

Page 76.   **make a speech on the House floor:** *Congressional Record,* December 5, 1963, 23473.

Page 77.   **"Bork is a jerk":** Tom Mathews, "The Point Man," *Newsweek,* August 30, 1976.

Page 77.   **"Dole out-Nixoned Nixon":** Personal interview with Norbert Dreiling.

Page 78.   **"Genghis Khan":** David E. Rosenbaum, "New GOP Chairman Robert Joseph Dole," *New York Times,* January 16, 1971.

Page 78.   **"Bonanza":** Quoted in Laurent Belsie, "Robert Dole," *Christian Science Monitor,* January 15, 1988.

Page 78.   **a plaque given annually** Rosenbaum, "New GOP Chairman Robert Joseph Dole."

Page 78.   **"Dole will do what it takes to get elected":** Personal interview with Norbert Dreiling.

Page 79.   **"It's a sad mistake to overlook . . .":** Lynne Holt, "Veteran Bob Dole Shuns Campaign Cards," *Wichita Eagle,* November 5, 1966.

Page 79.   **"I stayed to the bitter end . . .":** Holt, "Veteran Bob Dole."

Page 80.   **House colleagues:** *Congressional Record,* October 10, 1968, 30652 et seq.

### Chapter 7: "NIXON'S DOBERMAN PINSCHER"

Page 83.   **belonged in the government:** Personal statement by Dole.

Page 84. **"Is it a rule of the Senate . . .":** Loye Miller, Jr., "Dole Building Reputation as a Fighter," *Kansas City Times*, July 13, 1970.

Page 85. **Nixon's left-handed handshake:** Miller, "Dole Building Reputation."

Page 85. **"You don't question the orders . . .":** Personal statement by Dole.

Page 86. **"beer on a troop ship":** David E. Rosenbaum, "The GOP Chairman Robert Joseph Dole," *New York Times*, January 16, 1971.

Page 87. **the label was "unfair":** Personal statement by Dole.

Page 87. **"missionary":** *Topeka Capital-Journal*, December 26, 1971.

Page 87. **"If you liked Peter C. Stuart, Richard Nixon . . .":** "Bob Dole: Conservative Contradiction," *Christian Science Monitor*, September 10, 1976.

Page 87. **Nixon had inherited the Vietnam War:** See *Congressional Record*, March 5, 1971, 5235–36; April 22, 1971, 11489–90; June 10, 1971, 19357–58.

Page 87. **"I cannot leave unchallenged . . .":** Miller, "Dole Building Reputation."

Page 88. **"as painlessly as possible":** Gail Sheehy, "The Whole Robert Dole," *Vanity Fair*, April 1987.

Page 88. **"He sat with us for a family dinner . . .":** Personal interview with Phyllis Dole Macey.

Page 89. **"achieve maximum independence":** From *Congressional Record*, April 14, 1969, 8816–21.

Page 90. **Senator Bob Packwood:** Miller, "Dole Building Reputation."

Page 90. **Senator Barry Goldwater:** Miller; "Dole Building Reputation."

Page 90. **"younger and more aggressive leadership":** R. W. Apple, Jr., "Dole Is Selected to Direct G.O.P.," *New York Times*, January 6, 1971.

Page 90. **a storm of protest:** Apple, "Dole Is Selected."

Page 91. **Nixon-Dole ticket:** Personal statement by Dole.

### Chapter 8: A SUGAR-COATED STEEL MAGNOLIA

Page 93. **Nixon's running mate.** "Kansan of Achievement in 1971," *Topeka Capital-Journal*, December 26, 1971.

Page 94. **the divorce was granted on the spot:** "Dole's Wife Receives a Divorce," *Topeka Journal*, January 12, 1972.

Page 94. **"I'm still in shock . . .":** "Former Wife of Sen. Dole Still Shocked," *Topeka Capital*, January 15, 1972.

Page 94. **"I think you have to make a decision . . .":** Quoted in Myra MacPherson, *The Power Lovers* (New York: Putnam, 1975), 221. Reprinted by permission from the Putnam Publishing Group.

Page 95. **"I have no plans . . .":** Quoted in MacPherson, *The Power Lovers*, 222.

Page 95. **"We weren't programmed . . .":** Quoted in MacPherson, *The Power Lovers*, 222.

Page 96. **"I never saw any personality clashes . . .":** Quoted in MacPherson, *The Power Lovers*, 228.

Page 96. **"I don't think I really knew her well. . . .":** Quoted in MacPherson, *The Power Lovers*, 228.

Page 96. **"numbly unhappy":** B. Drummond Ayres, Jr., "Ex-Wife Says Dole Is a 'Perfectionist,'" *New York Times*, August 22, 1976.

Page 96. **"devastated by the divorce":** Personal interview with Phyllis Dole Macey.

Page 97. **"Phyllis was just too domestic for Bob":** Personal interview with Bub Dawson.

Page 97. **Russell Townsley:** Personal interview.

Page 99. **"Maybe I convinced myself . . .":** Quoted in MacPherson, *The Power Lovers*, 231.

Page 99. **"cold Arctic wind":** Personal comment by Dole.

Page 101. **"My goodness, he's an attractive man":** Quoted in Kandy Stroud, "Robert and Elizabeth Dole: America's No. 1 Power Couple," *Cosmopolitan*, January 1986.

Page 102. **first woman president:** According to a personal comment by Bob Dole.

Page 102. **John LeBoutillier:** Personal interview.

Page 103. **Maybe I convinced myself . . .":** Quoted in MacPherson, *The Power Lovers*, 231.

Page 103. **"sugar-coated steel magnolia":** Personal comment by Bob Dole.

### Chapter 9: THE MAN IN THE WATERGATE-PROOF VEST

Page 105. **"Thank goodness I only nodded"**: "The Droll Dole," *Russell Record*, November 5, 1987.

Page 106. **"an opportunistic politician"**: Stephen C. Fehr, "The Metamorphosis of Bob Dole," *Kansas City Times*, February 6, 1984.

Page 106. **announced that he was resigning:** Linda Charlton, "Dole Quits as G.O.P. Head, Bush Named as Successor," *New York Times*, December 12, 1972.

Page 106. **"execution at Camp David"**: Robert Scheer, "Dole Calls Afghanistan Carter Diversion," *Los Angeles Times*, January 19, 1980.

Page 107. **"See No Evil . . ."**: Gail Sheehy, "The Whole Robert Dole," *Vanity Fair*, April 1987.

Page 108. **"The memo suggested that . . ."**: Nicholas M. Horrock, "Dole's I.T.T. Role Could Be Fall Target," *New York Times*, August 29, 1976.

Page 108. **Dole's report on his 1971 travels:** *Congressional Quarterly*, August 5, 1972, 1938.

Page 109. **In mid-1971, according to the *New York Times* . . .:** Horrock, "Dole's I.T.T. Role Could Be Fall Target."

Page 110. **never known about any ITT offer at all:** Horrock, "Dole's I.T.T. Role Could Be Fall Target."

Page 112. **Norbert Dreiling:** "Dreiling Charges McCord Was on Dole's GOP Staff," *Wichita Eagle-Beacon*, May 3, 1973.

Page 112. **Two former top officials:** "Pair Says Dole Didn't Hire James McCord," *Wichita Eagle-Beacon*, May 4, 1973.

Page 112. **"It's an impossible dilemma"**: R. W. Apple, Jr., "For Dole, the Nixon Issue Is 'an Impossible Dilemma,' " *New York Times*, June 6, 1974.

Page 112. **"a legal case against the president"**: Apple, "Nixon Issue Is 'an Impossible Dilemma.' "

Page 112. **"wouldn't mind if Nixon flew over"**: Apple, "Nixon Issue Is 'an Impossible Dilemma.' "

Page 112. **Senator Edmund G. Ross:** John F. Kennedy, *Profiles in Courage* (New York: Pocket Books, 1956), 107.

Page 113. **seeing himself in the role of Ross:** Apple, "Nixon Issue Is 'an Impossible Dilemma.' "

Page 113. **"local recommendation"**: Personal interview with Bob Brock. Also see Stephen Darst, "How It Is Playing in Emporia," *New York Times*, October 20, 1974. Brock told me he was harassed by the IRS and lost his hotel's certification for a liquor license. He also said he did not know Nixon or anyone in Nixon's entourage, except Dole, who considered him a political foe.

Page 114. **"Dole's a great crier . . ."**: Personal interview with Dr. William Roy.

Page 114. **15 percent of registered voters:** Darst, "How It Is Playing in Emporia."

Page 115. **performed about ten abortions:** According to personal interview with Dr. William Roy.

Page 115. **fetuses in garbage cans:** Martin Tolchin and Jeff Gerth, "The Contradictions of Bob Dole," *New York Times Magazine*, November 8, 1987. Also personal interview with Dr. William Roy.

Page 115. **VOTE FOR DOLE:** Nicholas M. Horrock, "Anti-Abortion Ad Funds Accepted by Dole in '74," *New York Times*, August 25, 1976.

Page 116. **regained confidence in his ability to win:** Al Polczinski, "Dole—One Happy Man," *Wichita Eagle-Beacon*, November 6, 1974.

Page 116. **"I was flat out beat . . ."**: Polczinski "Dole Wins, Roy Blames Loss on Abortion Issue," *Wichita Eagle-Beacon*, November 6, 1974. Also personal interview with Dr. William Roy.

Page 116. **did *not* specifically disavow any ads:** According to Horrock, "Anti-Abortion Ad Funds Accepted."

Page 116. **The *New York Times* reported in 1976 . . .:** Horrock, "Anti-Abortion ad Funds Accepted."

Page 117. **Dole's brother Kenny says:** Personal interview.

Page 117. **Even Norbert Dreiling:** Personal interview.

Page 118. **"They said that since my opponent . . ."**: Tony Kornheiser, "Bob Dole Quipping and Questing for the Tall Cotton," *Washington Post*, February 16, 1980.

Page 119. **"a lady with heart"**: *Congressional Quarterly*, February 24, 1975, 4093.

Page 119. **"legislation to increase consumer representation":** *Congressional Record*, May 7, 1975, 13356.

Page 119. **Bob and Elizabeth's wedding:** "Dole Wedding Attracts Washington Celebrities," *Wichita Eagle-Beacon*, December 7, 1975.

Page 120. **According to Kenny Dole:** Personal interview.

## Chapter 10: 1976—GOP HATCHET MAN

Page 122. **"kick the ball away in the first quarter":** Peter C. Stuart, "Bob Dole: Conservative Contradiction," *Christian Science Monitor*, September 10, 1976.

Page 123. **"I've learned to respect McGovern":** Tony Kornheiser, "Bob Dole Quipping and Questing for the Tall Cotton," *Washington Post*, February 16, 1980.

Page 123. **Dorothy recalls:** Personal interview with Dorothy Voss Beecher.

Page 123. **Owen wrote:** "Owen Joins Dole's Team," *Wichita Eagle*, August 27, 1976.

Page 125. **What it seemed to come down to:** "The Dole Decision," *Time*, August 30, 1976.

Page 125. **only 1,921 of 2,259:** *The World Almanac and Book of Facts 1977* (New York: Newspaper Enterprise Association Inc., 1976), 37.

Page 125. **acceptance speech to the convention:** "Acceptance, Speech Criticizes 'Stranglehold' over Congress," *Wichita Eagle-Beacon*, August 20, 1976.

Page 126. **"Boy Scout":** Personal remark to author by Dole.

Page 126. **"If you want to start the campaign . . .":** *Wichita Eagle-Beacon*, August 21, 1976.

Page 127. **criticized nevertheless:** "Representative: Elizabeth Dole Should Resign," *Wichita Eagle*, September 9, 1976; *Topeka Capital*, October 22, 1976.

Page 128. **contribution to Dole:** Nicholas M. Horrock, "Dole Is Reported Linked to '73 Gift by Gulf Oil Aide," *New York Times*, September 6, 1976.

Page 129. **mysteriously missing:** Walter Pincus, "Dole Campaign Records Draw Renewed Interest," *Washington Post*, September 30, 1976.

Page 130. **Lyn Nofziger:** Quoted in Jules Witcover, *Marathon: The Pursuit of the Presidency 1972–1976* (New York: Viking Press, 1977), 613.

Page 130. **Richard Nixon:** Quoted in Sam Anson, *Exile: The Unquiet Oblivion of Richard Nixon* (New York: Simon and Schuster, 1984), 148.

Page 131. **"We're not on a leash":** Margot Hornblower, "Pitchman Dole Could Steal the Show," *Washington Post*, September 13, 1976.

Page 131. **"delegate responsibility":** Margot Hornblower, "Dole Gets Pro Campaign Help," *Washington Post*, September 22, 1976.

Page 131. **George Gilder:** George Gilder, "A Loner's Quest," *Life*, September 1987.

Page 132. **He attacked Carter . . .:** Hornblower, "Campaign Help."

Page 133. **"I thought of all the things I could have said":** Al Polczinski, "Dole: Important Thing Is How Viewer Judged Us," *Wichita Eagle-Beacon*, October 17, 1976.

Page 133. **"the jugular":** Quoted in *Time*, January 27, 1986.

Page 133. **"we will dredge up a few wars":** Polczinski, "Dole: Important Thing."

Page 133. **Elizabeth:** Polczinski, "Dole: Important Thing."

Page 134. **"but I never certainly thought of politics":** Forrest Hintz, "Dole's Mother on Campaign Trail," *Wichita Eagle-Beacon*, October 31, 1976.

Page 135. **"He was like a snake":** Thomas Edsall, "Dole's Transformations," *Washington Post*, March 9, 1987.

Page 135. **another sore loser, Richard Nixon:** David Frost's interview with Bob Dole on ABC-TV's "The Next President," January 3, 1988.

## Chapter 11: A QUIXOTIC QUEST FOR THE WHITE HOUSE

Page 140. **threats against his life:** Personal statement made by Ernie Garcia, Dole's chief aide during the cult hearing. Garcia left Bob Dole to work for Elizabeth Dole in the White House in 1981. He was appointed Senate sergeant-at-arms by Bob in 1986, when Bob became majority leader.

Page 141. **now turned to his wife for example:** The influence of Elizabeth Dole on her husband is evident to me from my own personal observation as well as that of longtime Dole aide Bob Lighthizer.

Page 142. **"We change behavior very, very fast"**: Thomas B. Edsall, "Dole's Transformations," *Washington Post*, March 9, 1987.

Page 143. **"I know I'll never be a Kennedy"**: Gene Murray, "Sen. Bob Dole . . . a Long Way from Russell, Kan," *Kansas City Star Magazine*, September 24, 1972.

Page 145. **In proposing his bill**: Dave Bartel, "Dole Acts to Aid Farmers, Blacks, Cities, Taiwan," *Wichita Eagle-Beacon*, January 16, 1979.

Page 146. **Exxon stock**: Dave Bartel, "Dole Sells," *Wichita Eagle-Beacon*, May 19, 1979.

Page 146. **Elizabeth also lent Bob**: Paul Wenske, Charles R. T. Crumpley, and Stephen C. Fehr, "How Closely Tied Was Dole to His Wife's Blind Trust?" *Kansas City Times*, January 18, 1988.

Page 146. **"Methinks the lady . . ."**: Dave Bartel, "Dole Would Shed Image of 'Hatchet Man,'" *Wichita Eagle*, May 15, 1979.

Page 149. **Dole announced his candidacy**: Speech printed in *Congressional Record*, May 14, 1979, 10859–60.

Page 150. **Gerry Mursner**: Tony Kornheiser, "Bob Dole Quipping and Questing for the Tall Cotton," *Washington Post*, February 16, 1980.

Page 154. **Johnny Carson**: Paul Corkery, *Carson: The Unauthorized Biography* (Ketchum, Idaho: Randt & Co., 1987), 137.

Page 159. **a reporter who had written critical articles**: Personal interview with the reporter who has requested anonymity.

Page 159. **Dan Glickman**: Al Polczinski, "Dole Fails to File for Primary," *Wichita Beacon*, February 12, 1980.

Page 161. **a report on the health status of each**: "Presidential Health Poll: How the Doctors Vote," *Medical World News*, February 18, 1980; Jane Floerchinger, "2 Doctors Dispute Dole Attack Report," *Wichita Eagle*, February, 12, 1980.

Page 161. **Computer Business Supplies Inc. filed a lawsuit**: Dave Bartel, "Dole Campaign Legal Problems," *Wichita Eagle*, October 12, 1979.

Page 161. **filed his own lawsuit**: Dave Bartel, "Dole Threatened with Defamation Suit," *Wichita Eagle*, February 1, 1980.

Page 161. **a defamation action**: Bartel, "Dole Threatened."

Page 161. **"tall men's clothing store"**: Kornheiser, "Bob Dole Quipping and Questing."

Page 162. **On March 15, at a news conference**: Melissa Cordonier, "Senator Dole Ends 'Long Shot' Quest," *Lawrence Journal-World*, March 15, 1980.

Page 162. **a Kansas newspaper printed a story**: According to the *Topeka Capital-Journal*, May 7, 1980, the *Johnson County Squire* reported that, at Elizabeth's urging, Dole would not seek reelection and would pick financial adviser Dave Owen to succeed him.

### Chapter 12: THE TAX MAN COMETH

Page 166. **settling for a Reagan bill**: Editorial, "Elizabeth Dole vs. Sex Bias," *Christian Science Monitor*, October 8, 1982.

Page 167. **sent it to Senator Paul Laxalt**: Jane Nevins, "Robert and Elizabeth Dole: The Powers That Be," *Family Weekly*, March 29, 1981.

Page 167. **the ball carrier**: Nevins, "Robert and Elizabeth Dole."

Page 170. **criticized him in an editorial**: "Where's the Dole Bill?," *Wall Street Journal*, May 15, 1981.

Page 173. **"Perhaps it's time to remind him . . ."**: "Where's the Dole Bill?"

Page 174. **"a very compassionate man . . ."**: Robert W. Merry, "Senator Robert Dole Plays Major Role in Future of Reagan Tax Bill," *Wall Street Journal*, July 15, 1981.

Page 175. **Reaganomics brought about . . .**: Stephen Weisman, "Reaganomics and the President's Men," *New York Times Magazine*, October 24, 1982.

Page 176. **a sensational article**: William Greider, "The Education of David Stockman," *The Atlantic Monthly*, December 1981.

Page 180. **"If I didn't know better . . .":** Robert Merry, "Tax Debate Seen Testing Sen. Dole, Who Is Leading the Fight Against Big Breaks," *Wall Street Journal*, June 23, 1982.

Page 180. **"There is a perception out there . . .":** Timothy B. Clark, "The Clout of the 'New' Bob Dole," *New York Times Magazine*, December 12, 1982.

Page 184. **"not trying to make a U-turn . . .":** Bob Dole, "Taxes: The Republican Identity Crisis," *Washington Post*, August 8, 1982.

Page 187. **lionized by Wall Street:** Haynes Johnson, "Bob Dole Redux," *Washington Post*, August 23, 1982.

Page 187. **Horace Busby:** Quoted in Juan Williams, "Bob Dole Wants to Raise Your Taxes Again," *Fortune*, October 18, 1981.

Page 187. **"We shouldn't favor big business . . .":** Williams, "Bob Dole Wants to Raise Your Taxes Again."

Page 191. **"I regret that I have but one wife . . .":** "Vote of Confidence," *New York Times*, January 27, 1983.

Page 192. **Newt Gingrich:** Andrew C. Miller, "Dole Makes Gains in Fight for Right Wing," *Kansas City Star*, September 8, 1988.

Page 193. **Joseph Rauh:** Thomas B. Edsall, "Dole's Transformations," *Washington Post*, March 9, 1987.

### Chapter 13: THE MAJORITY LEADER MAKES A U-TURN

Page 197. **four so-called last-man-out ballots:** "Dole Elected Majority Leader," *Garden City Telegram*, November 28, 1984; "Dole Is Selected Majority Leader, *New York Times*, November 29, 1984.

Page 198. **three tax increases:** "Dole Shakes Ruthless Image," *Garden City Telegram*, November 28, 1984.

Page 198. **"Senate interests":** *Kansas City Star*, November 30, 1986.

Page 198. **mobbed by dozens of tobacco company officials:** According to Chuck Lewis, producer for CBS-TV's "60 Minutes." For more on Dole's relationship with the tobacco industry 1985–1987, see David Corn, "Bob Dole and the Tobacco Connection," *The Nation*, March 28, 1987.

Page 200. **"shot at them":** Andrew C. Miller, "Dole Makes Gains in Fight for Right Wing," *Kansas City Star*, September 8, 1985.

Page 200. **Paul Weyrich:** Miller, "Dole Makes Gains."

Page 200. **Richard Viguerie:** Miller, "Dole Makes Gains."

Page 200. **"the Zelig of American Politics":** William Schneider, "The Republicans '88," *The Atlantic Monthly*, July 1987.

Page 201. **"political high-wire act":** Helen Dewar, "Dole Rides High After Budget Victory," *Washington Post*, May 23, 1985.

Page 202. **Caspar Weinberger:** "Dole Frustrated with Weinberger," *Topeka Capital-Journal*, January 26, 1985.

Page 203. **Howard Phillips:** Miller, "Dole Makes Gains."

Page 204. **"You've done too much good . . .":** Fred Barnes, "The Dole Moment," *The New Republic*, January 26, 1987.

Page 204. **$11.7 billion in 1986:** *World Almanac 1987*, 117–118. After the Supreme Court found the automatic spending cut process unconstitutional on July 7, 1986, Congress changed the law to give the Office of Management and Budget the final authority to determine the size of the cuts required to meet the spending cut targets.

Page 205. **the first eleven months of Dole's reign:** Stephen C. Fehr, "Dole Gets Results as Senate Leader but Angers Critics," *Kansas City Times*, December 9, 1985.

Page 205. **Nancy Kassebaum:** Fehr, "Dole Gets Results."

Page 215. **"I don't wait for the consensus":** Fehr, "Dole Gets Results."

Page 206. **Senator Jake Garn:** Fehr, "Dole Gets Results."

Page 206. **Senate veteran Democrat Thomas Eagleton:** Fehr, "Dole Gets Results"

Page 207. **GOP senator John Danforth:** Fehr, "Dole Gets Results."

Page 207. **"something he wants someday":** Jonathan Fuerbringer, "Temper, Temper, Temper," *New York Times*, March 11, 1986.

Page 208. **When Byrd rose to his feet . . .:** Steven V. Roberts, "Why Aren't These Men Smiling?," *New York Times*, August 11, 1986.

Page 208. **House Speaker Tip O'Neill:** David Rogers, "Dole's Leadership Role in Senate Helps Shape His Bid for Presidency," *Wall Street Journal*, August 15, 1986.

Page 208. **the controversial nomination of Daniel Manion:** See "Manion Confirmation," *Congressional Quarterly Almanac* 1986; Nadine Cahdas, "Controversy Surprises Manion, but Nominee Won't Withdraw," *Congressional Quarterly*, July 5, 1986, 1541.

Page 209. **Phyllis Schlafly . . . Paul Weyrich:** Symposium, "Who Should Succeed Reagan?," *Policy Review*, summer 1986.

Page 210. **The American Conservative Union . . . The Chamber of Commerce:** These groups' rankings can be found in *Politics in America* (Congressional Quarterly, 1987).

Page 211. **condones necklacing:** Anthony Lewis's syndicated column, *San Francisco Chronicle*, November 17, 1987.

Page 212. **In a statewide poll:** "Few See Dole for President," *Wichita Eagle-Beacon*, October 26, 1986.

Page 213. **dog . . . in a limousine:** According to Al Polczinski, "Hays Newspaper Feels Bite of Dole's Disgruntled Dog," *Wichita Eagle-Beacon*, August 29, 1986.

Page 213. **Lyndon Johnson:** See Doris Kearns, *Lyndon Johnson and the American Dream* (New York: New American Library, 1977). Johnson is reported to have threatened to quit his job and/or campaigns when confronting the specter of defeat. He has also been compared extensively with Dole in his ability and desire to be in control and in his ability to craft legislative compromises appealing to various factions on both sides of the aisle in the Senate.

### Chapter 14: THE 1988 RACE FOR PRESIDENT

Page 217. **running on "a record":** Albert R. Hunt, "Dole Launches Presidential Bid, Vowing a Balanced Budget, Touting His Record," *Wall Street Journal*, November 10, 1987.

Page 219. **George Wittgraf:** "Dole Denies Role in Bush Rumors," *Topeka Capital-Journal*, June 24, 1987.

Page 219. **"He's pretty good at that":** "Dole Denies Role."

Page 221. **"You've been playing quarterback too long":** Presidential candidates' debate on NBC-TV, December 1, 1987, hosted by Tom Brokaw.

Page 221. **"Central America wouldn't mind a three-day invasion . . .":** "Dumping on Dole," *Russell Record*, November 5, 1987; *Milwaukee Sentinel*, September 14, 1987.

Page 221. **on national television:** Presidential candidates' debate on NBC-TV, December 1, 1987.

Page 222. **Nicaraguan president Daniel Ortega:** Kenneth R. Lamke, "Dole Says Many Are Dubious of Ortega," *Milwaukee Sentinel*, September 14, 1987.

Page 224. **"What should we do?":** Story related in personal interview with Kenny Dole.

Page 224. **"I offer a willingness . . ." (Dole's announcement speech):** Bernard Weinraub, "Dole Makes His Presidential Bid Official," *New York Times*, November 10, 1987.

Page 226. **"not a racist bone in my body":** Weinraub, "Dole Makes His Presidential Bid Official."

Page 228. **When Bill Brock came on board:** Morton M. Kondracke, "Battleship Bush," *The New Republic*, February 8, 1988.

Page 230. **Dole was pilloried in the nation's media:** See, for example, David Corn, "Bob Dole and the Tobacco Connection," *Nation*, March 28, 1987; Martin Tolchin and Jeff Gerth, "The Contradictions of Bob Dole," *New York Times Magazine*, November 8, 1987; Jeff Gerth, "Top Insurance Officials Underwrite Dole Efforts," *New York Times*, December 24, 1987; Susan Page "Dole Frequent Corporate Flyer," *Newsday* September 17, 1987.

Page 230. **The allegations against Owen:** See, for example, Paul Wenske, "FBI Looks at Contract Won by Ex-Dole Aide," *Kansas City Times*, January 3, 1988; Anne Swardson and Dan Morgan, "Firm Paid Dole Associate After It Got Army Contract," *Washington Post*, January 24, 1988.

Page 233. **"a model of political decorum"**: Dorothy Collin, "Dole Goes on the Attack over Bush 'Distortions,' " *Chicago Tribune*, February 17, 1988.

### Chapter 15: BOB AND ELIZABETH—RIVALS AND PARTNERS

Page 236. **"using a stereotype about policitians' wives"**: Editorial, *Louisville Courier Journal & Times*, September, 18, 1987.

Page 236. **"This is a personal decision . . ."**: Mary T. Schmich, "Southern Strategy," *Chicago Tribune*, February 8, 1988.

Page 237. **"She's got my vote"**: "Elizabeth Dole Courts Voters as Senator's Southern Strategy," *Russell Record*, November 5, 1987.

Page 237. **undergone spiritual growth:** Kandy Stroud, "Robert and Elizabeth Dole: America's No. 1 Power Couple," *Cosmopolitan*, January 1986.

Page 238. **"It's really her room"**: Elizabeth Kastor, "Doles' Grace Shines Through at Convention," *Topeka-Capital Journal*, August 26, 1984.

Page 239. **suggested that his wife be appointed United Nations ambassador:** "Dole Backs His Wife for U.N. Post," *Kansas City Star*, December 14, 1984.

Page 240. **"in all three houses"**: "Doles Make History at Committee Hearing," *Topeka Capital Journal*, February 1, 1984.

Page 241. **Sea View Hotel:** Martin Tolchin and Jeff Gerth, "The Contradictions of Bob Dole," *New York Times Magazine*, November 8, 1987. Also Edward Pound, "Minority Leader's Backer Gains on Gasahol Issue," *Wall Street Journal*, September 25, 1987. Also "Minutes of the Annual Meeting of the Directors of Sea View Hotel, Inc., held March 27, 1982."

### Chapter 16: DOLE AS PRESIDENT

Page 246. **Jim Parrish:** Personal interview.

Page 246. **Norbert Dreiling:** Personal interview.

Page 246. **Professor James David Barber:** Quotations are from a personal interview with Barber, author of *The Presidential Character: Predicting Performance in the White House* (Englewood Cliffs, New Jersey: Prentice-Hall, 1985).

Page 247. **Bill Roy:** Quoted in Martin Tolchin and Jeff Gerth, "The Contradictions of Bob Dole," *New York Times Magazine*, November 8, 1987.

Page 248. **"Dole's history of anger is extensive . . ."**: James David Barber, "Candidates' Personalities, Not Their Promises, Are Key to Predicting Performance," *Atlanta Journal-Constitution*, November 29, 1987.

Page 250. **Russell Townsley:** Personal interview.

Page 251. **"I told him, 'Bob . . .' "**: Personal interview with Phyllis Dole Macey.

Page 252. **"He doesn't like to argue . . ."**: Personal interview with Phyllis.

Page 254. **Norbert Dreiling:** Personal interview.

Page 254. **John Woelk:** Quoted in James M. Perry, "Ferocious Ambition Drives Political Junkie Dole, But Candidate Lacks Carefully Fixed Philosophy," *Wall Street Journal*, September 25, 1987.

Page 256. **Tom Korologos:** Stephen C. Fehr, "The Metamorphosis of Bob Dole," *Kansas City Star*, February 6, 1984.

Page 259. **Helen Gurley Brown:** Quoted in Tolchin and Gerth, "The Contradictions of Bob Dole."

### Additional Sources

Baker, Bobby, with Larry King. *Wheeling and Dealing.* New York: Norton, 1978.

Barone, Michael, and Ujifusa, Grant. *Almanac of American Politics, 1988.* New York: E. P. Dutton, 1987.

Barrett, Laurence I. *Gambling with History: Ronald Reagan in the White House.* Garden City, NY: Doubleday, 1983.

Burns, James MacGregor. *Roosevelt, the Soldier of Freedom.* New York: Harcourt Brace Jovanovich, 1970.

Cannon, Lou. *Reagan*. New York: Putnam, 1982.

Canovan, Margaret. *Populism*. New York: Harcourt Brace Jovanovich, 1981.

Congressional Quarterly. *Almanacs 1961–86*. Washington, DC: Congressional Quarterly Press.

Goldwater, Barry. *With No Apologies*. New York: Morrow, 1979.

Greider, William. *The Education of David Stockman and Other Americans*. New York: Dutton, 1982.

Hodgson, Godfrey. *All Things to All Men: The False Promise of the American Presidency*. New York: Simon & Schuster, 1980.

Johnson, Lyndon B. *The Vantage Point: Perspectives of the Presidency*. New York: Holt, Rinehart & Winston, 1971.

Kalb, Marvin. Interview with Dole broadcast on PBS "Candidates '88," January 1988.

Leamer, Laurence. *Make Believe: The Story of Nancy & Ronald Reagan*. New York: Harper & Row, 1983.

Lukas, J. Anthony. *Nightmare: the Underside of the Nixon Years*. New York: Viking, 1976.

McGrory, Mary. "Robert Dole Pops Up as Liberal Hero." *Oakland Tribune* (May 9, 1982).

Miner, H. Craig. *The Fire in the Rock: A History of the Oil and Gas Industry in Kansas*. Newton, KS: Kansas Independent Oil & Gas Association, 1976.

Neustadt, Richard. *Presidential Power*. New York: Wiley, 1980.

Rich, Everett, ed. *The Heritage of Kansas: Selected Commentaries on Past Times*. Lawrence, KS: University of Kansas Press, 1960.

Roberts, Stephen. "The G.O.P.: A Party in Search of Itself." *New York Times Magazine* (March 6, 1983).

Ryan, Michael. "What Makes Senator Bob Dole Different? 'You Have to Try a Little Harder.'" *Parade Magazine* in *Topeka Capital-Journal* (November 2, 1986).

Ryan, Richard. "For Senator Bob Dole, 1982 Was a Very Good Year." *The Wichitan* (January 1983).

Smith, Hedrick. "Bob Dole's Big Gamble." *New York Times Magazine* (June 30, 1985).

Smith, Richard Norton. *An Uncommon Man: The Triumph of Herbert Hoover*. New York: Simon & Schuster, 1984.

Stockman, David. *The Triumph of Politics*. New York: Harper & Row, 1986.

Vexler, Robert, ed. *Chronology and Documentary Handbook of the State of Kansas*. New York: Oceana Publications, 1978.

Webb, Walter P. *The Great Plains*. New York: Grosset Universal Library, 1976.

Weinstein, Edward. *Woodrow Wilson: A Medical and Psychological Biography*. Princeton, NJ: Princeton University Press, 1983.

White, Theodore H. *America in Search of Itself: The Making of the President, 1956–1980*. New York: Harper & Row, 1982.

*The World Almanac and Book of Facts*. 1961–88. New York: Newspaper Enterprise Association, Inc.

Zornow, William. *A History of the Jayhawk State*. Norman, OK: University of Oklahoma Press, 1957.

# INDEX